My Life on Earth and Elsewhere

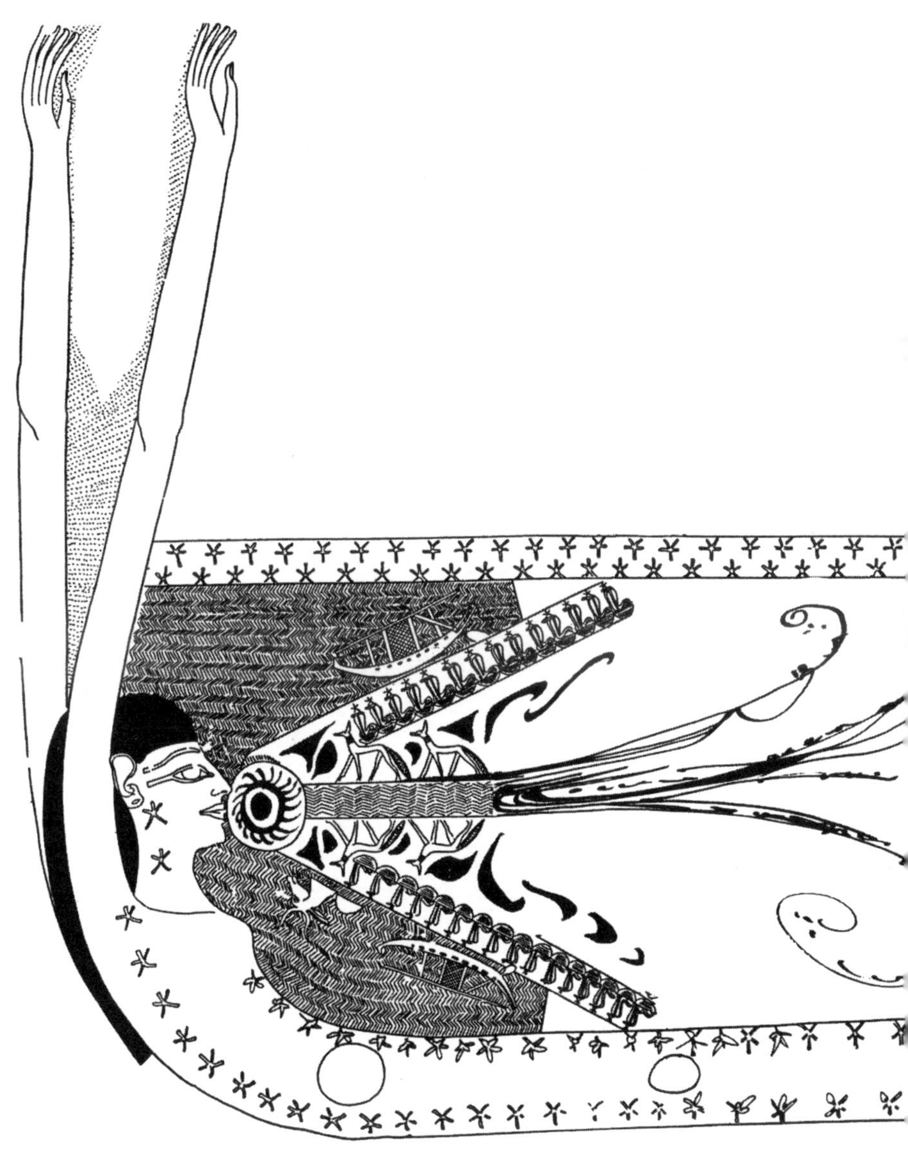

SELF PORTRAIT

MY LIFE ON EARTH & ELSEWHERE

R. Murray Schafer

The Porcupine's Quill

Library and Archives Canada Cataloguing in Publication

Schafer, R. Murray (Raymond Murray), 1933–
My life on earth and elsewhere / R. Murray Schafer.
– 1st ed.

ISBN 978-0-88984-352-3

1. Schafer, R. Murray (Raymond Murray), 1933–.
2. Composers – Canada – Biography. I. Title.

ML410.S25A3 2012 780.92 C2012-904348-6

1 2 3 • 14 13 12

Published by The Porcupine's Quill, 68 Main Street, PO Box 160,
Erin, Ontario NOB 1TO. http://porcupinesquill.ca

Readied for the press by Doris Cowan. Cover and interior images are courtesy of the author.

Represented in Canada by the Literary Press Group.
Trade orders are available from University of Toronto Press.

We acknowledge the support of the Ontario Arts Council and the Canada Council for the Arts for our publishing program. The financial support of the Government of Canada through the Canada Book Fund is also gratefully acknowledged.

CONTENTS

PART ONE

STUDENT, SAILOR, WANDERER

PART TWO

THE MUSIC OF THE ENVIRONMENT

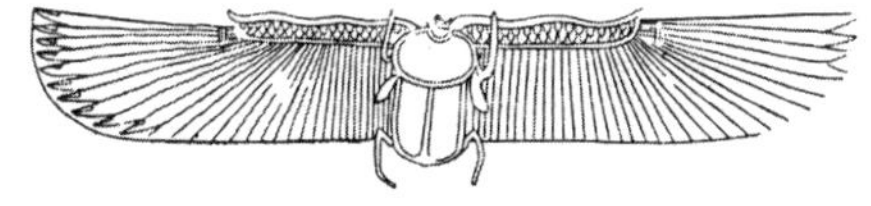

PART ONE

STUDENT, SAILOR, WANDERER

BEGINNINGS

I WAS CROSS-EYED and blind in one eye from the day I was born. My father held out hope that exercise might make vision possible, and when I was three or four years old he would cover my good eye and hold up various numbers of fingers before the bad one. I could only guess at them and then begin to cry. When I was eight years old I started to get aches in the bad eye and the doctors told my parents that I was suffering from glaucoma. Two operations followed in quick sequence. From the first, I remember only the smell of ether. On the operating table for the second time, I pleaded not to have ether and I remember the doctor hovering above me, knife in hand, and inquiring maliciously whether I'd rather have the operation without ether. 'No!' I screamed and the ether mask was clamped over my face.

When I returned to school a few weeks later with an artificial eye, the class had obviously been briefed on how to react. The girls were sympathetic, but some of the boys were not. 'You think you're smart because you've got a glass eye,' I remember one of them saying as he pushed me to the ground. Over the next few years I was beaten up frequently for no reason except that I looked different from other people.

Although I grew up in Toronto, my parents both came from Manitoba. My mother was born there in a sod hut. Her parents had moved west from Warsaw, Ontario, in the late nineteenth century to take up farming. My father was born in Erie, Illinois, but his family had moved to Hamiota after the wars with the Métis had been settled. My father had great respect for the culture of the native peoples and, many years later, I was to make friends with one of the members of the Manitoba Dakota reserve, Mike Hotain, and recorded many of his traditional songs and stories for a disc produced by Brandon University.

My father's parents ran a boarding-house, or hotel, next to the railroad where the crew would stay overnight, returning the next day to Winnipeg with grain from the local elevator. The hotel had a billiard table and my father became quite proficient at the game, playing with the train crews. In the winter, the engines had snow-ploughs and would attack the drifts by backing up and then surging forward full-steam. According to my father, they would sometimes jump the

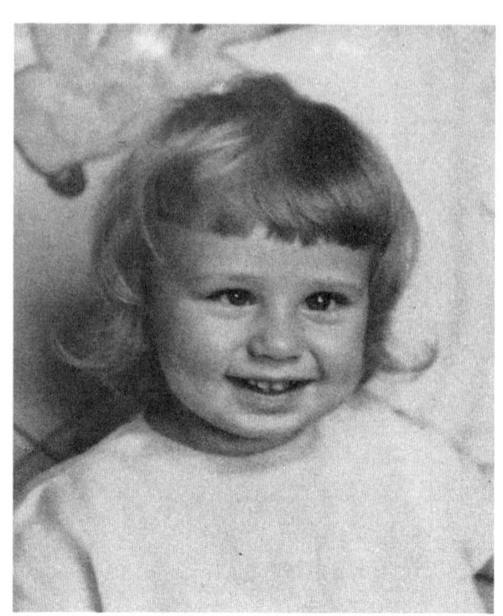

Murray at an early age.

Murray and his younger brother Paul.

tracks. Then they would have to dig the engine out and lay short rails beneath the wheels to get them back on line.

My father's first job as an adolescent was as a guard in the Hamiota bank where he slept all night with a loaded revolver under his pillow. During the winter months the snow would blow under the door to form a deep drift on the floor which he would shovel out after he had lit a fire and cracked the ice on the well to boil tea for the arriving employees.

From as far back as I can remember my mother used to take my brother Paul and me back to her Manitoba home each summer. We travelled by train, sharing a sleeper, though I'm sure my mother didn't get much sleep with two small boys in the same bed with her. The trains heading west all left at ten or eleven o'clock in the evening. There were three or four trains each night called 'sections' leaving at fifteen-minute intervals. I used to love to watch the lights flowing past our window until sleep would overpower my excitement. During the day, we could open the windows for fresh air, smoke and cinders. Later on, observation cars were introduced and we could sit there for hours looking out in all directions. Our destination was Brandon and we would spend a few days there with my grandparents before going to the farm near Souris, where we would spend most of the summer. We were given little jobs to do – picking peas or churning butter. My cousin Bob had a cart with a pony and we would harness it up every day and take the lunches out to men working in the fields. If there was nothing else to do, we used to lasso gophers when they stuck their heads out of their holes. The municipality gave us two cents for every gopher tail we brought in. They were a menace, but the gophers are still there long after the lassoing has ceased. One day I was actually thrown from a horse who tripped in a gopher hole.

I am grateful for the time I spent on the farm in Manitoba and several times I have gone back to visit whatever is left to see. Many of the villages have disappeared. But I never forgot those days and always thought that one day I would return to a farm. Eventually, when I was forty-two, I did. As more and more people crowd into the cities, we are losing contact with the earth, with birds and animals, with sunsets and starry skies. There is no distant viewing or distant listening in the city, only perpetual emergencies and promotional circuses.

Ever since I can remember I loved building things. While envious

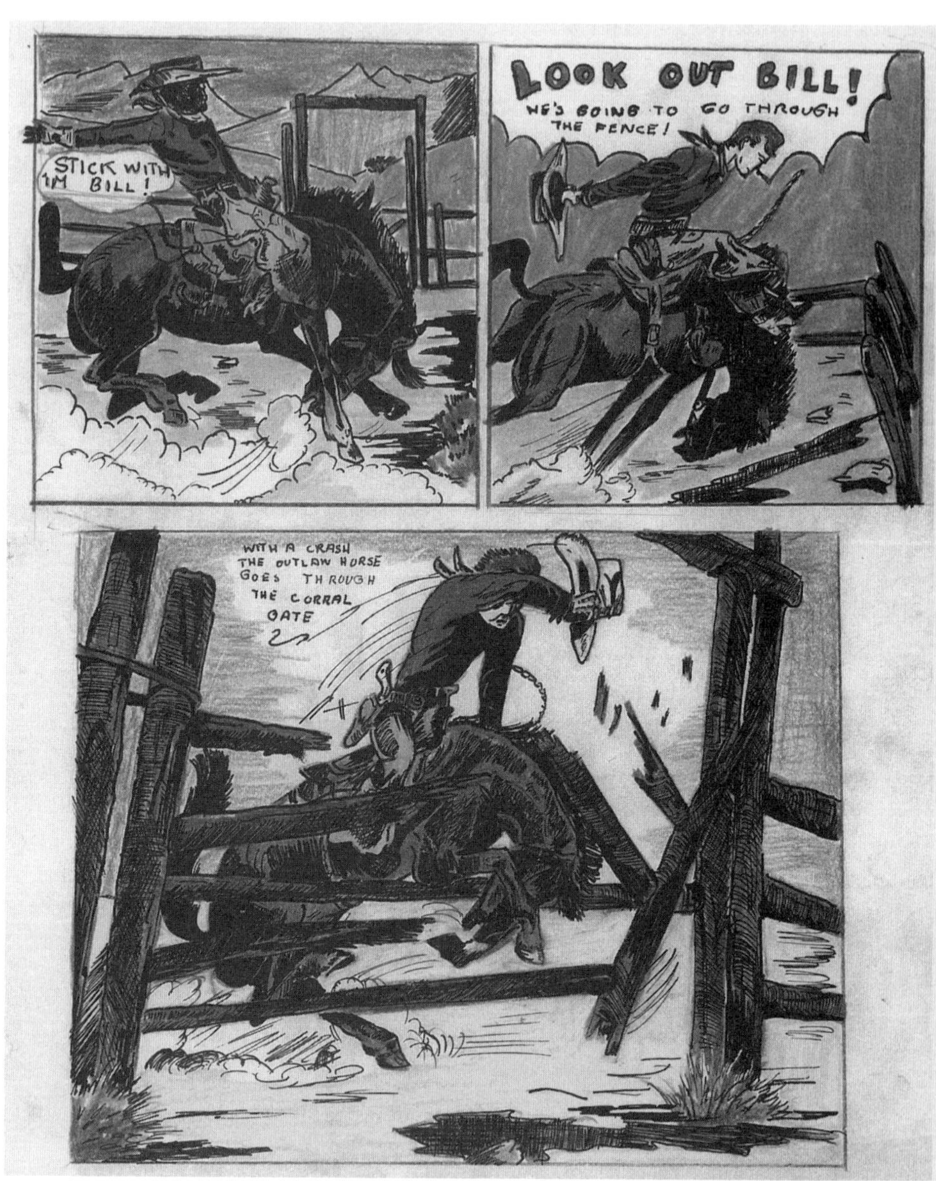

'Billy the Kid' from Murray's *Trigger Comics*.

of other children, whose richer parents bought them electric trains to play with, I built my own train, including the tracks, and pulled it around the basement floor. Later I built a beautiful church with celluloid stained-glass windows lit from inside which was brought out every year to decorate the mantel above the fireplace with drifts of cotton batting snow all around it.

Later I built a full-size racing car which never moved from the backyard, because my father wouldn't let me put tires on it. As an accountant for Imperial Oil, my father used to spend weeks and sometimes months on the road travelling across Canada; and on one of these occasions I built a full-size stagecoach with the intention of charging people to ride in it while some of my minions pulled the coach up and down the street. The stagecoach crashed on its trial run when the 'horses' let go of it as it rushed down Rushton Road.

Sometime when I was in elementary school I began to draw comic books. This was probably when I was eight or nine years old. I would rent them out for one or two cents a night and they were popular enough that I was able to buy chocolate bars with the profits. (Chocolate bars only cost five cents in those years.)

I called the books 'Trigger Comics' and each book contained stories about my heroes: the Black Doom, Billy the Kid, Two-Gun Manitoba, Whiz Sawyer, Oklahoma Kid and Hop Harrigan. 'You don't need a telescope! You don't have to look far', was my comic book slogan. 'Just look for the Trigger symbol, your guarantee of Top Entertainment in Adventure and Humour.' I continued to draw comic books for several years, hurrying home after school on winter nights to listen to the various serial stories on similar subjects in radio programs. After a few years I was able to draw animals and humans in various forms of activity as well as any of the illustrators of real comic books.

Of course, like every boy, I wanted to play sports, but my parents warned me to stay clear of rough games, so I never played hockey or football. Much later I coached young players in football – or rugby, as it was then called. For two or three years I coached a team in the under-100-pounds league at High Park YMCA. I had read many books by American football coaches and I knew all their strategies. Not only did my team never lose a game, we never had a touchdown scored against us. Other coaches would beg me to allow them just one touchdown but I was determined to hold on to our record – and we did!

I had been taking piano lessons from the age of six, as did my younger brother, Paul. Ours was definitely a musical household. My mother also played – mostly light music from the 1920s and '30s: 'Kitten on the Keys', etc. Although he had had no music lessons, my father taught himself to play the opening movement from Beethoven's Moonlight Sonata.

One of the sounds of my childhood that I'd almost forgotten about until I began to write this chronicle was the tinkling of the piano keys when my mother used to wipe them with a wet cloth. She did this almost every day to clean off the sticky substances after Paul and I had done our practising. Certain keys would sound over and over as the obstinate dirt refused to be lifted with the first light sweep of the cloth. In the early years the high and low keys would be passed over quite quickly while the middle notes got the heavy scrubbing. But this began to change after I began to attack Brahms and Beethoven – not to forget the improvisations, usually played with the windows open, in which I would attempt to impress the whole block by means of energetic arpeggios and glissandi across all limits of the audio spectrum. From this period I remember the girls in elementary school crowding around me as I played Rimsky-Korsakov's 'The Flight of the Bumblebee', and then would go on to 'Bumble Boogie', much to their delight.

In the days of my youth, young boys got jobs to help out at home. My contribution to the family economy was not absolutely needed but it was expected, and from the age of eight I had jobs either delivering prescriptions from drugstores on my bicycle or delivering newspapers – sometimes both. I delivered *The Globe and Mail* for several years. It was a large paper route and I was able to make ten dollars a week if I could collect all the money from subscribers, which wasn't always easy. 'Sorry, sonny, I haven't any change. Come back next week' was a familiar excuse. I will never forget VE Day in 1945 when I went to pick up my papers at the drop-off point only to discover that someone had snapped the wire binding and half of the hundred and fifty needed for my customers had been stolen by early readers. I probably could have sold a thousand papers that morning. Everybody wanted to read about the end of the war.

I worked at Farell's Drugstore for twenty cents an hour for several years. What I liked about that job was that when there were no prescriptions to deliver Mr Farell would send me to the basement to package candies! Later, I was offered a job at an apothecary, where there were no candies, but the rate was twenty-five cents an hour. In the apothecary basement was a large glass jar containing a pickled human brain. It had once stood in the window but was later removed, probably because it didn't attract customers. I was really terrified when the druggist would send me downstairs to fetch something.

In grade seven I won the gold medal for public speaking but I can't remember what I spoke about. I find it difficult to remember much about my years in elementary school, probably because I was so frequently beaten up in the schoolyard by boys who didn't like one-eyed classmates. 'Murray's got a glass eye! Murray's got a glass eye!' they'd holler and punch me in the stomach, or kick me until I fell down. Fortunately there were also some nice boys who would tell them to 'lay off' or chase them away. As for school, I remember receiving numerous vaccinations. We were all frightened of 'the needle' and I remember one boy passing out in anticipation. The day after the 'needle', a teacher swatted me on the arm with a ruler because I couldn't spell the word 'tolerant'. The scar is still there and I still have to check the word in the dictionary whenever I use it. In those days we had to line up each morning when the handbell was rung, the boys on one side of the entrance door, the girls on the other, and we would file into the classrooms like little soldiers. We were, of course, at war with Germany at that time. As part of the war effort all students were supposed to bring scrap metal, old clothing and newspapers to school on certain days. What I could never understand was that after VE Day the same materials we had brought to help England and the Allies win the war were now brought to help rehabilitate Germany and Russia. Many years later my brother Paul went to a students' reunion at Humewood Public School and was surprised to see, among the many photos of distinguished former students, one of me with the caption: 'Murray Schafer: famous composer of background music for television.'

HIGH SCHOOL PROVED to be a rockier experience than elementary school – though I blame no one for that. The guidance of a youth through his priapic years is a task that is often bungled. I began to fail almost every subject except art, though I notice from my report cards that by grade eleven I was even having trouble there. The marks that I

Ecclesia Dei.

received varied enormously from term to term as I tried to sort out my life. I didn't take music, because the course consisted of playing in a brass band and I had already done that, playing trumpet in a much better Boy Scouts' brass band while still in elementary school. Towards the end of high school I began to produce some quite respectable paintings including one entitled *Ecclesia Dei.* This was the explanation I wrote for it:

> I have attempted to portray the Church of God remaining supreme throughout eternity. The history of the world is represented in two phases. The building under construction in the upper left represents the prosperous years of history in which culture, economy and science flourished, while the burning building at the right represents the periods of depression, plague and war. Amid this strife and turmoil, even the smallest church remains supreme. The flood waters represent the end of the world approaching, carrying the church to an eternal home in Heaven, while the pyramid of mangled and bloody bodies, representing the sins of the world *(Pećcata Mundi)* quivers in fear. The broken wall at the left was their last attempt to stop the flood. The sole figure in the centre, clinging to the cross, is a redeemed sinner.

The painting was done in egg tempera and is now chipping away. The day I completed it my art teacher, Miss Higgins, anxious to prove that something of significance was being achieved in the art room, asked the principal, Mr Evans, to come and see it. To our mutual disappointment he stood before it for a moment then said, 'Yes, nice that someone can do that', and left the room.

During my adolescence I thought more seriously about a career in art than a career in music. When I visited the guidance counsellor and he asked me whether I'd given any thought to a profession, I said, 'Yes! I'd like to be a painter!' He said, 'You mean painting houses?' I said, 'No, painting pictures.' 'Oh, commercial art. There's good money in commercial art.' 'No, I mean pictures like Picasso and Van Gogh.' 'Don't be foolish,' he replied, and told me that within a few years I'd have a wife and family to support so I'd better get serious. Thankfully I never saw him again.

The academic subjects I enjoyed most in high school were history and English literature. In grade ten I read my first real book. It was Dickens's *Great Expectations,* and it opened the whole world of literature to me. The next year when *Macbeth* was our text, I memorized the whole play. In our history textbook there was a photo of the Lions' Gate at Mycenae which intrigued me so much that Mycenae became one of my first destinations when I finally visited Greece. Science, both chemistry and physics, as well as mathematics, was a struggle, but I drew nice clean charts and diagrams that substituted for comprehension.

In my final year I was given an assignment in English composition to write an essay about 'an interesting person you have met'. I decided to write an essay about a philosopher. I had begun reading Nietzsche so I spilled out what I could recall in the form of a conversation between the philosopher and myself. Across the bottom of the last page the teacher wrote 'Don't lie!' and failed me.

VAUGHAN ROAD COLLEGIATE INSTITUTE
GENERAL AND ACADEMIC COURSES
LOWER SCHOOL

Report of SCHAFER, Murray in Grade 10G

SUBJECT	Percentage Obtained: First Term	Second Term	Third Term	Promotion Standing	Initials of Teachers
English.. Composition	62	60	C		BN
English.. Literature					
Spelling					
Social Studies:					
(1) History	64	40	C		BN
(2) Geography	54	53	33		G.S.
Agriculture or Science	75	81	31	C	G.H.
Mathematics	30	35	33		WHE
Art	79	92	46	II	G.H.
Music					
Latin	62	54	08		HO
French	57	24	23		WB
German					
Greek					

SUBJECT	Percentage Obtained: First Term	Second Term	Third Term	Promotion Standing	Initials of Teachers
Business Practice:					
(1) Penmanship					
(2) Business Practice					
(3) Typewriting					
Defence Course					
Health & Physical Education Total	478	429	298		
Average Percentage	59.7	53.[illegible]	37.3		
Times Late	2	2	0		
Whole Days Absent	4	3	1		
Half Days Absent	1	8	3		

Failed.

Pass Mark — 50%
Credit Standing .... 50%—59%
Third Class Honours ..... 60%—65%
Second Class Honours .. 66%— 74%
First Class Honours .... 75%—100%

In the pupil's interest the parents are asked to study this report carefully, and to check particularly the pupil's attendance and punctuality. Without regularity of attendance, progress is seriously hindered. The report for the third term is complete for the year and should not be returned. In the first and second terms, however, the report must be returned to us as soon as possible after it has been examined and signed.

G. E. EVANS, M.A., B.Paed., Principal.

FIRST TERM
Signature of Parent Belle Schafer
Comments, if any

SECOND TERM
Signature of Parent H.J. Schafer
Comments, if any

Eventually I graduated from high school with a junior matriculation. In order to attend university one had to have a senior matriculation which would have meant another year (or, in my case, maybe three) to come out with proper grades. So I decided to leave school and pursue a course in music.

Throughout my high school I had maintained a mischievous love affair with the piano. I also joined a choir. My brother, Paul, had been singing as a boy soprano in the choir of Grace Church-on-the-Hill, an Anglican church in Forest Hill, one of the wealthier parts of Toronto. I don't remember how old I was when I joined but I do remember that I sang alto and that I was paid for it. Each choir boy made two or three dollars a month, which was a lot in those days. Of course, we were 'docked' for coming late to rehearsal or for any other misdemeanour. I remember that Paul once lost a month's pay for tossing a comic book across the chancel during a service.

My piano studies continued through my adolescence, to a point where a piano degree seemed to be expected. My teacher, Doug Bodle, preferred that I go to the Royal College and the Royal Academy of England rather than study for the degree offered by the Royal Conservatory of Canada. To earn a place in either school the student had to audition: pass a theory exam and also give a full-length recital from a syllabus repertoire. The only difference was that for the licentiate of the Royal Schools of Music degree the examiners came from England. My examiner was Sir William McKay, the organist at Westminster Abbey. I passed with distinction; but when Sir William asked me whether I had ever considered giving piano recitals I answered, 'Oh yes, especially of French music, "Les Six:" Milhaud, Honegger ...' 'Oh, *no!*' replied Sir William. 'Never!' I missed out on a scholarship to study in England, to the keen regret of my mother.

Having left high school early, I was faced with the problem of what to do next. My art teacher (who knew very little about my accomplishments or interests in music) recommended that I try to get into the Ontario College of Art. I obtained an interview and brought along several of my drawings and paintings. The interviewer looked at them and then looked at me. 'Do you have a problem with your right eye?' he asked. In those days I was very self-conscious about my eye. 'I have an artificial eye,' I replied. (I never used the term 'glass eye', because that was what the boys in elementary school called me before they beat me up in the schoolyard.) The interviewer replaced my art works in the portfolio and said: 'With sight in one eye only I wouldn't recommend a career in art.' I have often wondered since how many great artists have 'suffered' from imperfect vision – colour blindness or, in the case of El Greco, myopia.

That same year the Faculty of Music at the University of Toronto initiated a new project called the Artist's Diploma Program. It was a three-year undertaking for students of exceptional musical talent who lacked the credentials to enter university. The students worked with the same faculty and took many of the same courses as those seeking a music degree, but concentrated on musical performance. They would obtain a certificate, rather than a bachelor's degree. By this means I was able to study composition with John Weinzweig and piano with Alberto Guerrero while taking courses in history, theory and musicology. Attendance in the faculty choir or the orchestra was also obligatory.

Alberto Guerrero was the most respected piano teacher in the Faculty of Music at that time. He was the teacher of numerous Canadian pianists, including Glenn Gould, who had studied with him from childhood. Guerrero was born in Chile in 1886 and came to Canada at the age of thirty-two, after concertizing extensively in New York and elsewhere in the United States. I studied with Guerrero for a year and a half, beginning in 1954. Unlike most of his students I had absolutely no desire to become a concert pianist. What I learned from him was beyond music. Often I would go to him having scarcely touched the piano for a week. Then he would ask: 'So what did you do? Did you go to the art gallery or read a good book?' And I would eagerly reply that I had been studying the woodcuts of Dürer or had been reading Rousseau's *Social Contract,* and we would talk about that or whatever other things our discussion led to, after which he would say. 'Well, you'd better practise next week,' and he would shuffle down the corridor to the back of his house while I would let myself out the front door.

The other important teacher in my life was John Weinzweig. In order to appreciate John's significance in Canadian music history, one must understand that at the time, that is, post-Second World War, the Canadian music scene was still dominated by British organists – except for Quebec where it was dominated by organists from France, and nuns. These bastions of power were not immediately sympathetic to someone who had graduated from the Eastman School of Music in Rochester, New York, where he had been introduced to the twelve-tone music of Arnold Schoenberg as well as American adventurers like Charles Ives and Aaron Copland. Nevertheless, John was offered a job teaching theory and composition in the Faculty of Music at the University of Toronto.

The first works I wrote under his supervision were definitely not atonal, rather polytonal. My heroes were still Poulenc, Milhaud and Honegger; Jean Cocteau was their champion. My works were filled with sunshine and happiness. Some of them had an ironic twist such as the song *A Music Lesson,* in which the singer explains the technique of polytonality while the piano illustrates it. Although John was quite decisive in his own musical opinions and compositional style, he never tried to force his students to adopt his style or philosophy as do many European composition teachers. In fact, towards the end of my studies with him I wrote *Concerto for Harpsichord and Eight Wind Instruments,* in my polytonal style. After I played it through to him he picked up the phone and called a senior producer at the CBC in Montreal recommending it for broadcast and recording, which eventually came about. After I left Toronto my meetings with John were not regular although they continued to the end of his life.

While John Weinzweig and Alberto Guerrero were the principal influences on me during my student days, another luminary who would eventually have a significant influence over me was encountered at that time: Marshall McLuhan. One of the courses offered by the Faculty of Music was called 'Poetry and Music'. It had been taught by Lister Sinclair, a distinguished radio personality whose knowledge of English poetry and song was augmented by a sincere love of the song-cycles of Schubert, Schumann and Hugo Wolf. The course was filled with attractive sopranos and loud-mouthed tenors – and it remained full until the day McLuhan stepped in to take over from the ailing Sinclair. Of course, McLuhan knew English poetry well, but his knowledge of music was limited to the Detroit jazz scene and soon the students began to drop out until there were only about four or five of us left. Sensing the problem, McLuhan invited us to come over to his house one evening. In those days he lived in a house, now demolished, on the St. Michael's College campus. McLuhan had also invited a few

'Lucifer'

students from his English courses. Benches had replaced easy chairs in what would have been the living room. These were arranged against all the walls and McLuhan sat on a revolving piano stool in the centre. I remember the evening quite vividly. We were served beer and buttered toast and McLuhan invited us to ask questions or make comments. One of the first questioners was a boy with a bad stutter. 'Professor Ma-Ma-Ma-McLuhan, I, I, I'm having t-t-t-trouble with *Fin-fin-finnegans Wake*!' McLuhan wheeled about and said: 'The *Wake* is not a story, it's a radio program.' Then he recited the first paragraph, staring the student in the eye. 'Riverrun, past Eve and Adam's, from swerve of shore to bend of bay, brings us by a commodius vicus of recirculation back to Howth Castle and Environs.' 'Th-th-thank you,' said the student. I was so impressed that I went home and memorized the whole first page of the *Wake* in case the occasion should arise that I might find it useful; and it has proved useful at various drunken parties ever since. Actually, sometime in the sixties or seventies, the Irish radio did turn it into a twenty-four-hour radio program.

Despite the pleasure of working with Weinzweig and Guerrero, and meeting McLuhan, I was having difficulty in several other courses. Things were building to some kind of climax around Christmas time of my second year. In many ways, the university was a place that cared for authority rather than invention. For one thing, attendance was compulsory and a roll-call preceded every lecture. I hated these rules, which seemed the very antithesis of imaginative scholarship.

In those days the university choir was conducted by Dr Richard Johnston, a tempestuous Texan whose face burned red during the temper tantrums that he seemed incapable of controlling. We used to call him 'Furnace Face'. I resented having to sing in his choir since I had sung and was still singing more interesting music in the Grace Church Choir. The English choral tradition was still quite strong in Canada in those days, with a repertoire that extended back to Elizabethan times. When you've sung Thomas Tallis and William Byrd motets, or Handel's *Messiah* with multiple choirs and orchestra, as we did each year in Massey Hall, the prospect of drooling over sappy pop songs is not at all inspiring. So I used to take large art-books with me to the rehearsals and calmly inspect them while the choir floundered through a repertoire of tasteless and toothless choral music.

'Choir stand up!' commanded Dr Johnston from the top of the

chair he always stood on. The choir stood up. 'Choir sit down!' came the abrupt contravening order. The choir sat down. 'Choir and Mr Schafer stand up!' bellowed the commander. Schafer calmly turned the pages of his book on Rouault or Cézanne. 'Schafer!' screamed the doctor. 'Stand up!' Several girls began to swoon, recognizing the symptoms of the well-known tantrum that would sour the mood for the rest of the evening. 'Come up here!' Nonchalantly I wandered to the front carrying my precious book. 'Sit there!' ordered Il Duce, pointing to an empty chair directly in front of him. 'Now, once again, CHOIR AND MR SCHAFER, STAND UP!' The choir stood up. Schafer opened his book and began to read. 'SCHAFER!' It was the loudest sound the school had ever heard. The dust rose from the windowsills and the lights flickered. Dr Johnston leapt in the air, landing with such force that his feet went clear through the seat of his chair. I looked up to see him furiously waving his baton only a few feet in front of my nose. I did the only natural thing. I got up and ran away. He lunged after me but the legs of the chair trapped him and he came clattering to the ground. As I darted out the door, I saw girls hurrying to pick him up off the floor.

Now, before I go on, let me say that Richard Johnston and I grew to be friends in later years. We never spoke of that incident again. More important concerns united us. Chief among these was the fight to establish Canadian music as a subject fit to be taught and performed in Canadian schools and universities. The good doctor went on to establish an enviable collection of Canadian musical manuscripts and memorabilia at the University of Calgary and several of my manuscripts eventually found their way into this collection.

The other professor with whom I had a run-in at the U. of T. was Professor Rosy-Rear, also an American. Rosy-Rear was not his name but it is close enough. Of all the courses I had to take, his was the stupidest. Music education has never been distinguished by imagination but there are limits to how much stupidity a person can handle. It was during the Christmas exam that matters came to a head. I am not sure whether the questions on the exam were designed *by* a blockhead or *for* blockheads. I remember two of them. One was: 'What would you use rice for in cleaning a violin?' I have since asked many violinists this question without ever receiving a satisfactory answer. I even asked the famous violinist, Yehudi Menuhin, who didn't know either.

The other question was: 'How would you teach a hare-lipped boy to play the clarinet?' I answered this by saying I'd suggest another instrument. The rest of the questions were equally stupid and I rose to leave the examination hall after ten minutes; but the invigilator stopped me, by saying that I had to remain for a minimum of one hour. That was the rule. So I filled in the time by writing a little essay for Rosy-Rear on the subject of how music education might be more inspiringly taught. I didn't expect this to strike home and, in any case, it was probably a silly essay since I hadn't given the matter any advance thought. I recall that I concluded rather flippantly by telling him that it would please me greatly if he would give me zero on the exam because then, like Jean-Jacques Rousseau, whom I had been reading, I would have the distinction, if not of being better than my fellow man, at least of being different.

I expected to get zero on the exam but I suppose the essay was a little thick for the good professor with the result that he simply handed it over to the faculty director, Dr Arnold Walter. Dr Walter was a brooding Spenglerian sort of man who reserved his smiles for his dinner; at least, no one had ever seen him smile in the faculty corridors. He was, to be fair, an excellent lecturer, illustrating talks on Beethoven and Wagner with rhapsodic piano accompaniments. With him, after lectures, I would venture to talk about Martin Heidegger or Jean-Paul Sartre. I don't know what he really knew about these people but, to the sophomoric mind, he seemed to know a great deal and I admired the latitude of his learning. He and McLuhan were the only two lecturers who really set me thinking in those days.

Anyway, I was summoned that day to Dr Walter's office. When I entered he was clenching his fists into little balls and squeezing himself. Suddenly he pounded the desk and roared: 'I too haf read Jean-Jacques Rousseau!' The violence of the assertion was startling. It seemed to preclude any rational discussion of Rousseau's philosophy. I was told that I must apologize in writing to the two wounded professors or I would have to leave the school. A picture was painted of a young man forced forever to do menial work because he lacked a university education. A contrasting picture was sketched of an ambitious scholar going on to graduate school for which scholarships were tantalizingly touched on. Princeton University was mentioned. I was given twenty-four hours to think it over.

I returned the next day without having thought it over at all. I was hoping that, when his temper cooled, Dr Walter might be persuaded to discuss Rousseau's philosophy, and I hoped to learn something from him. It was a brilliant crisp day in mid-winter. The sun was shining brightly and the snow was sparkling. I entered Dr Walter's office and he said, 'Vell, haf you made up your mind?' I was just about to reply when I noticed the way the sun was shining through his ears. He had big ears – what the French call 'les étoiles'. I could see the little blood vessels in them. Then a strange thing happened. I laughed. It was one of those nervous little laughing fits boys get before they are to be punished. 'Get out!' said Dr Walter. 'I can see the sun shining through your ears,' I replied. 'Get out! Get out! GET OUT!' His voice echoed down the corridor as I left, never to return.

Years later I began to receive letters from the alumni association of the University of Toronto and began to think that somehow I had indeed graduated. Many years later the University of Toronto offered me an honorary doctorate and in my acceptance speech I told the story of my departure from the Faculty of Music more or less as I've just narrated it, to the merriment of the graduating class as well as the Chancellor and faculty.

My abrupt departure from the university opened up the big question – what next? Three things sustained me through this period of turbulence: the companionship of several members of Grace Church Choir, my love for Phyllis Mailing, alto soloist in the choir, whom I was later to marry, and two summers I spent at the Doon Art School – in spite of what I had been told at the Ontario College of Art.

Several of us used to go out for coffee after choir rehearsals. The general theme was music, in all its keys and declensions, though vocal music dominated. We also talked about literature and philosophy and, when the church initiated a philosophy study group on Sunday nights after the service, several of us attended. The philosophers chosen were religious philosophers – Duns Scotus, Kierkegaard, etc. – but the discussion was lively and was sustained in the village café until closing time. Phyllis Mailing also attended these meetings. She was a couple of years older than I was and engaged to be married, but that didn't stop me and soon the engagement was broken. We became lovers although we were not married until several years later in England.

ARTIST OR MUSICIAN?

DURING THESE YEARS I had lots of ideas for compositions but few works have survived. As I mentioned, I was enthusiastic about the French group known as Les Six and their pamphleteer, Jean Cocteau. In 1918 Cocteau published a pamphlet/manifesto, *Le Coq et l'Arlequin*, in support of their musical aesthetic. In *Le Rappel à l'ordre*, Cocteau said, 'Musical bread is what we want.' In other words, simplicity.

The first piece I let stand was *Polytonality:* a little exercise in three keys. Poulenc was my model. This was followed by *A Music Lesson*: I was the pianist, illustrating polytonality, and Phyllis Mailing was the singer, describing it. After our performance, I mouthed Stravinsky's credo that music is a non-emotional medium. 'Is that the way you feel about it?' someone asked from the audience. 'That's how I feel,' I said. Everyone laughed. I have never forgotten the humiliation of that day.

The work that followed was also largely polytonal, the *Concerto for Harpsichord and Eight Wind Instruments*. I had been studying harpsichord with Greta Kraus and hoped she would play it, but she never did. Her enthusiasm was exclusively for Baroque music and she used to give little concerts in her home. She also encouraged me to read C.P.E. Bach and Johann Joachim Quantz, from whom I learned a great deal about embellishments and rhythm. Greta Kraus came from Vienna and while playing through Bach preludes and fugues for her I used to admire the Kokoschka paintings on her wall.

The two summers I spent at the Doon Art School were important for me because neither of my teachers, John Martin or Carl Schaeffer, ever mentioned my eye as a handicap for an artist. On the contrary, they encouraged me to work in various media. They also introduced me to the great twentieth-century artists: Klee, Kandinsky, Matisse, Picasso and others. I had the greatest admiration for Paul Klee not only because of his paintings but also because I learned so much from his pedagogical writings. *The Thinking Eye* was the inspiration for *The Thinking Ear,* which I wrote after I became a teacher.

Doon had been the home of the Canadian painter Homer Watson, who in his day had been visited by Oscar Wilde and other luminaries

I was encouraged to work in various media.

I never thought I would make a living in art but I was later able to use some of the techniques I learned in art in my musical scores.

appreciative of the style of his Ontario landscapes. The school consisted of his large spacious house, a large yard and a row of barracks for the students. I actually spent a night in bed with a girl in this menagerie, but since nothing whatever happened, let me return to the world of artistic activity. Each day we were taken to a location, usually with a picturesque old house or barn on it and we fanned out to paint or draw it from all angles and distances while Martin and Schaeffer trotted around correcting our errors of perspective.

More important than the improvements I was making in my painting was meeting a person who was to become my best friend, and an influence on my work throughout my life. Bob Walshe was a young author who made his living as an advertising copywriter. He was extremely well read and, although he was only six years older than I was, had a vast library from which I was frequently to borrow books. For the next fifty years we were to correspond regularly and meet in England, Austria, Switzerland and, especially in France, where Bob finally settled, at first in Paris and later in Aix-en-Provence. At Doon I played him my early compositions on the rickety old piano in the living room, and sometimes, in the evenings, we would read and recite poetry with the other students. I remember John Martin one night reciting the whole of Rimbaud's *Une Saison en enfer* in French from memory.

Doon was a holiday. I never thought I would make a living in art but I was later able to use some of the techniques I learned in art in my musical scores. Returning to Toronto in the fall, I had to give immediate thought to making a living. My first job was in an ice-house, crushing blocks of ice for cocktail bars. It didn't last long. My father was still working for Imperial Oil and got me a job on an oil tanker. Some of the remarkable experiences I had over those nine months are as fresh to me as if they had just occurred.

ONE OF THE GREAT LAKES TANKERS was the S.S. *Imperial Windsor*. It was flat-bottomed like all Great Lakes ships and was therefore unsuitable for ocean travel, although it had occasionally sailed down to American ports on the Atlantic. I came on board as a deckhand in early March 1955. The deck crew took orders from the boatswain or 'bo'sun'. Our bo'sun was a tough Irishman whose career at sea had begun in the late days of sailing ships in the early twentieth century. He could tie a thousand knots and splice a rope or cable so that you'd never see the splice.

We worked forty-eight hours a week in shifts of four hours on, eight hours off, around the clock; but when the weather demanded or we were in port discharging or taking on oil, usually Bunker C, or were going through locks, we worked overtime, sometimes for stretches of twenty or even thirty hours with little or no rest. My starting salary was three hundred dollars a month, not including overtime, which might bring in another hundred each month.

The crew was made up of both rough and refined characters, some with twenty or more years of experience at sea. I was the only novice on board. My roommate, Dave Price, was a well-seasoned wheelsman from England who had an astonishing library of books: Schopenhauer, Kant, Giordano Bruno and Dylan Thomas among others. At the other extreme was 'Frenchie', a towering giant with the largest head and lowest brow I have ever seen. He took a strong dislike to me from the beginning and every time we met alone on a catwalk he would clutch the hunting knife that perpetually graced his belt and say: 'Someday I keel you!'

Sailors, I soon learned, had two topics of conversation: women and ships. While at sea they talked about nothing but women; when they hit port they headed for the nearest pub and talked about ships. There was a custom that whoever was the last to finish his beer had to pay for the whole round; or at least this was the custom as explained to me when we were in a pub in Toledo shortly after I came on board. At the end of the evening I had paid for a dozen rounds and still had six drafts in front of me before we staggered back to the ship and set sail into a terrible storm on Lake Erie. Lake Erie is the shallowest of the Great Lakes but is also the roughest. Lake Huron and Lake Superior have a bigger swell but the Lake Erie waves pitch faster and harder. I have never been so sick in my life.

But as the months passed, I began to be accepted by the crew. They were basically a good group of men. Our isolation from the rest of the world drew us together. Although half their vocabulary consisted of expletives, no offence was intended. Many of them read books since there was no television and radio reception was unpredictable.

Deckhands spent most of their time at sea chipping rusty paint off the decks and repainting them. When there was nothing more urgent to be done we would 'soogie' (i.e., scrub) the decks for no particular purpose that I could detect. The bo'sun would also make sure we knew our knots, and there were a lot of them: manila, bolon, stick bolon, and half a dozen different kinds of hitches. Many of these were used in working with the shore crew to tie up the ship in port or when going through canal locks. For instance, the bolon was used when tying heaving lines to cables. The heaving lines were then thrown to longshoremen and winches would let out the cables. The bolon could be undone with a yank and the cables would be put around the bollards. There was always a spare heaving line if the first didn't reach its target, but whoever threw it would be docked pay for inefficiency. There was always potential danger involved in manoeuvring a ship into its berth between other vessels, and a badly coiled heaving line could sometimes miss its target.

By far the hardest work a deckhand encountered was when we were going through the old St Lawrence canal system. There were twenty-two locks beginning at Iroquois, Ontario, then continuing to Morrisburg, Long Sault, Soulange and Lachine before reaching Montreal, and it all amounted to twenty-five or thirty hours of hard work with short breaks between the locks. The locks were just long and wide enough to take the ship so, as we approached each lock, the ship's engine would be cut and a snub cable, about an inch thick and as much as three hundred feet long, was let out for one of the deckhands to pull ahead and throw over a bollard. The windlass could then pull the ship forward slowly. Sometimes other ships were ahead of us and we had to wait, barely moving forward, for hours. The only rest the deckhands got was when the ship crossed Lac François – maybe a half an hour or so. The exercise went on day and night until we were through all the locks. I still have a vivid memory of entering Montreal via the Lachine Canal in the silence of the night when the only sounds to be heard were the water rats scampering around my feet as the black hulk of the ship inched its way through the water.

In the evenings of fair-weather days, the girls of all the villages around the locks would come and flirt, laughing, singing and sometimes throwing flowers at us. They knew they were safe since we couldn't leave the ship, but they liked to see us flexing our sun-tanned muscles and daring them to jump on board.

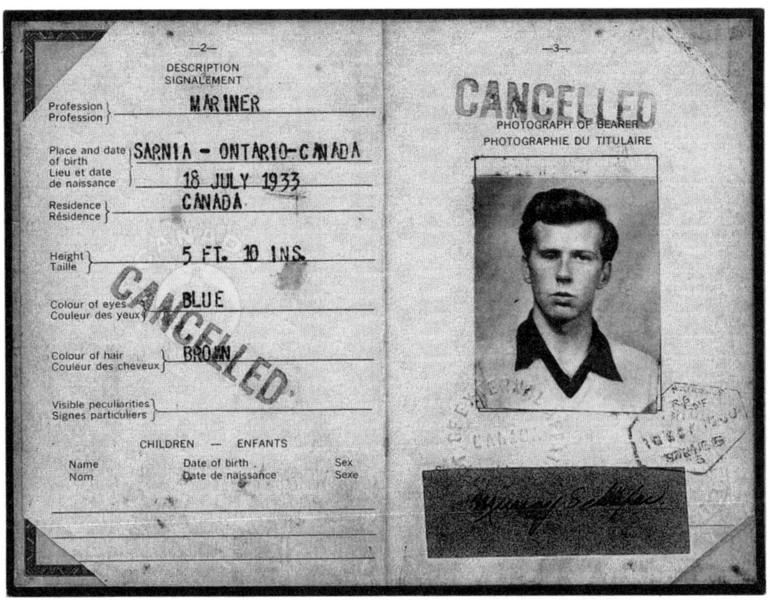
—2—

DESCRIPTION
SIGNALEMENT

Profession / Profession: MARINER

Place and date of birth / Lieu et date de naissance: SARNIA - ONTARIO-CANADA, 18 JULY 1933

Residence / Résidence: CANADA

Height / Taille: 5 FT. 10 INS.

Colour of eyes / Couleur des yeux: BLUE

Colour of hair / Couleur des cheveux: BROWN

Visible peculiarities / Signes particuliers:

CHILDREN — ENFANTS

Name / Nom	Date of birth / Date de naissance	Sex / Sexe

CANCELLED

—3—

CANCELLED

PHOTOGRAPH OF BEARER
PHOTOGRAPHIE DU TITULAIRE

One of the most amazing experiences of my time on the S.S. *Imperial Windsor* was to see the mirage of a ship that wasn't there. I thought immediately of the *Flying Dutchman*. It was a misty morning but overhead we could still see the outline of the sun. The mirage of the ship travelled with us all morning at a distance of about five hundred metres. It was startlingly real except that there was no smoke coming out of its funnel. A little before noon, when we changed direction, it faded away. The captain said the real ship, whose projected image we had seen in the mist, was probably five miles away.

Another memorable experience occurred one night on Lake Huron. I had by this time graduated to the position of watchman, and part of my duty was to spell off the wheelsman from time to time. It was always an indescribable thrill to take the wheel of this gigantic machine coasting over the waves under the moon and stars at night. In those days, the navigator plotted the course of the ship by listening to radio signals from transmitters at different points around the lake. Each signal had its own pitch and pulse: long-short-long ... short-short-short-long ... etc. On this night, as we were coming down Lake Huron, something went wrong with our receiver. The only signal we could bring in was that of a distant radio station playing Sibelius's Fifth Symphony. I will never forget that night: the foaming waves tossed over the fo'c's'le in the moonlight, blending with Sibelius.... No one spoke. We just listened to the symphony and the waves for a good half hour until the navigation signals returned. It was a good thing they did since we were nearing the shallow waters of the St Clair River where a lot of shipwrecks had occurred over the years. The position of these wrecks appeared on our maps and we had to keep clear of them, for some of the carcasses lay just a few metres below the surface of the water.

I left the *Imperial Windsor* at the beginning of November 1955, having saved a couple of thousand dollars, and returned home with the intention of going to Europe after Christmas.

EUROPE

I SET SAIL from Halifax on the S.S. *Ascania*, a Cunard ship, on March 3, 1956. Our destination was Portsmouth. The twelve-day crossing was rough and many people remained in their bunks, but my experience with storms had seasoned me and I remained upright. I liked to go on deck and watch the waves rush over the fo'c's'le. As we approached Portsmouth I had put on my suit, since I was to go directly to London to stay with my cousin Scott Medd. I was standing on the deck as the ship docked, and a seagull pooped on my starboard shoulder. I knew at once that I would not remain long in England.

My cousin, whom everyone called Medd, was a painter, still a bit under the Victorian influence. He also spent considerable time restoring paintings and church murals. I had known him from family picnics in Canada and he encouraged me to come and stay with him while I looked for 'digs' in London. He lived in Chiswick in a large Victorian house with his wife and daughter, two sisters of his wife and his wife's brother, also a painter, allegedly of great talent, who was housed in a room upstairs which he never left. I never met him but got used to his hammering on the floor when he wanted his dinner, which one of his sisters would dutifully take up to him.

Medd took me to most of the London galleries, and I could not have had a better guide. He also took me to operas and the theatre and got me a pass for the Reading Room of the British Museum – which was not easy since this famous citadel was reserved for great scholars and writers. I am sure I saw Robert Graves there or was it W.H. Auden? At the door was a very old man who carefully examined one's pass. It was said that he began working there when Karl Marx used to visit the library. When a BBC interviewer asked him if he remembered Karl Marx he said, 'Oh yes, indeed! What ever happened to Mr Marx?'

Inside the famous circular library there were rules about access to the books. One filled out cards and took them to the centre desk where they were checked over by the librarian; then one returned to one's carrel and waited an hour or two for the books to be brought up from the depths. There was no talking in that library. The only sound one heard was the swishing of pages and the snoring of exhausted readers.

While I was there I resolved to write a book about the history of aesthetics, but I am glad the public was spared the valueless document it would have been had I completed it.

While I was in England I proposed to the CBC, through their London office, to do a series of radio interviews with British composers. To my surprise, they accepted the proposal and so I bought a portable tape recorder† and wrote letters to most of the better-known composers requesting interviews. I was to interview sixteen of the most prominent, from John Ireland (born 1879) to Peter Maxwell Davies (born 1934). In those days a lot of British music was played on the CBC and in Canadian concerts. The British Commonwealth was still intact, and the Canadian music scene was both enriched and enfeebled by the presence of British organists and theory teachers.

The interviews were later published as a book by Faber and Faber, and it received many favourable reviews. This was because my interviews concentrated on the compositional process rather than discussing career highlights. What is inspiration and how large a role does it play? When a composer says he hears music in his mind what is he actually hearing – a theme, a texture, a shape? Beethoven once said he heard a work mentally 'in its breadth, its narrowness, its height and depth … from every angle.' Does a composition sometimes get put together completely in the mind before it is written down? Is a piano or another instrument useful when composing, and if so, how might this affect the texture or the colour of the piece, for instance, in chordal spacing or tessitura?

I had almost finished the book but one important figure had not been interviewed: Benjamin Britten. I had written him but received no reply. So I did something very un-British: I took the train to Aldeburgh, where he lived, and knocked on his door. When he opened it I introduced myself as the young composer-interviewer who had written to him. He was obviously embarrassed and kept doing funny things with his legs. I could hear chatter in the dining-room. He and

---

† In those days 'portable' tape recorders weighed about twenty kilos and recorded on five-inch reels that had to be changed about every twelve minutes. They also emitted sounds and had to be positioned at least ten metres from the microphone to eliminate running noise.

Michael Tippett

his companion, Peter Pears, were giving a dinner party. I did eventually get the interview, though not on tape. I sent him the questions and he replied in written form.

Of all the composers I met in England, two in particular made a lasting impression: Michael Tippett and Alexander Goehr. Tippett lived in the country near Corsham, west of London, and he was kind enough to invite me several times to lunch, after which we would take long walks in the country and return for tea. Then I would catch a train back to the city. Tippett was my favourite British composer at the time. His was a music of complex energies that often seemed to be going in several directions at once. His orchestrations were often plethoric but, at the core, his music was pellucid.

My relationship with Sandy Goehr was different. He was giving a course in analysis at Morley College on the south side of the Thames and I attended it. Sandy was the most exegetic critic of contemporary music that I have ever met. Our classes hovered between acceptance and dismissal of all forms of modern music, but his illumination of the structures of music in pieces by composers as divergent as Chopin and Stravinsky was a revelation to me. I was later to work with Sandy on a production of Ezra Pound's opera, *Le Testament,* for the BBC Music Department.

'Yesterday I walked in the Vienna Woods.'

THERE WERE MANY THINGS about England that I liked, but I had my heart set on going to Vienna. I knew that Schoenberg was no longer living there, and that Berg and Webern were dead, but I felt that there must still be a legacy of students who could instruct me in twelve-tone and atonal music, so in April of 1956 I departed for Vienna. Like Berlin, Vienna had been occupied by Allied troops after the Second World War. In fact, they had just departed a few weeks before my arrival. My harpsichord teacher, Greta Kraus, had given me her brother's address in Vienna and I wrote to him with the hope that he might help me to get settled. To my surprise, he informed me that his son Uli, a medical student, had an apartment in Hietzing, a district near the outskirts of the city, and was looking for someone to rent one of his rooms. I went to look at it. The room was small but I liked it and immediately took it. Uli had no objection to my having a piano and within a few days I had rented a Bechstein grand for about a dollar a week! It was very cheap to live in Vienna at that time and my total expenses worked out to be about forty dollars a month. Shortly after my arrival I wrote to my family:

> My first impression of Austria is nothing short of wonderful. Yesterday I walked in the Vienna woods. The city is in a plain surrounded by hills and mountains. The buildings are all old but the streets are clean and everyone seems happy. The Austrians have a word, *Gemütlichkeit,* which is untranslatable and a Canadian wouldn't understand it if it were, for it means fullness of life, hospitality and happiness. When I enter a store the storekeeper looks up brightly and begins to talk of whatever is current. When I try to answer in German it makes him more good-natured than ever. Everyone I meet seems anxious to help me.

Tickets to concerts were then as low as sixteen cents in the 'gods' and about three dollars for good seats at the State Opera. I had mistakenly thought that the audacious spirit of Schoenberg would still be present in Vienna, but aside from an occasional performance of Berg's *Wozzeck* at the opera house, the anti-modernist spirit of Hans Pfitzner was more evident. Mozart dominated every concert that year, because it was the bicentenary of his birth.

During these early days in Vienna I was alone most of the time. Uli was at the medical school and didn't come home until seven or eight o'clock in the evening. Frau Jutta, who inhabited one of the smaller rooms and was our housekeeper, also worked all day at a hospital. So I spent a lot of time practising the piano, trying to get my technique back into shape. The rest of the time I spent trying to read German poets – Goethe, Hölderlin, Heine. Some of these were on the reading list of the German course I had enrolled in at the university. In those days, German was taught as a literary rather than a conversational language. To begin with, one had to learn how to read the Gothic script in which all books were printed; and then one was plunged directly into the work of the masters. There was no conversation in the class. One listened to the lecturer read from the books, and since many of the texts were esoteric I soon dropped the course and tried to improve my conversational ability by talking to shopkeepers.

Hietzing was a district that my mother would have called 'a very good address'. The window of my room looked out on a garden flanked by a row of elegant houses belonging to members of Vienna's 'upper ten thousand'. Schönbrunn, the palace and garden of the Empress Maria Theresa, was not far off, and I would often walk there in the afternoon. In the evening, I would walk the quiet streets under the pastel light of gas-lamps that made a faint hissing noise. My insufficient German made it impossible to find friends and I was perpetually lonely.

So it was that within a couple of months I decided to take a trip. We were quite near the *Autobahn* leading west to Germany and Switzerland. West was the only direction one could travel since Austria was then surrounded on three sides by Communist states: Hungary to the east, Yugoslavia to the south and Czechoslovakia to the north. So, with no particular destination in mind, I began to thumb rides to whatever places drivers took me. Nights were spent in youth hostels, which were quite numerous in those days; or sometimes farmers would give me a dinner and a bed at no charge. After a few days I found myself in Cologne, where I spent a lot of time in the cathedral. I had read Goethe's essays on Gothic architecture; they had helped to inspire the completion of this great building, begun in 1248 but still only half finished in his day.

I then went west to Aachen to visit Charlemagne's very different and much smaller Romanesque cathedral, where one can also see an unusual sixteenth-century altarpiece showing thirteen disciples seated with Christ at the Last Supper – the thirteenth member wearing glasses! He was the donor of the altarpiece and, since glasses were as costly as diamonds in those days, he is naturally anxious we should notice that he could afford them.

I then moved on to Brussels to visit Nicole, a young woman I had met on the boat-train on my way to Vienna. We had already corresponded, as young people often do. We went to Oostende where she had relatives and walked the strand for several days in animated conversation with intermittent kisses. Eventually, she had to return to school in Brussels and I made my way back to Vienna obsessed with my beautiful muse. Just to think of her inspired melodies, and many of them found their way into the *Minnelieder*, a cycle of love songs for soprano and wind quintet, which was probably the best work I wrote during my Vienna days.†

The absent lover was the theme of much or most of the *Minnesänger* poetry of the twelfth and thirteenth centuries; but in order to understand the lyrics of Walter von der Vogelweide or Dietmar von Eist, I needed to find a teacher of Medieval German. Eventually I located a woman who was a specialist in Mittelhochdeutsch. She taught me how to read and pronounce the language in return for my helping her to improve her pronunciation of English, which had somehow been arrested around the time of Chaucer.

As Christmas approached, the weather turned colder. It was time to fire up the *Kachelofen*. Each room in the house had its own oven reaching from floor to ceiling and covered with tiles, often in very attractive patterns. Each tenant in the building had a little bin in the cellar and would descend each morning to scoop up enough coal to last until the evening. The tiles would stay warm until late at night, long after the fire had gone out. The only problem was that at that time there was a severe shortage of coal. The coal came from Poland, a Communist country, and imports fluctuated with political tides and turns.

---

† Many years later I was to make an arrangement of the *Minnelieder* for full orchestra which Eleanor James recorded for ATMA Classique.

Austrian peasant.

When my friend Bob Walshe arrived just before Christmas, there was no more coal available in Vienna. Uli was happy to rent him a large handsome bedroom at a cheap rate, but without heat it was a pretty dreary space. Bob would spend entire days propped up in bed with a bolster wrapped around his shoulders, his pencil wiggling under his nose as he laid out the plot of a new novel. The background of the novel was to be the Hungarian Revolution, which was unfolding before us just a few kilometres away. We were informed that the Hungarians were escaping the Communist regime by walking across the Neusiedler See, a quagmire three or four feet deep that separated Austria from Hungary. It was the only escape route free of land-mines. So Bob and I went down to Rust, a village on the Austrian side of the lake, where we did indeed see clusters of refugees with their children or their possessions on their shoulders wading through the muddy lake to Austrian freedom. Tents had been set up by several Western countries to interview potential immigrants. Canada was one of these countries and I remember standing near the entrance to the Canadian tent where an official from the Canadian embassy was questioning a water-soaked refugee. He asked him, 'Have you applied to any other country before coming here?' 'No,' said the man. 'Liar!' said the official. 'I saw you at the US tent. We don't want liars in Canada!' That's how the decisions were made on a cold night in a foreign country.

Bob didn't write the novel he had begun, though he did manage to interview one or two Hungarian countesses during his stay in Vienna. He did, however, later write a novel about life in the book publishing world that was to be nominated for a Booker Prize. He was the most influential person in my life, aside from certain women. He directed my reading towards great literature, though he never succeeded in teaching me how to spell. Later, after he moved from England to Paris, he was tireless in the promotion of my music and arranged for *The Tuning of the World* to be translated and published in French, with substantial consequences for the soundscape movement in Europe.

Bob didn't stay in Vienna long enough to learn much German. I sent him out one day to buy some frankfurters. There were going to be four of us for dinner so I reckoned two each and told him to buy eight. He went to the butcher shop and, pointing to the circles of *Knackwurst* hanging from the wall, said *'Acht.'* The butcher proceeded to take down eight strings while Bob kept repeating, *'Nein, acht! Acht!'*

'Ja, ja,' replied the butcher as he wrapped up eight strings of sausages. We ate them every day for three weeks.

On the other hand, Bob was very lucky with women. He was either visiting some Hungarian countess for information concerning his novel, or taking out some Argentinian music student to a concert. Once or twice, he even lured me into attending by telling me that his girlfriend was bringing along a Bolivian or a Costa Rican friend, but whoever it was never provoked any itchy desires on my part. I preferred to spend my nights reading Franz Kafka or listening to concerts on my short-wave radio.

One night Bob and Uli managed to get me to go out for a walk with Frau Jutta. When I returned and went to my room, I was startled to see an enormous beetle hanging on the wall near the ceiling, complete with feelers and many little legs. It was the beetle of Kafka's *Metamorphosis,* which I had been reading and enthusiastically discussing with my friends. They had made quite an accurate artifact out of pillows, buttons and knitting-needles.

Bob Walshe left Vienna at the beginning of April 1957, and my social life came abruptly to an end since I had taken no trouble to cultivate friends of my own. I finished writing the *Minnelieder* and didn't know what to write next. So I resorted again to hitchhiking throughout Germany, and even went as far north as Copenhagen.

My German had improved and I could now carry on a half-decent conversation, so I decided to look up my German relatives who lived in Hildesheim. To my surprise, I discovered that I had a cousin, Marlis by name, a couple of years younger than me and quite attractive. My uncle Georg was happy to take me to the cemetery where generations of Schafers were buried but I was less happy to discover that they were all *Bauern* (farmers). I had secretly hoped that perhaps Charlemagne might have been a member of the family. Years later I was somewhat cheered when I read an article in a magazine by a genealogist who demonstrated mathematically that the whole population of the Western world is distantly related to the famous emperor.

Back in Vienna, I immediately planned a trip to Greece. For the sake of young readers I should point out that in those days there was little travel by plane and it was terribly expensive. One travelled by ship or by train.

THE TRAIN FROM VIENNA to Athens took forty-eight hours, and went through Yugoslavia. One had to take one's own food since the coaches were locked from the Austrian border to Thessaloniki. One was not allowed even to descend onto the station platforms, Yugoslavia being a Communist state. There were no sleeping cars in tourist class and the seats were made of wooden slats. I debated whether to take such an uncomfortable ride but the prospect of seeing the Parthenon and the Lions' Gate of Mycenae soon convinced me so I packed my duffel-bag with six bottles of beer, a lot of rolls and cooked sausages, and went to the station.

The poverty was evident as soon as one left Austria. At first, there were plenty of seats, but as we moved south the train began to fill up with Turks who were being thrown out of Yugoslavia, whole families of them, including dogs, chickens and other living creatures. Many of these were stashed in the lavatories, there being no room in the carriages or aisles for them. The costumes of the Turks were colourful and the women, whose hands were covered with henna, just smiled as I tried to explain where Canada was by drawing a map of Europe and the Americas, and they went on smiling while their husbands tried to explain that Canada was on the other side of a huge ocean.

I remember standing in the corridor eating a chocolate bar, closely observed by a little boy. I offered him a piece and rubbed my stomach to indicate that it tasted good. He took the chocolate, ate it, and rubbed his stomach as if that was a necessary part of the operation.

Passing through Serbia, one saw many shepherdesses: large, rugged women standing motionless like fortifications on the hills. They held branches across their breasts and seemed to be the omens of some tragedy. Occasionally a fire burned before them, for it was cold and damp.

We arrived in Thessaloniki late on the second day. I left the train and was immediately enchanted by the town, strung out around the north shore of the Aegean. The weather was balmy and outdoor seafood restaurants were spread out on the shore. I don't remember what fish I ate that night, but it was the best fish I had ever eaten. In the morning I tasted Greek honey for the first time in my life – another wonderful gastronomical experience. Then I took the train to Athens and booked into a hotel full of American tourists. The next day, I slipped out to hunt for the Acropolis. I could have asked the tourists where it was but I wanted nothing to do with them. I wandered the streets for half an hour, and then, there in the distance a mile or so away, was the Acropolis with the Parthenon shining in the golden morning sunlight!

I walked towards the Parthenon, transfixed, and spent the whole day sitting on its steps reading about it from the guidebook I had purchased. I even chipped off a little piece of the stone with my pen-knife and still have it, together with a few potsherd fragments and some Byzantine coins which young boys had found in the ruins of the Agora and would offer to tourists for a few drachmas. I need hardly say that in 1957 the famous sites were not under such strict custody as they are today. There were few tourists, most of them English or French. I also visited the Areopagus, where St Paul once preached to the Athenians, and the Pnyx, meeting-place of the Athenian assembly and the cradle of modern democracy. In an old notebook I find these lines, written while resting on the Acropolis:

On my back in the grass
between the marble colonnades,
drinking the Corinthian sun
in the endless quiver of the day.
Evenings I walk among the green pillars
reading the inscriptions,
or occasionally recline
by the windless sea
taking thrusts with my spear
at vows as elusive as fish.

I spent several days in these sites wandering around or reading Thucydides' *Peloponnesian War*. One afternoon, while I was sitting in the shade of the Parthenon, a young woman approached me and asked if I would mind her sitting with me. Some Greek soldiers had been bothering her. Of course I had no objection and after we had chatted and walked around the famous sites for an hour or two, she asked me whether she could buy me dinner by way of thanking me for protecting her. At dinner she gave me her address in Paris and told me that, if I ever visited that city, I might look her up. She and her husband had a large apartment with a spare room overlooking the Jardin de Luxembourg.

After several hot, sunny days in Athens, it began to rain, and I was forced to take my studies indoors to the library of the British School of Classical Studies. At first, they denied me the privilege of entry into the school since I was neither British nor a student of classical studies, but eventually they relented when they saw me sitting under a porch in the rain reading Thucydides. I had nowhere else to go. I was sharing a room in a cheap hotel with six men and we were not allowed to enter the room until evening.

One day as I was walking down the street in the rain a girl was about to pass me when she said, 'It's raining again.' I was surprised that, despite all my efforts to look 'native', she immediately spotted me as a tourist. We talked a while under her umbrella; she then invited me into a coffee house and we spent an hour or two chatting. We exchanged addresses as young people do, or used to do. It was dark when we left the coffee house and she led me up a lane where she stopped and kissed me. It was a tongue-sucking kiss of a duration and passion I had never experienced before. She kept saying, 'Let me smell your breath!' That was all. We exchanged addresses and wrote to one another for some time. I have never forgotten her, or to be precise, I have never forgotten the way she kissed. One day I received a letter from her which consisted simply of the following line: O MIKROS ANTHROPOS POU THA GINEI MIA MERA VASILIAS. (The man who will one day be king.) The play is on the word VASILIAS (King). She is VASILIKI (Queen). It is a disguised marriage proposal. Underneath it she wrote, 'How nice. I say yes!'

Here is what I wrote in a letter to my parents during my visit to Crete:

> I see now why Mediterranean civilization was the first to arise, and why it was able to flourish everywhere with so much colour and brilliance. All societies here live with an eagerness unknown to us in the North. Goethe somewhere remarks on the essential difference between Mediterranean and Northern architecture: the South Europeans could get along with pillars and a roof while Northerners had to fill the spaces with heavy walls as a protection against the winter weather. In the North so much is hidden that is displayed in the South, usually in its highest and happiest state. People

> talk loudly. There are no secrets in the streets or in the shops and coffee houses. Men walk together holding hands or often only two fingers. Priests in their black cassocks smoke and play cards with wagon-drivers in the taverns. Children pee and poop under trees at the edges of the streets.
>
> The monologue is unknown in Greece. Cyclones of dialogue are the rule. If you leave your seat for a moment on a train or in a tavern, it will quickly be occupied by someone else and if they do give it back to you they will either start a conversation or, within minutes, they will put their head on your shoulder or set a child on your lap and both will go to sleep.

As the rain continued in Athens, I decided to go to Crete to see the Palace of Minos – a trip that was to have a profound effect on my future work, since Theseus, Ariadne, the Minotaur and the labyrinth were to invade my imagination and appear in several of my works.

There are few secrets in the Mediterranean, which makes it all the stranger that the brightly coloured mosaics and painted pillars of the Palace of Minos should be bound so closely with one of the darkest myths of all time: that of the Minotaur and the labyrinth. I became fascinated with this myth during my daily visits to the palace. Books have been written (for instance, Hans Georg Wunderlich's *The Secret of Crete*) attempting to show that the Palace of Minos, despite its colourful frescoes, was actually a necropolis. But that is hard to believe when one visits the palace as restored by Sir Arthur Evans. My memories of the week or so I spent visiting the site every day were strong enough to provide the principal characters and themes of the *Patria* cycle, particularly *Patria 5: The Crown of Ariadne* and *Patria 7: Asterion*.

I was fascinated by the wells and cisterns of the Acropolis. Staircases leading down into a mysterious darkness have always attracted me. *Asterion* consists almost exclusively of corridors of darkness, interrupted by simple but very startling episodes of light. It was the cisterns of Athens, Mycenae and Crete that inspired these themes in my work.

While in Greece I also visited Troy, where I spent a day almost alone reading Heinrich Schliemann's *Troy and Its Remains* and wondering which of the nine levels of rubble was that of the Trojan War.

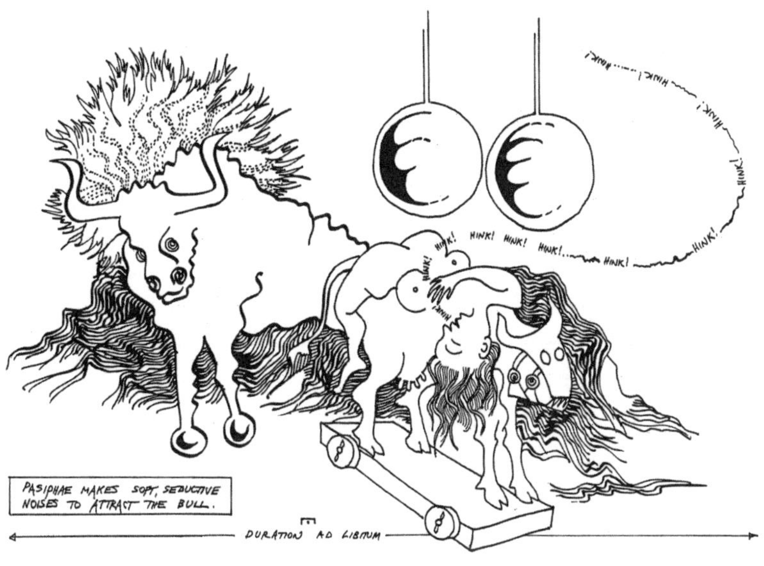

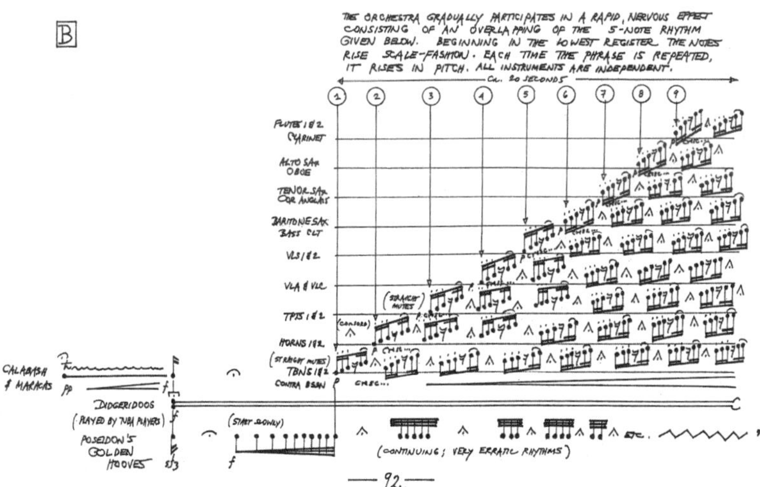

Pasiphäe entices the Bull – score from *The Crown of Ariadne*.

Schliemann thought it was the ninth level, but later archaeologists concluded it was the seventh. I spent the day quite undisturbed except once, when a peddler attempted to sell me a stick of wood he claimed came from the original Trojan horse. He had stacks of it at the roadside awaiting tour buses of which there were only one or two a day at that time. One arrived while I was there. 'Where are we now?' I heard a weary voice ask. 'This is Troy,' replied the tour guide. A few people descended to view the ruins, which consisted of a few disintegrating stone walls. 'We've got a Troy in America that's bigger than this one,' said a voice.

Following my visit to Greece, I returned to Vienna but didn't stay long. In June I again hitchhiked to Brussels to see Nicole but she was ill when I arrived so I circled back to Duisberg where I visited the Schiffahrtsvermittlung (Marine Agency) to inquire whether my seaman's card from Canada would allow me to work on a barge in Germany. It would, though I had no immediate intention of finding a job. I still had enough money for another year saved from my work as a seaman in Canada.

Back in Brussels a couple of days later, I did see Nicole, but it was clear that something was going wrong in my relationship with her. She took me to a jazz nightclub where the music was so loud we could scarcely converse. She wanted to dance, while I was trying to explain Goethe's dictum to her regarding the two forms of music: that which impels us to dance and that which inspires us to pray. (Hardly the right place to bring that up.) Nicole introduced the word *désinvolture* and explained that it means participation without empathy, in other words indifference or slackness. I was not sure whether she was accusing herself or me of this fault. I was afraid that this would be our last meeting and that, if so, I would miss her desperately – as a bird misses wings. She was going to spend the summer in Lebanon where her father worked for UNESCO. I never saw her again and she stopped answering my letters. But she remained my muse for a long time and danced in my dreams on her perfumed little cat feet. Lesson: 'He who puts his trust in muses will be greatly deceived when dawn ascends.'

I spent the rest of the summer of 1957 hitchhiking aimlessly around northern Germany. I paid another visit to Cologne cathedral and stayed in a *Bunker* hotel in Deutz, just across the Rhine. It had been built as a bomb shelter for German officers during the Second

World War. What a strange feeling to be in a little cell without windows in a building with walls of cement six feet thick. The only contact with the outside world was a tiny air-shaft with a slight spot of blue somewhere in another world.

I revisited my relatives in Hildesheim then set out for Lüneburg where Bach studied the organ with Georg Böhm. The organ is still there in the thirteenth-century *Backstein* Gothic church with its heavy, crooked tower. My reading consisted of Hesse's *Steppenwolf* and Kafka's *Diaries,* both of which had a profound influence on my work.

With nothing else to do, I pushed north to Hamburg where I remained for a few days. While there, I wrote a poem in German celebrating this city of ships, soot and grime. It began:

> Waren Sie einmal in dem Hafen zu Hamburg?
> Im Hafen zu Hamburg?
> Wo alle die Schiffe liegen gleich Toten,
> liegen gleich Toten,
> Waren Sie dort?
> Wo die Kräne spannen die Därme und Fäule
> Kreist durch die Luft wie ein Rauschmist,
> Und das Magazin steht mit offenen Mäulern
> Und lacht ein tierisches Lachen und frisst.

Despite its obvious mistakes, it pleased me to attempt to write poetry in German after having spoken the language for little over a year.

It was to be a long summer without Nicole either in person or in letters. Here is a description in my diary of a typical day:

> July 26. Rain, gloom and headache. Went back to bed after lunch, slept a little, woke, thought of where I could travel to kill a few days, slept again, dreamed of women with burned-out breasts (only craters remaining), thought of how absurd some of Novalis's aphorisms are, slept again, then woke up with a distinct premonition that I shall be blind by the time I am forty. Finally got up about 6 pm. Went to the station and bought a ticket to Flensburg then sat in the park and watched the night come, choking everything in its path. I wept internally but no tears came to my eyes.

Eventually I returned to Vienna, but not for long. It had been my intention to spend a year or so in France learning the language and seeing the country. I had had three or four years of French in high school, which was not encouraged by my father, whose solution to the French 'problem' in Canada was to 'make them learn English'.

ON SEPTEMBER 17, 1957, I arrived in Paris and was wandering the streets looking for a cheap hotel when I recalled the young woman I had met in Athens, and her invitation. I found the address and was astonished when I approached the concierge, who said: 'You must be Monsieur Schafer! Madame Delvert has told me all about you! Madame and Monsieur are on holiday in les Vosges but you are welcome to stay in their apartment. May I show it to you?'

It was a magnificent apartment overlooking the Luxembourg Gardens on the fifth floor, high enough to cut most of the traffic noise. I stayed there for a couple of weeks then, one night, just after I had gone to bed, I heard a key in the lock; Madame Delvert and her husband had returned. There were brief introductions as they were both tired. We would have dinner together tomorrow – and we did. But it was evident that Monsieur thought that we had done something more than just talk together in Athens, so the following morning, I departed.

I checked into a boardinghouse while I looked around the Rive Gauche for a studio-apartment – perhaps one abandoned by a famous painter or writer. My heroes had all been here in the twenties and thirties: Pound, Joyce, Cocteau, Stravinsky, Les Six, Picasso, Matisse, Kandinsky and dozens of others. While I was waiting for the ideal atelier to appear, I shared a room with a workman from Brittany whose favourite pastime was throwing knives at a target just above my bed. Fortunately, he had to report to work early so that the knife-throwing gymnastics were usually over by ten o'clock.

A few weeks passed without anything significant happening except that a very gentlemanly black man from Chad permanently borrowed my overcoat. In this and other ways I found Paris to be significantly colder than Vienna. People rarely spoke to you in shops and restaurants. Paris was also more expensive than Austria. I began to wonder whether a smaller city might be more friendly: Dijon, Lyon, Rheims…?

So one day I packed a small bag and began to hitchhike south with no particular destination in mind. As I moved further south the scenery improved and after about three days I found myself approaching Barcelona where I knew there were some important works of Antonio Gaudí so I kept on until I got there. Anyone who has seen Gaudí's works in their original setting will never forget them. They are so different from the shaggy buildings of ordinary city streets. I visited and revisited Gaudí's works until a slight tragedy occurred in the cheap hotel in which I was staying.

In the middle of the night my alarm clock rang unexpectedly and as I reached out to my dressing-table to stop it, I felt my hand push slightly against something polished. It crashed to the floor with the sound of a light-bulb exploding. Instantly, I knew what it was. I had smashed my glass eye. The self-consciousness of living with an artificial eye, from my childhood on, had never left me. I was cross-eyed during the day and one-eyed at night, since the prosthesis had to be removed and carefully washed. I was aware that my eyes did not look the same or move the same shortly after my right eye was removed; and for years I practised turning my head so that I would be looking straight at the object or the person and not sidelong, which would reveal my handicap. I was also aware that my artificial eye did not get red when tired and didn't even completely close in sleep or even in normal blinking.

Why did I keep up this deception? Why didn't I wear a patch over my eye like the man in the famous Hathaway Shirt ad? I have often said that a handicap, if not too severe, gives one an advantage in life because it forces the handicapped to work harder. But this was not the right moment for philosophizing. I had a spare eye somewhere in my trunk, but that was in a railway station locker in Paris. I would have to return immediately to Paris and search for it. So I wrapped a black stocking over the cavity, checked out of the hotel early in the morning to avoid inquisitive people and walked to the station where I took the first train heading north.

The problem was eventually solved, but I was still faced with the question of whether to remain in Paris or go somewhere else – London perhaps, where my friend Bob Walshe was now working. One day, I was walking down the Boul' Mich when I was suddenly surrounded by a group of university students singing songs. The fall term at school had begun. They dragged me off the street to join them in a terrace bar.

The Tivoli House in Angers.

When they found out that I was a musician they decided they wanted to form a choir, and I was to be the conductor. We vacated to somebody's room, nine of us, and commenced singing French folk-songs, aided by a bottle of *eau-de-vie*. At about five o'clock, we broke up and, as each person departed, they called to me – *jusqu'à ce soir!* Now where we were to meet that evening, I was never told.

I did, however, keep in touch with one of the students, or rather he kept in touch with me. François Tivoli was from Angers and in mid-October he invited me to come to his home for a weekend. I was surprised by the size of his parents' ancient house situated a few kilometres outside Angers. The house had the strange name of 'Feneu'; by way of thanks, I did several drawings of it, which I gave to them, keeping the poorest for myself.

François had two younger brothers and a sister who spent the weekends at Feneu and weekdays in a small stone house in Angers, where they were completing their studies in high school. I also met François's friend Bernard, whose father was the owner of a large hotel just across the road from the train station. Before the weekend was over, I was to move to Angers with the younger members of the Tivoli family, where I would stay free of charge in a small room on the top floor of the hotel. I was also invited to eat dinner each night prepared by François's sister, Madeleine, in return for giving her and the brothers an hour of conversation in English. Certainly, it was going to be cheap to live in Angers. The only problem was my unheated room. If there was any heating at all in the hotel, it did not reach the top floor and as November approached I was forced to do all my reading lying fully dressed under the bedcovers.

As usual, I was involved in heavy reading: Carlyle's *On Heroes and Hero Worship*, Frazer's *Golden Bough*, and Maritain's *Creative Intuition in Art and Poetry*. I also fashioned my itinerary for the next few years. Here is the list I made while lying in bed in the Hotel Angers one November evening in 1957.

1. Angers until Christmas
2. Toronto, January to May 1958. Earn some money, read the Bible and read Spengler's and Toynbee's studies of history.
3. France, May and June. Study French.
4. Travel to Italy in summer. Learn Italian.

5. Autumn till November in Berlin and Vienna libraries studying aesthetics.
6. November, south to Cairo. Study Arabic.
7. Spring 1959: At least two months on Mount Athos absorbing Byzantine culture.

Where was music? Evidently, nowhere. Nor did I receive much encouragement from the BBC jury to whom I had sent scores of my *Partita* and *Minnelieder*. The remarks of the adjudicators were as follows:

'Ingenious but doesn't amount to much.'
'Enterprising but neither orthodox nor truly modern.'
'Interesting ideas but the texture doesn't suit the style of musical thought.'

My reaction? I wrote in my diary: 'I probably agree with them though I have never given it much thought. I'm free and that's all that matters for the present.' I have no idea what happened to the *Partita* but I'm glad that the *Minnelieder* have survived as my first decent composition.

The weather continued to get colder. In my diary I find entries such as 'Twice to the cinema to try to keep warm.' 'Cold! My room unheated. Brings back thoughts of Brecht's *und die Kälte der Wälder wird in mir bis zum meinem Absterben sein*.'† In one sense the northern poet has an advantage, for he understands the poetry of winter. He learns to love the hearth as the southerner loves a gentle breeze. His poetry has more intensity. He doesn't write to entertain but because he is cold and wants to create warmth.

A postcard from Bob Walshe: *It's filthy with fog here so that all women look like Helen of Troy. Better come while it lasts.*

December 10, from Paris to London. Glad to see Bob again. His misfortunes in the advertising industry and his persistent family troubles seemed to be crippling his best years. His book was refused in both London and New York. But his conversation was still clear and

† . . . and the cold of the forest will be in me until I die.

brilliant. We talked of the Canadian culture we had both escaped. 'We should realize,' he said, 'that the people who created our country left the old world precisely because they didn't like its culture. What should we expect when our grandfathers were confirmed philistines. To them, life was all hammers and nails.'

December 15. Took a ship back to Canada. Lying in my bunk while the waves clattered against the bulkhead like an endless row of noisy feet, I wondered when or whether I would ever return to Europe.

SO I ARRIVED IN CANADA just before Christmas 1957, but according to the list my plan evidently was not to remain there for long. Although I have no diary to provide specific dates, my memory tells me that I returned quite quickly to England where for several months I shared Bob Walshe's basement apartment. Phyllis Mailing also came to England that year to study singing, and I remember her giving at least one recital of *Lieder* for which I provided the accompaniment in the spacious living room of the Hon. Wynn Godley, in whose basement Bob and I had our 'digs'. At some point in the spring of 1958, I went to Trieste, with the intention of taking a ship from there to Egypt. I was deliberately running away from Phyllis who had begun to discuss marriage.

I didn't go to Egypt but remained in Trieste where, for a few weeks, I taught conversational English at the Berlitz Language School – a job that James Joyce had performed in the same school forty-odd years before. Each day I would chatter away with my students until lunchtime (they all wanted to speak with an American not a British accent) and then I would eat spaghetti somewhere and enjoy a cappuccino. One day I got into conversation with a young man at the next table named Riccardo.

'To know Italiana language, you must reada Dante,' he said.

'I was intending to do so,' I replied.

'I helpa you find a nice copy of *La Divina Commedia*. My uncle own a bookstore.'

'Thank you.'

'But first you need a Dante jacketa. You cannota reada Dante in those clothings. I take-a you to nice shoppa owned by my brother.'

So we bought the perfect Dante jacket, then the Dante shirt, then the Dante socks. Finally we were ready to buy Dante's book. And we

The fountains in Trieste are delightful
except for the ugly nymphs that inhabit them.

The Prince's Villa, Trieste.

did buy a nice green cloth-bound volume of *La Divina Commedia* which I still have. Riccardo and I read faithfully after lunch each day, but one day he told me that tomorrow he was not able to come but was sending his friend Carla to read with me. I looked forward to meeting Carla but when she appeared she was a pudgy fifteen-year-old with glasses and the reading sessions soon drifted into oblivion. But I have read my Dante over the years and have set passages of it in Italian to music from both the *Inferno* and the *Paradiso* sections.†

Trieste had once been the most important city on the Adriatic. Her harbour had been full of ships. Banks had flourished. Bankers grew rich and their wives ate strudel with rococo manners. Now the banks – ugly buildings with pouting statues – were crumbling, for Trieste had been totally cut off from its inland markets by the Yugloslav and Austrian borders. Duino, where Rilke wrote *The Duino Elegies,* was only about ten miles west of the city. And Walter Pater describes affectionately the innocent diggings of Winckelmann around Trieste, trying to reveal the priceless legacy of Greece and Rome without success. There are Paleolithic remains, Neolithic remains, Celtic remains – the name Trieste (Tergeste) is Celtic, but of Roman times nothing remains but a toppling amphitheatre and a few collapsing arches. But I liked the relaxed atmosphere of Trieste and in 1960 I was to return with Phyllis Mailing on our honeymoon.

Later in the spring of 1958 I returned to Canada. Phyllis was to perform *Three Contemporaries,* a work I wrote for her shortly before I had left Vienna. The contemporaries, or almost contemporaries, were Benjamin Britten, Paul Klee and Ezra Pound. The style was very different from that of the *Minnelieder,* especially in the depiction of the latter two personalities, both of whom had influenced me a great deal. The concert was reviewed by John Beckwith in *The Canadian Music Journal* (Summer 1958): '*Three Contemporaries* was the success of the concert, and is as original a work as this commentator has heard from the pen of a Canadian lately.'

---

† *'Lasciate ogni speranza voi ch'entrate ...'* is the text of the choral section in *Patria 1: Wolfman,* and a lengthy text from Dante's *Paradiso* is the text for *The Love That Moves the Universe,* a commission from the Vancouver Chamber Choir in 2009.

BEHIND THE IRON CURTAIN

SOMETIME AFTER THE CONCERT I returned to London, staying again with Bob Walshe while I tried to figure out my future. I transcribed the interviews I had done with British composers and sent each composer a transcript of what had been said in the radio interview, asking them to amplify or change anything they wished. I also sent all composers a number of general questions, such as: Do you compose at the piano? Do you revise extensively? How many hours a day do you work? And so forth. Faber was to publish the book, but not until 1963 and I needed to find some immediate projects that would bring in some money. One day I read that the International Folk Music Council was planning a conference in Romania. Perhaps I could attend the conference with my 'portable' tape recorder and make some radio programs that I could sell to the CBC or perhaps the BBC. Aside from the folk music I could perhaps interview people about life behind the Iron Curtain. I was very sympathetic towards socialism at the time and felt that some programs favouring the better side of socialism (such as massive funding for the arts) might have some influence over the intelligentsia of my own country. The folklorist Maud Karpeles, president of the Folk Music Council at the time, suggested that the Romanian Embassy might fund my travel and living expenses at the conference and perhaps set up some interviews with artists and politicians. So I visited the Romanian embassy and laid out my credentials before one of the senior secretaries.

'So you are with Canadian radio,' said the secretary. 'What other organizations do you represent?'

'Well, I am a member of the Canadian Music Council and the International Folk Music Council.'

'Yes, yes, what else?'

'I represent the University of Toronto Press.' (Actually I had written some articles for the student newspaper.)

'Good, and...?'

'*The Globe and Mail* newspaper.' (I had once had a letter to the editor printed there.)

'Very good! More?'

'The Toronto YMCA and the Kiwanis Club and –'

The secretary had been attempting to write all this down. Suddenly he stopped and said, 'Comrade, you will be guest of the People's Republic of Romania!'

Filled with euphoria at my good luck, I spent the next days visiting the Hungarian, Bulgarian and Yugoslav embassies, where my petition met with similar success. I would visit Budapest before travelling to Sinaia, where the folk music conference was to take place, then Bucharest, Sofia, Belgrade and Zagreb before returning to Vienna.

I began to keep a diary of the trip. These are the opening pages of it.

> Departure Vienna, 23:00 hours, Monday, August 10, 1959. Hot and humid day, so that even the buildings, with trickles of water oozing out of the cracks, seemed to be perspiring. Evening, still warm until about an hour before departure time.
>
> In the compartment a Russian who lives in Paris, and a Hungarian girl who had just had a five-week holiday in Italy. The Russian will visit his sister in Kischinev, but must go all the way to Bucharest to make train connections. When he arrives in Kischinev he must stay in a hotel and eat there and will only be allowed to see his sister between meals. The Hungarian girl only got the holiday by courtesy of relatives in Italy. They paid for the whole trip. She is not allowed to take any money other than silver change with her out of Hungary. Her father is a novelist and is supposed to be well-known in Hungary. His name is Karinthy, son of the famous Hungarian humorist. While in Budapest I am to interview Lazlo Laita and Zoltan Kodaly.
>
> Budapest, August 13: Train sat in station from 5 a.m. until 9:15 a.m. I stretched out and had a sleep. From Budapest the compartment was full of Hungarians. Afternoon: The man across from me stares at me continually over a Hungarian novel he is reading, especially when I smoke my pipe. Later we talk of politics and he says that he is satisfied with the politics here – says it was much worse before, when the king was alive. His wife has a thrombosis on her leg which seems to hurt for she puts it up on the seat beside me, her leather boot practically on my knee, and winces every time I look over at her.

Talking with Zoltan Kodaly in Budapest (1959).

Later the whole compartment tries my can of cashew nuts and seems pleased with them; in return, they offer me a few kernels of pepper. At the border, a loudspeaker plays Romanian folk tunes and then comes out with 'Begin the Beguine'. We have to leave the compartment and stand in the aisle to allow soldiers to search for weapons or explosives (in case anyone is trying to smuggle them to Hungarian malcontents inside Romania). One chap with a flashlight looks under the seats and, coming up with a French matchbox cover, looks back at me over his shoulder from his position on his hands and knees and smiles sheepishly as he puts it in his pocket. Outside, a train loaded with pigs is waiting beside us and everyone makes a joke in his own language about 'pig-perfume'. Guards stand about the train, young men with their hands on their revolvers, but otherwise looking as if they would rather be swimming.

By evening we are climbing up through the foothills of the Carpathians, stopping finally at a junction to add two extra engines for the final haul up over the mountains. The station attendants come out and stand at attention with signal flags in their hands as the train passes, and at night they stand at attention with a signal lantern held out at arm's length.

Here the diary narrative ends. What follows could not be written down at the time. The experience remains vivid in my mind even at this distance, and though some details may get twisted slightly I shall tell the truth as I recall it. I warn the reader that at times the story may seem like the plot of a B-grade movie – but that's the way it happened.

I am on the train from Budapest, riding through the Carpathian mountains to Sinaia. The compartment is full of travellers, and among them is an attractive girl of eighteen or so who boarded the train in Budapest. As the night progressed, everyone got off somewhere except the girl. When we were alone I attempted conversation but she spoke no other language than Hungarian. Still we conversed with gestures and by drawing pictures and scribbling names on paper. I gathered that she was going to a town named Tusnad Bai, which must have been somewhere near Sinaia judging from the picture she drew of the railroad track connecting them. She had relatives there. There were a great many Hungarians in that part of Romania and, as I later learned, the Romanians were very suspicious of them, not only because of the Hungarian Revolution three years previously, but because the Hungarians had once ruled the mountainous region of Transylvania and had treated the Romanians badly. For instance, no Romanian was allowed to build a house with a window.

Erzsébet and I – for I learned that was her name – whiled away the night with our scribbles and our jokes. Dawn was breaking when the conductor came and told her Tusnad Bai was the next stop. I helped her to carry her things to the end of the coach. She had written her address and drawn a little map on a sheet of paper. Now she made a big gesture with her arms, meaning that I should come and visit her. I caught her arms and we embraced as the train came to a shuddering stop. She descended in the dawn light. I never thought I would see her again.

The train travelled on to Sinaia where I was met by one of the conference organizers, who explained that the conference was to take place in one of Romania's most important 'Houses of Creation' – that is, a place where artists, composers and writers come to live and create art, obviously according to socialist models. I was impressed with the organization of the conference, though less impressed with some of the papers delivered by the delegates. They were boring. It was during a lecture on the Chinese three-hole flute by Dr Lawrence Picken of Cambridge University that I took out and unfolded the paper where Erzsébet had written her address. Dr Picken was a great authority on ancient Chinese music; in fact, he wrote the chapter on it in *The New Oxford History of Music* (1957). But he was not much of a performer on the three-hole flute. He couldn't even negotiate the third hole, and I quietly left the assembly while he grappled with whistle tones.

Now what? More lectures or...? *Faute de mieux* I packed a little bag and walked to the station where I pronounced the name 'Tusnad Bai' to the clerk at the ticket counter. To my surprise I was handed a ticket. I really hadn't expected to get away with it in a country where officials were constantly demanding documents, permits and letters of authorization.

The train, packed full of peasants, arrived at the village of Tusnad Bai towards evening. I got off and was quickly surrounded by a group of villagers astonished that there were people in the world who spoke neither Hungarian nor Romanian. I showed them Erzsébet's note and someone who could read accompanied me down the dirt road and pointed to a cottage where the girl's relatives lived. Of course, Erzsébet was overjoyed to see me. I was led into a darkish room, the only one in the cottage, and made to sit down. The aunt immediately filled a bowl with goulash while the uncle smoked a long-stem clay pipe and tried to make conversation.

And so I remained there for the next several days, eating the same delicious stew each morning and evening. During the days Erzsébet and I hiked in the mountains and ate the paprika sandwiches her aunt made for us. The Carpathian Mountains are not so high really (the highest peaks are only about 2,500 metres), and the lower slopes are rolling and grassy. We flirted, hugged, kissed and attempted to learn each other's language, all quite innocently as we walked the paths and rested in the pastures. Nor did Erzsébet's aunt or uncle show any suspicion that we might be misbehaving. They seemed proud that their niece had a suitor from an exotic country like Canada. One night we all went to the village restaurant where I was the centre of attention. I drew a vague map of Canada on the tablecloth and everyone looked on amazed while I tried to explain the size of my country. Drinks were ordered and everyone toasted 'Canada' repeatedly.

Carpathian Village.

Romanian shepherd.

I only left Erzsébet when I realized that the conference in Sinaia would be concluding soon and would move on to Bucharest where the delegates were to attend several concerts of folk music from various parts of Romania. Romania is (or was) an exceptionally rich country in music and folklore. Even at Tusnad Bai I was frequently entertained by musicians and singers, and I once remember an extraordinary quartet consisting of a violinist, a cymbalom player and two men who created a percussive accompaniment by tugging a thick rope back and forth through a barrel – a sort of mammoth *cuica* (a Brazilian friction drum) with the barrel bottom serving as a drum head and the barrel as resonator. The violinist sang and narrated for well over an hour, sometimes playing, sometimes allowing the others to illustrate his story, for it was evident from the reactions of the listeners that he was narrating a well-known tale. At times they participated by asking him to repeat certain episodes or reminded him of other episodes he had forgotten. I was later told that the *Iliad* and the *Odyssey* were probably narrated and sung in the same way as these Balkan epic stories. Certainly the experience at Tusnad Bai was never to be forgotten or repeated, and though I promised Erzsébet we would meet again in Hungary, I knew how unlikely that was.

Returning to the conference I was greeted by Mr Ioanid, one of the organizers, who asked me where I had been the past few days. I knew that if I told him the truth it could spell real difficulty for Erzsébet's relatives. In those days, all visitors had to check into an Intourist hotel and have their visa stamped each night. I answered Mr Ioanid casually that I had been visiting some friends.

'Oh, so you have friends in Romania?' He seemed almost amused by my reply. 'What were their names?' I made up a name; and when he asked me where they lived I said I couldn't remember. It was just someone I had met on the train.

The matter seemed to rest there. I knew that Mr Ioanid was a Communist official, not only responsible for the welfare of visitors, but also spying on them for any information that might be useful to the Party. He asked a few more questions, but didn't press the point, at least, for the time being.

The next day we were to visit the city of Brasov, which at that time was called Orasul Stalin. Actually, it was a city of many names. The Germans called it Kronstadt because it was founded (in 1211) by the Teutonic Knights and became a Saxon colony. German was still spoken by many of the inhabitants, though the Romanians mistrusted them as much as they mistrusted the Hungarians. We had been taken there to visit some beautiful Teutonic churches and towers. Returning to the bus a young woman came and sat next to me. I had seen her at the conference where she was one of the translators, but I had never spoken to her.

'We missed you the past few days, Mr Schafer.'

'I was visiting some friends.'

'Oh, you have friends in Romania?'

'I met them on the train.'

'Where do they live?' she asked with seeming innocence.

It was beginning again. I said I didn't want to say anything about them because I didn't want to make trouble. Could we change the subject?

We did and began to talk about the history of Brasov. She said she noticed that I had been talking to some of the German residents. 'Practising my German,' I replied and said that the German spoken there sounded distinctly medieval. I recited a few medieval German poems for her to hear the sound. It turned out that the young lady was a student of literature.

The following day the conference moved to Bucharest. I was not exactly surprised to find the young interpreter seating herself next to me once again, nor was I surprised when she again inquired about my absence, but I continued to be evasive and managed to twist the conversation over to literature once more. She seemed fascinated when I quoted some poems by W.B. Yeats and Ezra Pound, authors she had never heard of though she had studied English literature at university. She asked me if I would write them down for her.

'Have you ever heard of James Joyce?' I asked, 'or William Faulkner or D.H. Lawrence?' All unknown. 'Then what modern authors have you read?' She mentioned the names of some English socialists, most of whom were complete unknowns to me. Those, she had been taught, were the great English writers of the twentieth century. Her curiosity about the figures I had mentioned was strong; also about Kafka and Rilke and Proust and almost anyone I could tell her about. We chatted all the way to Bucharest. From time to time she asked questions about my disappearance, but I continued to be evasive.

The next couple of days consisted of concerts of folk music and visits to museums and other cultural attractions. Corina Dosios, for that was the name of my interpreter, stayed close to me most of the time. My memory of those days is that we often had dinner together alone, though I don't really know how this would have been possible. Perhaps it was after evening concerts that we would sneak off for some wine and a barbecue. It was in the Balkans that I was introduced to barbecued meat, long before it became fashionable in the Western world.[†]

One night Corina began to weep. 'You really must tell me where you were, otherwise I will lose my job.' What was I to make of that? Was this a trick or...? Of course I had seen her talking with Mr Ioanid frequently during the Bucharest days, making her reports, I supposed. But my conversations with her convinced me that this emotional outburst was a genuine appeal for some information that would clear us both of conspiring against the state.

'There are things you don't realize,' she said. 'When you were missing, the police rounded up all the young men with beards in the whole Carpathian region for questioning. They're afraid of a revolution like the one in Hungary. You came from there and they think you visited Hungarians in Romania and brought them something – news or money.'

I knew Corina was telling the truth. I decided to confide in her. 'Look,' I said, 'I was visiting a Hungarian family, relatives of a girl I met on the train. They are poor illiterate peasants. I wouldn't want harm to come to them. I'm not interested in politics, and I certainly didn't bring anything from Hungary.'

Corina dried her eyes and looked at me. They were beautiful dark eyes, for her father was Greek. I may have kissed her then. I did kiss her for the last time a couple of days later.

The conference was over and we decided to visit a small lake in a park on the outskirts of Bucharest, where one could rent a rowboat. Corina seemed more relaxed than usual that day, though I do remember her looking around carefully before asking me if I recognized the

---

[†] I remember reading Kafka to Corina on a park bench somewhere in Bucharest. The sunlight drenched her light dress as she listened eagerly as if to prophecy.

name Ionesco. I said of course I did. He was a famous playwright in Paris. Again she looked around cautiously, even though we were in the centre of the lake, and told me to keep my voice down. Ionesco, she explained in a hush, had defected to France. She wanted to know something of his plays, which were, of course, banned in Romania. Speaking quietly I told her what I could.

It was dark when we returned the boat and began to walk through the park toward the streetcar that would carry us back into town. Suddenly Corina whispered: 'We're being followed!'

'Nonsense,' I said, 'you're following me, so who…?' But I did hear boots on the gravel some way behind us. Corina let go of my hand and we walked on in silence towards the tram stop. She was very nervous. We could see a streetcar taking on passengers and preparing to leave. 'Come on,' she whispered, and we ran for it. Behind us I could hear heavy boots running also. Breathlessly we climbed aboard. Behind us I heard the closing door wrenched open and two men entered. I don't remember what they looked like or whether they wore uniforms. I just remember Corina's terror. 'You get off at your hotel. I'll go home alone. I don't know who they'll follow.' It was impossible to calm her. When my stop came she pushed me out the door into the dark street. Like all eastern European cities at the time, there was almost no street lighting.

The two men got off behind me. The hotel was only one block away. I could even see a little pool of light from the lobby on the pavement ahead; but at no other time in my life have I been as frightened as I was that night walking that dark street with the clicking of heavy heels behind me. I reached the hotel and entered. The two men loitered about outside for a moment and then disappeared.

I saw A.L. Lloyd, the English folklorist, seated in a chair in the lounge reading. He had been at the conference and I liked him, though I strongly suspected him of being an English communist. I told him the whole story. 'Don't talk to anyone about it,' he cautioned. 'Go to your embassy tomorrow morning and tell them the whole story.'

But we had no Canadian embassy in Romania in those days, not even a legation. I could disappear and no one would know about it. I scarcely slept and the next morning I went to the British embassy and explained what had happened. The young man took down the particulars and said they would try to speed up my departure as I still had several days remaining on my visa and at that time no one could enter or leave an Eastern bloc country except on the day written on the visa.

I returned to the hotel, where, to my surprise, another young lady was waiting in the lobby to see me.

'Good morning, Mr Schafer. My name is …' – I can't remember what it was – 'and I'm your new interpreter. Today you wished to visit the George Enescu museum?'

'Where's Corina?' I demanded.

'She's not feeling well today. Shall we go?'

We went of course, but I kept demanding to see Corina or at least speak to her, and at lunchtime my new interpreter went off, allegedly to call her. She returned and said that Corina would meet us at such-and-such a restaurant that evening at seven o'clock. I don't remember anything about what we did that day.

Now here's where my story may seem to degenerate into the plot of a grade B movie, if it hasn't already; but I swear I am not inventing the following scene.

My new interpreter and I were seated at a table in the appointed restaurant. Corina entered the door, shook her head slightly and sat down alone at a table on the far side of the room. There was a gypsy orchestra in the restaurant as there was in many Balkan restaurants in those days, and the lead violinist was moving from table to table soliciting favourite tunes. He had played at Corina's table and now he was favouring ours with a sticky-sweet tune when he leaned towards me smiling and deftly dropped a folded piece of paper onto my lap. Corina then left the restaurant.

When I was later able to open the note it said: 'I'm being followed, but I'll come to the train tomorrow to say goodbye.' I hadn't been told I would be leaving tomorrow. Even today I can't unravel the mystery. If my departure date had changed, how did she know? It is possible that the British Embassy had arranged it and had informed the Romanian authorities – but how would Corina know? The one thing I am certain of, however, is that this was the message on the note and that I received it exactly as described.

There is little more to tell. The next day I was taken to the station and my bags were placed above the seat that had been reserved for me. I then returned to the platform and searched up and down. Moments before the departure I saw Corina running towards me. We embraced,

A deserted church near Sofia.

we kissed, we embraced … and then we parted. I never saw Corina again.

My next stop was Sofia, where I was to be a guest of the Bulgarian Composers' Union. The idea of a union of composers seemed strange to me, even stranger when I was ushered into a large building where the union president greeted me with open arms while outside his office at least a dozen men were loitering around, smoking. Yes, they were all composers and I was introduced to some of them, who immediately asked me how much a composer in Canada was paid to write a symphony or a film score. Having written neither, I found it impossible to stimulate either envy or admiration. I was asked to give a presentation of Canadian music and as I had brought two or three LPs with me, I was able to play them Weinzweig's *Red Ear of Corn*, Somers' *North Country Suite* and my own *Concerto for Harpsichord and Eight Wind Instruments*. The big hit was Harry Somers' *North Country Suite*, and with good reason; it is a strikingly original work. I knew that my harpsichord concerto was pale by comparison with Weinzweig and Somers, but the indifference with which it was received by my Bulgarian critics, together with the events in Bucharest, plunged me into one of the worst states of depression I have ever experienced. Neither was this abated by the gloomy city of Sofia with its drab streets and rattling trams. The whole city reeked of garlic. In the Hotel Sevastopol where I had been billeted, one had the choice of bowls of yogurt with garlic buds or bowls of yogurt without garlic buds for breakfast – and that was all. In the shop windows, instead of merchandise one saw pictures of merchandise. To order a watch or a vacuum cleaner one signed up on a waiting list.

The rich musical life compensated for the material deficiencies, particularly the uniquely wonderful folk music, which I recorded for my projected series of radio programs. But it was while recording a service in the Alexander Nevsky Cathedral that my recording activities came to an abrupt end. In those days the substantial hum of the tape recorder made it necessary to position it many metres away from the microphone. I had placed the machine behind a pillar and was recording the magnificent singing when I chanced to look around and saw the tape spilling out all over the cathedral floor. The take-up reel was not functioning. Technicians at Bulgarian Radio attempted to fix it, but they simply didn't have the parts necessary for the British-made

EMI machine. That was the end of my work and of the income I could expect from it. So a day or two later the composers' union arranged for my departure for Yugoslavia.

The station in Sofia was so crowded with people that the two assistants who were to help me onto the train had to raise my suitcase and my defunct tape recorder high over their heads to make passage through the multitude. But I was dumbfounded when I saw the accommodation that awaited me on the train. I had half a car to myself. A door from the corridor led to an enormous compartment. In one corner was an ornate wooden desk. Beside it were two plush armchairs. A real bed (not a bunk) lay at the other end of the compartment, behind which was a private bathroom. I uncorked the first of the four bottles of cheap cognac I had bought with the per diem the composers' union had paid me. The allowance had been generous; the only problem was that there was nothing to spend it on but cognac or wine. I was nicely drunk when I heard the click of boots in the corridor followed by the sharp military rap at the door. I knew that we were approaching the Yugoslavian border. Before I could get out of my chair, the door was flung open and two border guards, one armed with a rifle, peered in at me. Noticing my inebriated state and the deluxe accommodation, the officer pronounced the words, 'Ah, *diplomatichka*!' and gently closed the door without even inspecting my passport.

Yugoslavia was passed through as quickly as possible because of my defunct tape recorder. I carried the heavy machine all the way back to the EMI factory in England.

Corina and I corresponded for a while. Knowing that our letters would be opened and read, I had rigged up a code in which every fifth word constituted a secret message. It was fun constructing messages using this code, but what was it that we wanted to say in secret anyway? 'I love you? One day we'll meet again?' Eventually the correspondence ceased. The last I heard she was working for a Mr Popp at a folklore institute in Bucharest. That was now many years ago.

IT MUST HAVE BEEN IN 1959 that I received a grant from the Canada Council to study composition. A previous application to study the influence of Middle Eastern music encountered during the Crusades on troubadour and trouvères songs was wisely turned down by

Phyllis Mailing and I on our wedding day, London, England, June, 1960.

the jury. Obviously, there was an influence but I was not the person to reveal it. My second application was successful but carried the proviso that I was to study with a well-established teacher. My first choice had been Michael Tippett, but he did not teach composition so I chose Peter Racine Fricker. Many of our lessons took place in a London pub where we analyzed scores by contemporary composers such as Berio, Dallapiccola and Boulez. The principal work I wrote at this time was *Brébeuf,* a cantata for baritone and orchestra.

I had been looking for a cantata subject with a Canadian theme but it was Harry Somers who suggested Brébeuf, one day while we were walking in the Jardin des Tuileries in Paris. In constructing the libretto I drew on Brébeuf's own account of his voyage up the St Lawrence to establish his second Huron mission in 1643. Other works written at the time show a greater influence of Fricker and the works we were analyzing: *Canzoni for Prisoners, Five Studies on Texts by Prudentius* and *Untitled Composition for Orchestra.*

In June of 1960 Phyllis Mailing and I were married in the Town Hall of Chelsea. It was a double wedding; Bob Walshe was married to an English girl on the same day.

THE 1960S

PHYLLIS AND I went to Trieste for our honeymoon, then to Verona and Merano, where I was determined to see Ezra Pound. (I had met his wife, Dorothy, in Rapallo the year before.) Pound had recently been released from St Elizabeth's Hospital in Washington after fifteen years of detention for remaining in Italy during the Second World War and participating in Fascist propaganda. At the end of the war he was brought back to the United States where he was to be tried for treason, with a penalty of the death sentence. An international rally of protest by writers managed to get the penalty commuted to insanity and for the next thirteen years he was confined to St Elizabeth's Hospital (really a lunatic asylum) in Washington. In 1958 he returned to Italy to live at Schloss Brunnenburg, which perches on the side of a mountain high above Merano. The castle was the possession of Prince Boris de Rachewiltz, his daughter Mary's husband. Following his release, I had written to him to ask him whether I might discuss reviving his opera *Le Testament* for which he wrote the music to a text by François Villon, the fifteenth-century poet. Through Sandy Goehr, now a part-time music producer at the BBC, my proposal had generated substantial interest in such an undertaking.

Pound wrote back: 'Your proposal sounds unvenomed and innocuous. Don't come.' Well, I went. Leaving Phyllis at a hotel I took a bus up the winding road to the village of Tirolo a short distance from the castle. I knocked on the door. No answer. I knocked again, louder and a man in shirtsleeves appeared high in a tower. It was Pound. 'So, you've come!' he said. And he told me to come up. He was alone in the castle that afternoon. I apologized for disturbing his nap. He waved his arm. 'I have learned from my wife that you are one of the few people who ought to be let in here,' he said, and we immediately began to discuss the subject of music and poetry. 'Don't mind if I take to the horizontal,' he said and he lay down again, shading his eyes. We talked, first of his opera, then of his Chinese translations, and finally, inevitably, of politics. He complained: 'I'm supposed to be an animator, but what you observe now is a bit of derelict wreckage. It's a damn shame to outlive one's intelligence.' I insisted he was doing remarkably well. He bounced out of bed and sang a few strains from his opera, complained that he couldn't recite without his false teeth, located them and read me a few unpublished poems. 'I've just been lying here thinking things out, but they don't cohere. Your visit has revived me somewhat.' He lit incense and we talked about music. 'I'm only sorry that you didn't meet me while I was still alive,' he said, smiling. He invited me to bring Phyllis next day and stay for tea.

When we arrived Dorothy, his wife, as well as his daughter, Mary, and the prince were there. As the tea-hour was protracted by conversation he suddenly snapped: 'Schafer came here to discuss poetry, and the whole thing has descended into a God-damned tea party!' He then told Mary to fetch the books. Instantly dishes were cleared away and a pile of books brought in. He had marked each book with passages he wanted to read. He thought that the Chinese Odes could be very effectively set to music and I agreed with him. He now repudiated his famous style of ranting recitation, but he still had a strong voice for singing and sang most of the arias from *Le Testament* from memory, quite accurately, as I looked at the score. He was most keen on the intricate rhythms of the arias and I was amazed that he still retained most of them thirty-five years after he had sung them to George Antheil who wrote them out for him. This was to become a problem with the new production since the BBC wanted them simplified in order to save rehearsal time. But later Bob Hughes was able to restore the original rhythmic complexity in his excellent recording of the work and publication of the score.

He wanted us to remain there longer but an impending storm in the Alps and an interview I had previously arranged with Sir William Walton in London led to the decision that we should depart. I asked him how I would get hold of the score of *Le Testament* and he immediately sat down and typed out a letter to the Director of the Library of Congress as follows:

Give Schafer microfilm of *Villon*

Ezra Pound

As we were leaving he handed me a brown envelope and said,

'When you get to London give this to Tom.' Of course, one was supposed to know that Tom was T.S. Eliot, who was then an editor at Faber and Faber. The envelope was open and during the long train ride I discovered that it contained the latest instalment or perhaps the conclusion of the *Cantos*. Naturally, I read it. The day after I got to London I went to Faber hoping that I might meet Eliot but he was not in, so I was obliged to leave the envelope with one of the editors who assured me Mr Eliot would receive it.

The envelope I carried to London in 1960 was the conclusion to the *Cantos*, but it was not destined to be published for another twelve years. Pound was still 'legally' insane. His wife, Dorothy, was his guardian. Evidently, the family thought that there was more to come, or that the crumbling conclusion was an unsatisfactory ending to one of the greatest poems of the twentieth century in the English language.

At this point I was perhaps the *only* Pound enthusiast who had seen the conclusion of the great work. Can you imagine how many EP scholars contacted me over the next few years to find out how the *Cantos* ended? Researchers and critics phoned and wrote, asking for details. But details were all that I could recall from a cursory reading on the train:

> Yet to walk with Mozart, Agassiz and Linnaeus …
>
> …
>
> The Evil is Usury, *neschek* the serpent … the defiler …
>
> …
>
> Over Portofino 3 lights in triangulation.

The last line I remember because I had seen the lights on my previous visit to Rapallo. 'Why didn't you photocopy the manuscript?' the young reader will undoubtedly ask me. Because in 1960 there were no photocopiers and I preferred to admire the Alps, rather than copy a manuscript by hand on a bumpy train.

PHYLLIS AND I RETURNED to Toronto some time in 1961. Phyllis was able to make a living as a soloist and as a member of the newly formed Festival Singers, conducted by Elmer Iseler. I picked up some work from the CBC music department and also for a time worked as librarian at the Canadian Music Centre. But my principal enthusiasm was Ten Centuries Concerts. In a program note Harry Somers described how it started:

> It all started on a drizzly evening early in the spring of 1962. The place, of *all* places, Toronto. The exact location: the basement apartment of the composer Norm Symonds, alias the Skull, so called because of the gleaming condition of his scalp. Anyway, a number of composers had gathered to talk of all things. Skull was plying his colleagues with their favourite beverage, as usual, with the result that the conversation, as usual, got pretty animated. You see, to composers Toronto's musical life is like an enormous restaurant that serves only fish and chips, which is fine if you like fish and chips but even then, you can get sick of the same dish day after day, year after year. So naturally we got to thinking that there might be other people around who felt the same way we did.

The founding group of Ten Centuries Concerts in Toronto, 1961.
Left to right: Harry Freedman, Norm Symons, Harry Somers,
Gordon Delamont and R. Murray Schafer.

By the end of that evening, Gordon Delamont, Harry Freedman, Harry Somers, Norm Symons and I had hatched the idea for a series of miniature concerts featuring unusual pieces of music drawn from varying periods and in varying styles. Soon other musicians were to join us; but the rule was to be that non-musicians would never be on the board. Our initial meetings were beautifully anomalous, but before long we had our first promotional sheet ready, with our aims stated at the top:

> The institution of a regular series of chamber music concerts dedicated to the performance of rarely heard music of all kinds from the Middle Ages to the present day ... including various styles of jazz and works by contemporary Canadian composers.
>
> Groups and soloists of distinction will be invited to perform in combination with one another, and by means of imaginative and experimental policies in programming, various periods, styles and instrumental groupings will be compared and contrasted.
>
> The point of view of the series is that music is of primary importance; it will be chosen in collaboration with the groups and soloists and will represent what they themselves express an interest in performing.
>
> A further aspect of the concerts will be the attempt to relate music to the other arts. It is hoped in future that this aspect will be broadened to include the graphic arts, modern dance, puppetry, etc.

An attractive recital hall was just opening in the new Faculty of Music building at the University of Toronto. I went to see Dr Walter about renting it for our series. The events during my student days that had led to my dismissal from the Faculty of Music had been tranquillized by that time. The hall (which one day was to be known as Walter Hall) would be made available, but the good doctor was apprehensive about our proposed programs since his usual experience with recitals involved plump, graduating contraltos who drew audiences of no more than a dozen or so.

But we were determined and figured that, if we could sell the series out on a subscription basis to an audience of five hundred, we could survive. And by means of a diligent telephone campaign we did sell the series out.

What made Ten Centuries Concerts unique was that the choice of music always came first, above the performers and the tastes of the audience. In a lengthy article on Ten Centuries Concerts† I tried to explain how putting two pieces of music together on a program is like a montage in film. That law was formulated by Sergei Eisenstein and it states that two agglutinated pieces of film combine to produce a third effect different from the sensations produced by either piece in isolation. As examples from the first year of Ten Centuries Concerts I might mention the thirteenth-century *chant fable, Aucassin et Nicolette* paired with Schoenberg's twentieth-century *Pierrot Lunaire.* I might also mention that in the 1960s Toronto audiences were as ignorant of medieval music as they were of twentieth-century music. Another flamboyant experiment was a performance of Bach's *Musical Offering,* based on a tune that Frederick the Great had given to Bach, followed by compositions for jazz band based on the same tune.

Elsewhere in the series we performed Schumann's *Kreisleriana* interspersed with readings from E.T.A. Hoffmann's stories about Johannes Kreisler, the mad composer who inspired the work. The entire concert was presented in costume by candlelight. All music from the Baroque and early Romantic periods was originally illuminated by candlelight, a feature that definitely contributed to its appreciation, but has been extinguished from all performances since that time. In fact, one could say that electricity killed Romanticism. This concert interested me a lot since I was in the process of writing a book about E.T.A. Hoffmann and music at that time.‡

Ten Centuries Concerts survived for six years. There was no board of directors. It was entirely run by musicians, who chose the music, sold the tickets and operated all aspects of the series, backstage and front of house.

IN 1962 I APPLIED for and succeeded in obtaining a position as artist-

† See *On Canadian Music,* Arcana Editions, 1984, pp.2–35.

‡ Published by the University of Toronto Press in 1975.

in-residence at Memorial University in Newfoundland and in the fall Phyllis and I moved to St John's. From Port aux Basques to St John's we travelled on the legendary 'Newfie Bullet', a narrow-gauge railway that rocked and jolted across the island, taking about twenty-four hours for the crossing. In winter it often took many more hours, and I remember hearing weather reports on the radio in which the announcer would say 'Tuesday's train has been delayed and will be arriving sometime on Wednesday.'

Snowstorms are frequent and ferocious during the winter in Newfoundland. I remember one that descended so quickly that people walking in the streets finally gave up and knocked on the door of the nearest house for shelter. We lived on St Elizabeth's Avenue, normally a quite busy street, and by nightfall six or eight people had come to our door to sleep in chairs or on the floor of our living room. By the next morning the snowdrifts were six feet high and we dug a tunnel to the street where the ploughs were endeavouring to clear a path so that people could walk home.

At that time, there was no program in music or any of the arts at Memorial. I recall my visit with the university president shortly after my arrival. 'Just what have you come here to do?' he asked. 'I assumed you would tell me what you would like me to do,' I replied. 'Well, you have your office in the library. I'm sure you will find it comfortable.' And that was that. But there were some faculty members who had more definite ideas and within a couple of months I had started a music appreciation club and Phyllis had given a couple of *Lieder* recitals to a very appreciative audience. We also obtained a little money to invite some performers from the mainland to give recitals and chamber concerts. Of course in Newfoundland the weather was always a threat. I recall one concert in which a group was coming from Halifax, but they had not yet arrived as the audience had begun to assemble. About fifty hopeful people from both 'town and gown' stood outside the Arts Building and listened to the drone of the aircraft circling the airport (in those days there were no jets) for half an hour before the plane was directed back to Halifax. No problem. The audience returned the next evening for an excellent concert.

St John's had no symphony orchestra at that time, but it did have five eager conductors who used to meet periodically to discuss forming one. I was asked by the university to join the committee and it was

In my office at Memorial University, Newfoundland.

there that I met Ignatius R. Rumbolt, or 'Nish', as he was known. Nish knew nothing about orchestras but he was a wonderful choral conductor, particularly of folk songs. He had a great sense of humour and his choirs always smiled as they sang, although none of them were ever taught how to read music. This made him a target of ridicule by some of the British faculty at the university but he knew that I respected his talent and he often dropped into my office for a friendly chat.

In those days all schools in Newfoundland were denominational and there were seven boards of education. The music program consisted of brass bands and some of the performers were excellent. I can't recall exactly the circumstances, but before long I had formed an ensemble of brass players, most of whom were Salvationists, to play the *canzoni* of Claudio Merulo and Giovanni Gabrieli and the *Turmmusik* or tower music of the German Baroque composers. We gave several recitals in Gower Street Methodist Church with Dave Peters, the church's organist. Meanwhile, Phyllis had formed a small madrigal group, mostly of faculty members and their wives.

My appointment was for one year only but as the year drew to a close a campaign was mounted to try to have it extended. Fortunately, it was successful, for neither Phyllis nor I had any prospect of future employment elsewhere.

Phyllis had made a great sacrifice to come to St John's. To pursue her career as a singer, she needed to be in a metropolis. She decided to give her career as a singer one last chance and entered a competition for *Lieder* recitalists in New York. She won! And was immediately signed up for a tour in the USA. But after a few weeks of hectic travelling, she carefully considered her future and decided that she preferred the quiet environment of St John's to the frantic life of a touring singer.

Sometime in 1963 the Montreal composer and television producer Pierre Mercure called me with a proposal to write an opera for television. Pierre had a television program on Radio Canada entitled *L'Heure du concert*. It was an excellent program full of invention and variety. I recall one program featuring a piano recital by Claudio Arrau. The entire program was done with one camera in an empty studio. The camera followed the pianist from his entry at the far end of the studio to the piano, where he sat down and the title of the Beethoven sonata he was about to play was displayed on the screen. The camera then traced the form of the work, returning to the same

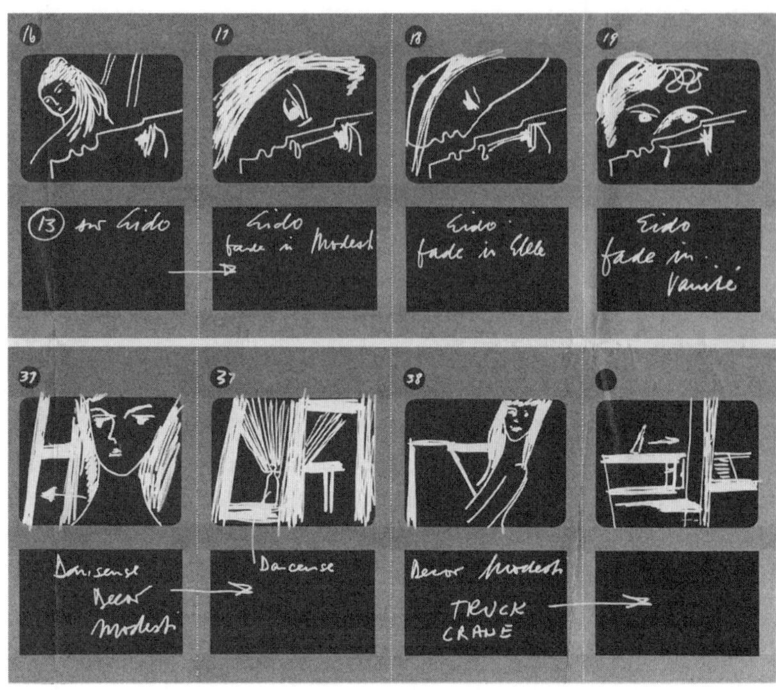

Pierre Mercure's sketches for scenes from *Loving*.

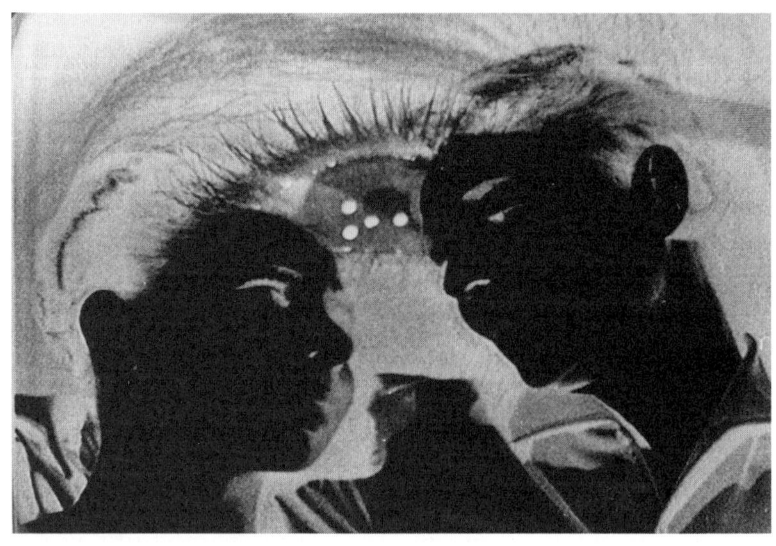

The opening scene from *Loving* on CBC Television.

position for each recapitulation and angling to new positions when the music diverged in an unexpected direction. The program was simple but brilliant.

I went to Montreal to discuss the opera proposal with Pierre and his assistant, Gabriel Charpentier. Pierre had taken a work of mine for soprano and several instruments titled *The Geography of Eros* to a conference of radio broadcasters in France and it had been well received. I was surprised that they would commission an anglophone to compose an opera for television in French. I suggested that we might consider a bilingual opera and that the subject might be two lovers, the man speaking French and the woman speaking English, in which the man imagines the woman as various personae: Modesty, Vanity, Eros and Ishtar, and the woman sings arias suggesting these characters. With this rough plan in mind I returned to St John's to begin framing the text by mail with Gabriel Charpentier, who was to translate the French portions of the libretto.

On January 8, 1965, I addressed the Humanities Association of Memorial University and my subject was *Aspects of LOVING: A Work in Progress*. During the course of the talk I played a recording of *The Geography of Eros*. The secretary of the Humanities Association described the event in the minutes of the meeting as follows:

> The work proved to be a highly unconventional type of opera – sans plot, sans characters, sans beginning, sans scene-divisions, sans conclusion, sans curtains, sans programs, perhaps even sans audience … A previously recorded excerpt of the sound was played back to a somewhat startled audience of about fifty members and friends who had not understood that to appreciate the jangles and screeches, the clangings and the swishes, it is necessary to divest oneself of all prejudice.

I didn't mind this childish sarcasm because I was about to spend considerable time in what was then Canada's most cosmopolitan city.

PIERRE, GABRIEL AND I worked closely together in Montreal for several months. I flew in from St John's for several days at a time. The

Music education exercises with children in Montréal in 1963.

Teaching students at l'Université de Montréal
at the time of *Loving* in 1963.

collaboration was not regarded without suspicion by Pierre's administrators. I recall I was once asked to refund $1.21 of my *per diem* allowance because I took a flight home an hour earlier than planned. On another occasion, I recall one of the administrators coming across the word *putain* (whore) in the libretto. For a moment his pasty face snapped to attention. Gabriel was instructed to find a euphemism, and a few days later, he produced the delightful expression *dévergondé*.

The problems were subsequently more complex. Pierre began to behave in a peculiar way, disappearing at times for a day or two and missing rehearsals. One day he called me to meet him in a hotel room. 'You see,' he said, 'I mess up the sheets on the bed so they will think I sleep here, but I don't.' I begged him to return since we were going into production but he didn't show up and the filming was put on hold. When Pierre called me next, his supervisor insisted on coming with me to a new hotel. We entered a darkened room. On the walls, Pierre had pinned up cartoons from the daily newspapers. He led us around laughing at the jokes in them. His supervisor immediately called for a doctor and Pierre was taken to a hospital.

The next day the music was recorded without the filming in order to preserve something of the production. The music, at least, had been beautifully prepared by the composer-conductor, Serge Garant. Months later (by this time I was in Vancouver being interviewed for a job at Simon Fraser University), Pierre called to tell me that the filming of the production had been completed and that he was going to France for a holiday. A few days later I was informed that he had been killed in an automobile accident in France.

It turned out that the filming had not been completed. Several scenes were missing. To fill out the allotted program time I was asked to go before the cameras to discuss the work. When the abbreviated version was shown, the French critics, perhaps more out of respect for Pierre than comprehension of the work, were generous in their appraisals; the English management of the CBC and the English critics were more critical. The work was regarded as 'experimental' and since that time in 1966 no further experiments in new music have been produced by the CBC on television.

Loving was presented in concert version by Bob Aitken's New Music Concerts in 1978 and was recorded at that time but it has never been staged in Canada. With music departments and opera schools springing up all across the country one might have expected a little curiosity but the opera schools are still slavering after foreign fare. Even Harry Somers' opera *Louis Riel*, which was commissioned and performed by the Canadian Opera Company to great success with the critics and the public, has rarely been remounted.

MY SECOND YEAR in Newfoundland came to an end, and we spent the summer of 1965 in Toronto. I had been approached by Bruce Altridge about joining a Centre for Communication and the Arts at the new Simon Fraser University in Burnaby, BC. While waiting to find out whether they would take me, since I had no university degrees, I taught at a music summer school organized by Laughton Bird, the director of music education in North York. I had worked with Laughton before, at conferences he and Keith Bissell had organized in Toronto. Peter Maxwell Davies had been invited to one of these also, and together we had pushed the theme of creativity forward, demonstrating that creativity did not mean chaos, as many teachers had feared. Later I was to write a series of booklets based on my experiences in music education, eventually gathered together under the title *The Thinking Ear*.† About this time the National Film Board of Canada made a documentary film about my work with a class of nine-year-old children over a week of activities. By the end of the week the children are composing, performing and conducting their own music.‡

At that time I had hopes that creative music education would be welcomed with excitement across the country, but this did not happen. The choral and instrumental programs were too well-established. Most teachers apparently felt that making music from found sounds – what the anthropologist Lévi-Strauss would call *bricolage* – was unworthy, poor man's music. While in Mexico or Brazil people make

---

† *The Thinking Ear*, Arcana Editions, 1986. The individual booklets were originally published by Universal Edition under the titles *The Composer in the Classroom*, *Ear Cleaning*, *The New Soundscape*, *When Words Sing*, and *The Rhinoceros in the Classroom*.

‡ The title of the film was *Bing Bang Boom*.

remarkable music from bones and shells and tin cans, in Canada and the USA the first requirement of a music program is that it should *look expensive,* with a lot of gold and silver instruments and costume flummery. I say this now after extensive experience teaching music in Central and South America. If you ask children in Latin America to bring an interesting sound to school you will be amazed at the variety and ingenuity of material that will be produced. Very good. That will be our orchestra. Let's get busy and make music. In North America one will get a lot of puzzled faces and the following day some students will confess that they couldn't find anything interesting to bring.

It is only now, forty years later, as *all* music programs in North America are being pushed out the door, that the low-cost Schafer method is being investigated. A little booklet like *A Sound Education,*† consisting of a hundred exercises in listening and sound creation, sells thousands of copies in Japan, Brazil, Mexico, Germany and elsewhere. Perhaps, one day, North America will rediscover that music can be made with the simplest materials and a little imagination.

In September 1965 I began my duties in the Communication Centre of Simon Fraser University. The bulldozers were still ploughing the cap off Burnaby Mountain where the university was being built. The noise was at times unbearable. I think the 1960s must have been the noisiest decade of the twentieth century. Jet aircraft had just been introduced for commercial flights, expanding the noise profile around airports enormously since they were much noisier than turbo-prop planes. Cities were growing rapidly to the unmuffled sounds of construction noise. Rock bands were pushing the amplified volume of music to levels well over a hundred decibels, louder than music had ever been before. It was also the age of what the Detroit manufacturers called 'muscle cars' – with more low-frequency vibration than in any cars before them. I also discovered when I went looking at houses in Vancouver that they were penetrated by more outdoor noise than houses in Ontario or Newfoundland because they required much less insulation for heat and were without storm windows.

---

† *A Sound Education,* Arcana Editions, 1992.

Students conducting and performing their own compositions at Simon Fraser University, 1966.

All these developments were to have a profound influence on my future work. I joined a noise abatement society but soon found that unsatisfactory because noise was an exclusively negative preoccupation. What chance did fifty or so people have against the multimillion-dollar organizations that were building our cities and expanding our economy? Over the course of the next few years, I was to develop a totally different approach to environmental sound by shifting the focus of research from noise to soundscape.

The Centre for Communications and the Arts was an experimental department very much inspired by Marshall McLuhan's media studies. The original staff consisted of a composer, a painter, a dramatist, a former television producer and a social psychologist (the chairman of the department). Later we were joined by a mechanical engineer. Although not all of the faculty embraced the concept of uniting media with the arts, I welcomed the opportunity to explore the new territories suggested by our mandate. I was able to build an excellent electronic music studio, which later, with the purchase of sound analysis equipment, permitted research in acoustics and psychoacoustics.

Our department was originally in the Faculty of Education, so I was able to continue my work in music education; but by 1972 we had moved to the Faculty of Arts and the dean of education wasted no time in appointing as my successor someone whose concept of music education was inspired by campfire sing-songs.

But our department's removal opened up new opportunities. My teaching methods have always been heuristic, encouraging the student to discover solutions to problems for her or himself. In doing this, the teacher should never be too explicit about the desired goal. In fact, the goals of a course should be as numerous as the students.

Sometimes I would limit my role to choosing a location and allow the students total freedom with their projects, provided they originated in the selected place. One such location was the corner of Hastings and Carroll streets in downtown Vancouver. The intersection of these two streets was in a slightly seedy part of downtown Vancouver. There was always a great variety among the projects undertaken by the students. One student might produce a portfolio of drawings or photographs, another might interview some of the old men who were often sitting on the benches there. The more ingenious their investigation of the site, the higher the grade, which was sometimes decided following an open discussion in the class. Once a student pasted a leaf on a piece of cardboard. 'What's this?' I asked. 'It's my project. I found the leaf at Hastings and Carroll.' 'You fail.' He got angry and said he'd go to the dean. 'Then don't forget to show him your project.' He dashed out the door with his leaf and never returned. The other students were pleased that they had received honest grades.

On one occasion I chose a block in Burnaby as the research site. It was a quite ordinary residential block with an empty church or chapel at one end that was rented out for meetings or parties. The subject of the course was to make a study of some aspect of the block that would be exhibited in the church hall at the end of the course, and to which the local inhabitants would be invited. I remember one boy making a detailed study of the architectural styles of all the buildings. Another boy made a scale model of all the underground wires, pipes and sewers, obtained from the public works department. A pair of girls requested recipes from all the women on the block, many of whom were Italian immigrants, and cooked up some of the recipes for the little gathering of students and residents that was the final event of the course.

On another occasion a seminar class of eight or ten students was given the assignment: 'You may do anything you want in this course provided you all do it together.' 'Anything?' asked the dismayed students. 'Anything.' 'Well, let's all go to a movie. Will that qualify?' 'If you all do it.' 'I don't want to go to a movie. I came here to learn,' said one student. 'Then what do you want to do?' Suggestion after suggestion followed without consensus. After about five weeks of discussion the students were getting desperate. 'What happens if we don't find something we can all agree on?' they asked. I didn't know. I'd never taught such a course before but I told them it would seem I would have no alternative but to fail them all. At the height of the desperation someone suggested they might make a movie of themselves and their frustration. 'Would that be legitimate?' 'If you're all in it.' None of them had made a film before so they were going to need some technical support. I invited a technician to the class from the audio-visual department to show them how to operate the necessary equipment. They were about to go out on their first shoot when another problem arose: one of the students was a paraplegic. I reminded them that they all had to work together. 'Can you get out of that chair?' they asked her. 'If you carry me,' replied Merle – for that was her name. So, awkwardly at first, two boys lifted Merle out of her chair and off they went. They returned to the class each week to give me a report on the state of the film. They were beaming with excitement and so was Merle. The movie was completed in about eight weeks. The subject was the frustration they had first suffered in class followed by the liberating activities each student would prefer to be doing.

I invited them all to my house for a little party at which the movie would be premiered. I will never forget watching one of the boys, who happened to be the captain of the university swimming team, park his car in front of my house then go around to lift Merle out of the car. She was nothing but smiles that night and so were we all as we ate pizza and watched the movie together.

Now, was that communication?

I gave them all A, and of course the dean came to see me about the grades but I talked him into letting them stand.

In February 1967 I invited John Cage to visit Simon Fraser University. Merce Cunningham was also present and gave a performance with his dance company in the theatre. Cage gave his 'Lecture on Nothing' to a rather dismayed audience of faculty and students. At the conclusion he asked for questions. There were many of them, and to each he replied by shuffling a pack of cards and giving a prepared answer that had nothing to do with the question. That soon irritated the questioners and by the end only half of the audience remained.

But I will always remember how, when we returned to my house for a reception, Cage strode through my living room to a wall on which I had pinned up a few graphic scores of my own and declared, 'Oh, did you do that? It's very interesting.' Although we met seldom, John was always very kind to me and followed my work in trying to revise music education methods with much interest.

The other celebrity I brought to Simon Fraser University in the early days was Buckminster Fuller, who was probably at the peak of his fame at that time, having just designed the famous geodesic dome at Expo 67 in Montreal. 'Bucky', as he was called, gave a three-hour lecture with his eyes closed to an entranced audience, but when he was finished speaking he left the stage without giving the audience any opportunity for questions. He displayed a similar hauteur the next day while I was interviewing him for the CBC, stopping in mid-sentence when I had to change the reel on my portable tape recorder and continuing only when the tape was running again. Without an audience or a microphone he had nothing to say.

THE YEAR 1967 was Canada's Centennial and there were lots of commissions and gala concerts that year. I provided music for two of the exhibits at Expo 67: the Man and Life Pavilion and the Chemical Industries Pavilion. Both of these consisted of electronic music soundtracks to accompany films. I don't know what happened to the soundtracks and imagine they would sound quite jejune compared to advances made in that medium since those days. That is the problem with all electronic media: what dazzles us one year bores us in the next. Written music can still be brought back to life by live musicians whereas electronic music begins to pale almost immediately after creation.

I wrote one work in 1967 that includes some electronic sounds yet still makes an impact when performed today. This was *Threnody*, conceived originally for the Vancouver Junior Symphony. I wanted to write a piece for those young performers that would make them think about social issues. The Cold War was in high gear in 1967 and stockpiles of nuclear weapons were expanding. The text of *Threnody* consisted of eyewitness accounts of the bombing of Nagasaki on August 9, 1945. I knew that these extremely graphic accounts of suffering and death would affect both the performers and their parents, forcing them to consider seriously the consequences of nuclear war. The narrators were children and young people and there were tears after the performance. *Threnody* has been performed many times since 1967 and in 2007 the Newfoundland Youth Orchestra took the work to Nagasaki, site of the original bombing.

Another work written about this time was *Requiems for the Party Girl* for mezzo-soprano and nine instruments. This work, written for Phyllis Mailing, consisting of ten short arias, was later to become the source of *Patria 2*, the first of the *Patria* works to be completed. The narrator is a young woman, very disturbed, describing various states of her existence including, in the end, her own suicide.

Shortly after the performance of *Requiems*, John Roberts, then director of music for the CBC, commissioned me to create a one-hour radio drama as Canada's submission for the Italia Prize, then the world's most coveted prize in radio. I was grateful to John for his faith

From *Requiems for the Party Girl* at Stratford.

in my work. He was certainly the most daring and dedicated music director the CBC ever had. John put much more money into commissioning composers than any director before or since him and he was open to experiments; for instance, he gave Glenn Gould a studio and a technician to create whatever he wished.

The work I proposed to John for the Italia Prize was to be called *Dream Passage*, a one-hour drama incorporating *Requiems for the Party Girl*. The singer was to be trapped in an asylum or hospital, surrounded by doctors and psychiatrists; but the doctors and psychiatrists spoke only foreign languages so that a cure was impossible. John allowed me to be director and producer of my own work, much of which was put together in the electronic music studio at Simon Fraser University. *Dream Passage* did not win the Italia Prize but, with a little more editing and a restored title, *Requiems for the Party Girl* became the second part of the *Patria* cycle and the first to be staged live. In 1972 it was performed on the Third Stage of the Stratford Festival, directed by my colleague at SFU, Michael Bawtree. Phyllis Mailing performed the role of Ariadne, the heroine.

I was afraid that a production at the Stratford Festival of an atonal opera in several languages with electronic sounds would be beyond the comprehension or interest of the regular Stratford Festival audience, so I conceived a plan to buy all the tickets myself and resell them to students and new music enthusiasts at a reasonable price. I sent a letter to the Stratford Festival box office as follows:

> Stratford Festival
> Box Office, Stratford, Ontario
>
> Dear Sirs:
>
> I should like to order all the tickets for all three evenings of Murray Schafer's *Patria* 2 as advertised in your brochure. I enclose a cheque to cover the purchase of all tickets. Should you receive orders for tickets in the future, I would be grateful if you could turn them over to me.
>
> Yours sincerely,
> R. Murray Schafer

I thought the ticket price they had set was too low and I intended to scalp the tickets at double the price. Needless to say, they refused to sell me the tickets.

The production was excellent. Phyllis gave a superb performance as the poor, deserted 'party girl'. The orchestra was conducted by Serge Garant.

ONE DAY IN 1970 I received a telegram from the Montreal Symphony Orchestra. It read: 'Congratulations! Have been awarded commission by the MSO. Wire acceptance immediately!' I wrote back that, flattered as I was by their surprising offer, no discussion had taken place concerning the length of the piece, and of course, the fee they were offering.

I have always liked the music of Richard Strauss. And one evening, just after the details had been worked out with the MSO, Jack Behrens and I were listening to Strauss's tone poem *Don Juan*, counting the number of 'erections' of the main theme. The next morning I awoke knowing that I wanted to do a rewrite of one of Strauss's tone poems. This was not a particularly original idea. Several composers had done rewrites of classical works. Nevertheless, I had a clear idea and the work I chose was *Ein Heldenleben* (A Hero's Life). The hero of this work is not just Strauss, but Man, at the centre of the universe, dominating all other living creatures. I saw in *Heldenleben* a typical nineteenth-century idealization of human imperialism, and so *Son of Heldenleben* would have to be, to some extent, a send-up of Strauss's ideas.

I decided to use the main theme of *Heldenleben* as an elongated *cantus firmus* at the rate of a half note per sixteenth note in the original score. There would also be a tape of electronic sounds, mixing with the orchestra.

I sent the entire package – score, tape and program notes – off to the MSO and heard nothing for some time. Then one day I got the summons to come to Montreal to meet Maestro Franz Paul Decker, one of those majestic foreigners to whom we have entrusted all our major orchestras. I went (at my own expense) and waited outside the door until Maestro could spare the time to see me. Everywhere Decker went he was followed by two stooges who punctuated all his statements with 'C'est juste' or 'C'est cą.' 'You know, Mr Schafer, only last veek ve are performing ze rrrreal Heldenleben! Now zis ... foolish joke vill not reflect vell on us, not at all.' 'C'est juste,' etc. 'First I vould ask you to consider changing ze title.' 'No.' 'But zis is impossible title!' 'Impossible, impossible,' echo the two stooges. 'Audience vill laugh, but ze vill not be laughing at me, ze vill be laughing at you, Mr Schafer.' 'At you, at you, c'est juste, c'est juste!'

At one point one of the stooges asked Maestro whether he would like a cup of coffee and went and returned with (true, so help me) three cups of coffee, which they drank. It then emerged that Decker hadn't looked at the score yet. He opened it and asked, 'Vat is zis at bottom of page?' 'That's the notation for the tape of electronic sounds. I sent it to you four weeks ago.' 'I have no tape recorder.' 'That's right, Maestro has no tape recorder.' 'C'est juste, c'est cą.' 'Well, get him one,' I announced with sudden impatience.

A very strange thing happened at the first rehearsal. The MSO manager, Pierre Béique, came up to me and said, 'Monsieur Schafer, Maestro is ill today. You will have to take the rehearsal.' 'Me? I'm no conductor. The orchestra will kill me.' 'Then we will have to change the program and perform Tchaikovsky's *Francesco da Rimini*.'

'I'll do it.' And I step up to the podium. With the concertmaster beside me we begin the rehearsal. 'There's a mistake in my part,' says the bassoonist. 'And in mine,' says the clarinetist.

I know they're trying to unnerve me but I address their concerns patiently and accurately, scarcely looking at the score. The atmosphere calms down, grows intensive. Everyone works hard. By the time we get to the outbreak of the *Heldenleben* theme in its original form I am sweating enthusiastically.

A break. And then what happens? Maestro miraculously appears and without a word to me, steps up on the podium. Obviously, one of the stooges had called to tell him that the piece wasn't that difficult and the orchestra wasn't in revolt.

The night of the concert, Montreal is hit with a blinding snowstorm. The concert is cancelled. The premiere will take place tomorrow. The next evening I am to fly to England. I go to the airport. The flight is delayed one hour, two hours, four hours ... I phone István Anhalt to see how things went. He is ecstatic. He reports that he listened with four ears and all ears enjoyed it.

And finally: a few years after the printing of *Son of Heldenleben,* Strauss's publisher in Munich got in touch with Universal Edition in Vienna, demanding royalty compensation for borrowing the Strauss theme. Eventually a deal was struck by which 50 percent of all performance royalties go to the Strauss heirs; but I doubt they've been able to buy much beer with the proceeds.

A commission from the Toronto Symphony Orchestra followed that from the MSO a year or so later. The contract read: 'It is agreed that the work shall have a minimum duration of approximately seven (7) minutes and no longer than ten (10) minutes.' That is, the work was to be what Canadian composers call a 'pièce de garage', intended for performance while the patrons were parking their cars.

The sociologist Emile Durkheim, has somewhere said that in order to define the law we must break the law – therefore crime is necessary. *No Longer Than Ten (10) Minutes* defines the ritual of the concert by breaking it. I have often wondered why a work of art must be finished and framed, why, on the contrary, it might not proceed out of chaos, gradually emerge into clarity, then return again to chaos.

I had been informed that the new work would have the distinction of being first on the program 'when the audience was fresh'. I determined to confuse them by agglutinating my piece to the next piece on the program so that there would be no opportunity to open the doors between numbers, and latecomers would have to wait outside until the intermission. As the second number on the program was to have been Brahms' B Flat Minor *Piano Concerto* played by Claudio Arrau, I was quite pleased with this plan. My piece would be a vast introductory modulation to it, and at the same time would leave the Brahms fans standing in the foyer. I went around and carefully explained the situation to all the ushers.

No Longer Than Ten (10) Minutes begins out of the tune-up. The conductor enters and begins beating time, but nothing much changes; only gradually does the work gain definition. The climax is reached after a long crescendo precisely at ten minutes. Then the conductor signals the orchestra to cut and turns to leave the stage. But the orchestra continues to hold the last chord, only gradually fading down. Now the instructions are to go back to the beginning of the crescendo if there is applause from the audience and to continue repeating the crescendo to the climax for as along as the applause continues. When the applause finally subsides, the last desk of each string section is instructed to sustain very softly a dominant-seventh chord in the key of the following piece until the conductor returns and gives the down beat.

Smelling trouble, the management altered the program, saving the Brahms until after the intermission and substituting Kodaly's *Peacock Variations*. The percussionists, who were my friends, were totally on side, but the conductor, Victor Feldbrill, had reservations. He said, 'It's a great idea, Murray, marvellous, but there's just one thing – when do I return to take my bow?' 'You don't,' I replied. I think his interest in my music, if there ever had been any, flickered out at that moment.

The performance was hilarious. The orchestra tuned up. The conductor entered. A smattering of applause. Only gradually did the piece gain coherence out of the tune-up. As ten minutes approached, the huge crescendo of sound grew, and Victor managed to get it building up effectively. When he turned to leave, the patrons reacted predictably by applauding, and the huge wall of sound began again. Just to make sure that things went according to plan, I had brought about thirty students from York University and instructed them carefully to keep the waves of applause coming. Also, my friend Arnold Rockman, anxious to demonstrate the Durkheim dictum, had brought along another thirty students from his sociology class, many of whom, to my delight, had come with garbage-can lids and other objects to beat.

From my seat in the first balcony, I could see everything. I stood up, bowed and began to bravo vociferously. The percussionists began a third crescendo. Rockman was now running around the upper balcony leading the claque in more stormy rounds of applause. By now, several of us were bravoing at the tops of our voices. The percussion rose to another climax. In the centre of the orchestra I could see the puzzled faces of several violinists, continuing to noodle their instruments, because the score required them to continue playing, but not, of course, playing what I had asked them to play. The audience had by now quite realized the cybernated situation and were beginning to join in the fun too. More crescendi from the orchestra. More applause. The offstage door opened a crack and I could see someone through the crack gesticulating desperately towards the percussionists, trying to get them to stop. It was the orchestra manager.

At length Victor Feldbrill returned, waltzing along, trying to look normal and buoyant again. The regular subscribers applauded. This triggered another final crescendo from the percussion but Victor had by now reached the podium and plunged right into the *Peacock Variations*. Kodaly's music unfolded sullenly. It occurred to me that the Kodaly should be renamed 'A Lot Longer Than Ten Minutes'. It was curious how thoroughly contaminated it was by my prelude, and I am sure every member of the audience must have felt it, for there was a lot of shuffling and coughing.

Of course the critics were unkind. They attacked me for being insincere. Not a word about the fraudulence of others. Bang! Schafer gets it right over the head. One critic even suggested that I appeared to be finished as a composer. My poor mother almost believed him.

THE SOUNDSCAPE

THE 1970S WAS THE DECADE of my most ambitious orchestral works and the largest of these was *Lustro*, composed between 1970 and 1972 – inspired by a trip to the Middle East. In 1969 I had applied for and received a Canada Council travel grant which allowed me to visit Iran and Turkey for about two months. Phyllis accompanied me. We arrived in Tehran late at night on March 29. Tehran was a terrible disappointment. There were American signs everywhere in the familiar colours of Coca-Cola, Pan Am, etc., with a little Persian scribbled in one corner. Most of the women in the city had traded their veils and traditional clothing for American and European styles. The traffic was terrible. Iranians drove their cars with the same malignant cruelty they once inflicted on their animals. But the people were handsome with noble features, not disfigured or blemished like the faces of many Turks and Arabs. The bazaar quarter of town was surprisingly quiet. Few voices were raised. There was often singing in the narrow alleys. The pre-Islamic Zoroastrian religion was vividly upheld. The fire temples were kept burning at all times with the sacred flame. A holy fire must be compounded of sixteen different fires, all purified after a long and complicated ritual. One fire is obtained from the cremation of a corpse. Then, above the flame, chips of sandalwood are ignited in an openwork metal spoon. This is repeated ninety-one times, to the accompaniment of recited prayers. Fires from other temples are purified in a similar manner. Finally sixteen fires are brought together by priests, who wear coverings over their mouths so as not to render the flames impure; the fires are placed in the fire urn of the temple. The worshippers come individually at any time of the day or night. Each worshipper washes the uncovered parts of his body, recites a prayer, takes off his shoes, and then moves to the threshold of the fire chamber, where he offers the priest sandalwood and money in return for some ashes of the sacred fire, which he puts on his forehead and eyelids. He then retreats backwards out of the temple. I was so inspired by this ritual that I later wrote a work entitled *Zoroaster* for multiple choirs and soloists illuminated solely by candlelight.

I preferred Isfahan and Shiraz to the metropolis of Tehran. The

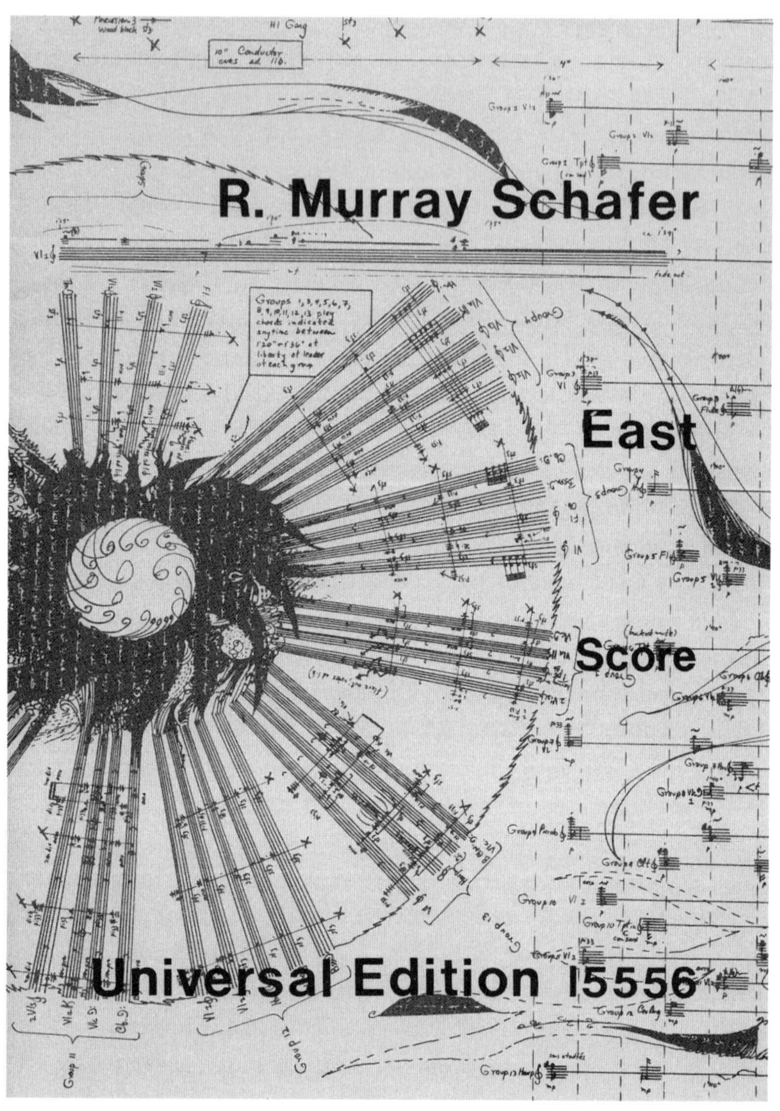

'East' is a meditation on a text from the Isha Upanishad.

Shah Abbas mosque in Isfahan is surely one of the most beautiful buildings in the world. The azure tiles of its cupolas may be equalled by those of other mosques but none can match the famous seven-fold echo. Stand in a small circle directly under the main cupola and a handclap will receive precisely seven echoes – no more, no less. Stand outside the circle, and no echoes will be heard. Many years later I was to write a lengthy work for brass instruments entitled *Isfahan* in which I preserved the famous echo.

Incidentally, the mystery of how the cupolas of the Persian mosques are so exquisitely shaped was revealed to me by one of the tour guides in Isfahan: a stake was driven into the ground at the centre of the proposed cupola and strings the length of the radius were tied around the wrist of each builder so that, as they moved around and upward, the distance from the centre of the cupola would always remain constant.

I believe it was in Shiraz that I was allowed to listen to a lesson given by a blind *santour* player to a class of students. (The Persian santour is an ancient wooden-hammered dulcimer.) The master would play a phrase and then nod to a student who was to repeat it back perfectly. If he did so, the master would play another phrase and nod at a different student. If he failed to play it accurately the teacher would repeat it again as many times as it took to get a perfect reply. 'You see,' explained the teacher, 'our music consists of hundreds of different phrases and ornaments. I know them all and the students will be masters when they also know them all.'

I discovered Jalal ad-Din Rumi's poetry while I was in Iran. Later I was to set some of it in a large orchestral work entitled *Divan i Shams i Tabriz*. The work also includes seven solo singers who chant passages from Rumi's *Masnavi* in Persian. The same year (1970) I also wrote a work entitled *Music for the Morning of the World* for solo singer and quadraphonic soundtrack also on texts by Rumi but in English, which Phyllis was to sing a number of times.

From the Middle East I returned directly to Chicago where I had been offered a job at the University, though I decided to turn it down because Chicago was not a very safe city in those days. I had dinner with the celebrated patron of new music, Paul Fromm. Ernst Krenek was there but all I remember was his bright, cobalt-blue eyes and rather sullen face. On another evening I attended a reception where I

Schafer in his Persian period.

met Saul Bellow and the psychologist Bruno Bettelheim and then – Guity Nashat, a princess from Telloh with jet-black, geometrically cut hair and lovely black eyes who took me home to her apartment to read to me from the *Masnavi* until 3:00 a.m. It being too dangerous to go home at that hour, we slept the night together. How strange that one should travel half the world seeking a sympathetic soul with whom to discuss the religion of the Sufis and the poetry of the Middle East, only to discover that person in the depths of Chicago. Guity and I met on one or two other occasions but a year or so later she decided to return to Iran and I never heard from her again.

My two pieces inspired by my trip to the Middle East, *Divan i Shams i Tabriz* and *Music for the Morning of the World,* were eventually combined with another work, *Beyond the Great Gate of Light,* a setting of Rabindranath Tagore's poem 'Light, my light, the world-filling light', to form the triptych *Lustro,* which was performed in Toronto, May 31, 1973. The CBC recorded the performance quadraphonically thanks to John Roberts, the music director.

During these years I occasionally saw John Weinzweig. We would have lunch and laugh at some of the absurdities of our profession. John's wit and intelligence are evident in much of his music, as well as in the chapbooks he published over the years and circulated to friends. On John's sixtieth birthday, *The Canada Music Book* gathered together birthday wishes from several of John's colleagues and students. My tribute was written from the S.S. *Arcadia,* on my way to New Zealand.

> John Weinzweig was the first florescence of genius to become visible on the Canadian musical scene. This occurred about 1950; by that time there was no doubting his talent, which had marched out of the rheumatized closet in which Canadian music had up to then been kept. This is not to say that many people participated in his discovery; and still today, when his music ought to be played weekly, daily, hourly in all the concert halls of the country, the best his few admirers can do is to mount a verbal apotheosis for his birthday.
>
> Back in 1950 most of John's colleagues were busy composing music for those over fifty who had never been under fifty, and so he became the only teacher to whom those who were under fifty could go while they still remained under that

John Weinzweig's eightieth birthday. Left to right: Harry Somers, Phil Nimmons, Victor Feldbrill, John, Murray Schafer and John Beckwith.

age. Toronto musical life was then still run by the pommies. John was more cosmopolitan; a Jew who had studied in the USA, had imbibed something of Stravinsky and the Neo-Viennese school, and who was fascinated by the northern and western sweep of Canadian geography; and each of these factors has at one time or another influenced his lifeline as a composer. Toronto critics called him the Donald Duck of music, and preferred the oscitations of Brahms; but for us he was a Parnassus of one, and all the young men who wanted to know about the newer things burst into his office between 1945 and 1960. I do not know if he was a good teacher, I only know that he was considerate and that the things he had to offer were not purchasable anywhere else in Canada at that time.

If I were asked to name his principal service to Canada it could be this: that he rode out the first storm of criticism alone, until he could educate enough other composers to offer him the companionship of the Canadian League of Composers. His refusal to admit that music was at a standstill ('e pur si muove') gradually won a more benign attitude for the reception of our music.

Most of John's contemporaries have long since entered the diminuendo phase of their composing careers, while his music still leaps with vitality; and I have no doubt it will still leap even after the indulgent dotage of these tributes.

R. Murray Schafer

IN LATE SPRING 1970, the Canadian Music Council held a conference in the newly opened National Arts Centre in Ottawa. The weather was warm; flowers were out; it was late spring. The theme of the conference was 'The Performer in 2001'. To begin, Hugh LeCaine had set up his computer music system in the Arts Centre lobby, but since it just sat there blinking and powerfully suggesting that there would be no performers in 2001, its effect seemed more to inhibit than to stimulate discussion. Serge Garant had come up from Montreal with his new music ensemble. Gilles Tremblay produced an improvisatory composition with the delegates. I took them on a sound walk in Ottawa, trying to suggest that the performer of the future might be required to expand his listening habits to include all the sounds of the environment.

Cathy Berberian came to perform several works of her own and of her former husband, Luciano Berio. There was worry over that fact that the culminating dinner lacked a distinguished speaker. For some reason this has always seemed necessary at all conferences. What would be more appropriate than to invite one of the world's leading composers? Berio happened to be on his way from London to New York at the time and agreed to speak for a fee of five hundred dollars. However, when he arrived he said he was too tired. Some confusion resulted, at the end of which it was agreed that Berio would answer a few questions put to him by Maryvonne Kendergi. Maryvonne prattled through a long, adulatory introduction then asked the first question. I don't remember what it was. Berio stood up slowly and answered as follows: 'One of the Dadaist poets once said that life is composed of two things: roses and shit. I'd sum up the contemporary situation this way: we are looking for the roses and we're covered with shit.' Then he sat down. There were no more questions. There was no applause. Maryvonne got up and expostulated for a few moments on the profundity of this observation; then she sat down. The guests finished their coffee and left quietly.

Later, backstage, Berio asked for his money. The president of the CMC sheepishly presented him with a cheque. But Berio wanted cash. So the executives went into a huddle, pulled out their wallets to produce whatever cash they had until at last the full amount was assembled. Berio opened his hands to receive a pile of ten- and twenty-dollar bills. I'm not sure whether he considered them roses, but it seemed to be what he was looking for.

In 1970 I composed another work, *Okeanos,* which I put together with Bruce Davis and Brian Fawcett in the Sonic Research Studio at SFU. *Okeanos* is a study of the sounds and symbolism of the sea, using natural and electronic sounds with voices reciting texts by various authors who had written about the sea – Homer, Hesiod, Melville, Pound ... When I first approached the CBC with the idea of creating a portrait of the sea, I was asked how long the program would be. I thought twenty-four hours would be suitable. How could we suggest the limitless magnitude of the ocean in a stingy half-hour show? John Roberts intervened and gave us ninety minutes. He also talked the technical department into broadcasting the work quadraphonically by using the stereo systems of both CBC networks. This was the first and perhaps the last time that a quadraphonic work was presented on the CBC. At the outset the announcer asked listeners to arrange two stereo receivers on either side of them; and to relax, perhaps even lie down on the floor between them. Then the deep, underwater sounds began to swirl around them, gradually rising to the surface where voices were heard narrating the legends of the sea from many cultures.

I HAVE BEEN DISCUSSING some very large-scale works but I don't want to give the reader the impression that all my works were of such magnitude. During these years there were many small pieces, both instrumental and choral. One of the choral pieces was *Miniwanka,* a recital of the various sounds produced by water from raindrops to ocean waves.

The composition was derived from an exercise I used to do with school children. I would ask them to make up words for raindrops, stream, waterfall, lake, river and ocean waves in their own private language. Then we would perform the sounds all together in sequence. This little exercise inspired me to write *Miniwanka,* which is now performed by choirs all over the world. The premiere was given by the Canadian Children's Opera Chorus before Queen Elizabeth and Prince Philip during their visit to Toronto in 1973. The conductor, Lloyd Bradshaw, sent me a script of the royal reaction to this sound-poem.

The Queen said, 'How do you do, Mr Bradshaw?'

Lloyd said, 'How do you do, Your Majesty?'

Lloyd looked at the Queen.

The Queen said, 'They were singing Indian words, were they not?'

Lloyd said, 'They were words describing the forms of water such as rain, stream, lake, waterfall, and so on.'

There was a pause.

Lloyd said, 'The last time we sang this out of doors, it brought on a rainstorm. I'm glad it didn't do that today.'

Pause.

Lloyd continued with, 'We thought you might like to see the score since the notation is not traditional.'

The Queen said, 'Oh, yes, I saw some of the children moving like that.'

Lloyd replied, 'That is the storm at sea, and those are the chords demonstrating it.'

There was a brief pause, then Philip said, 'Will you please extend our congratulations to the choir,' and Lloyd said, 'I will, thank you.'

That seemed to be the cue to end the conversation and Lloyd turned and left the platform as he had been instructed.

MY IDEAS CONCERNING creative music education were not appreciated by the Faculty of Education at SFU, even though I was beginning to receive invitations to many other schools and universities across Canada and the United States. I also had made two tours of schools in the United Kingdom and an extensive tour of Austria and Germany organized by my publisher Universal Edition. I had signed a contract with them to begin publishing my orchestral pieces as well as my booklets on music education.

Universal Edition is one of the most distinguished publishing houses in Europe for contemporary music. They have a most impressive list of twentieth-century composers in their catalogue: Schoenberg, Berg, Webern, Stockhausen, Berio, Boulez and a great many more.

For some time the London branch of UE had been handling my educational booklets and they had been doing quite well. The question of a German translation came up and I was invited to come to Vienna to discuss the matter. They had booked me into one of Vienna's better hotels. This didn't work out too well, however, since two roads were simultaneously being torn up at the front and back of the hotel, so I complained that the noise made the place unbearable. UE was dismayed. 'Stockhausen never complained!' But at length I managed to persuade them to find a quieter hotel. Tickets appeared at the hotel for the State Opera and the Burg Theatre. Evidently, I was to amuse myself until they were ready to see me. On about the third day of my stay an appointment was made for me to see Herr Direktor Schlee, the top man.

The secretary asked: 'Wen soll ich melden?'

'Schafer aus Kanada,' I replied.

She disappeared, then returned to tell me that Herr Schlee was busy for a few moments. György Ligeti was in Vienna and had dropped in. Could I please wait? I did for some time. At length Ligeti came out of the 'Direktor's' office. He had a sullen face, not so much sad as just sour. I was not introduced. I was ushered into Herr Schlee's office, a large, chocolate-coloured room with inadequate light but comfortable furniture.

'Ein sehr grosser Komponist,' said Schlee, who didn't speak English. 'Dass war der Ligeti.'

'I recognized him,' I said. 'Certainly a great composer.'

'Sehr grosse Talent.'

'Very great.'

The conversation cruised around for a while before settling on my own work. Schlee said that they were so far behind in their publishing commitments that he doubted whether they would be able to do anything for me, but in any case, Herr Direktor Harpner would like to meet me on Sunday to determine whether anything could be done.

'Sunday?' I inquired. It was probably only Wednesday or Thursday. I was told there would be more tickets for concerts to fill in the interval. Ligeti's *Requiem* would be performed tomorrow night, and so forth.

On Sunday Stefan Harpner picked me up at the hotel and proposed that we should go swimming at Baden bei Wien. My four little music education books came along, but they remained most of the time in the sand while we sipped our drinks and sunned ourselves. Occasionally, Harpner picked them up and thumbed through them muttering things like 'Your style is very difficult to Germanize,' or 'I don't know just who we could get to undertake the translations,' or 'I'm not sure our schools are ready for this type of approach.' When we were parting after a sumptuous dinner Harpner asked, 'How long will you remain in Vienna?'

'I thought I would leave tomorrow.'

'So soon? Well, goodbye then.'

I thought it was a polite rejection but marvelled at the courtesy of my hosts who had put me up for a week in order to reject my music.

I left and went back to Vancouver. But just after I arrived, I received a communication from Friedrich Saaten who wrote, 'I have been commissioned to translate your books into German. I have already begun on the first one and have the following questions …' Later, UE was also to publish a number of my orchestral works.

IN JULY 1971 I WAS SEPARATED from Phyllis. I had met Jean Elliot, a secretary in the university president's office, and almost immediately fell in love with her. Jean was Welsh and had just arrived in Canada after being divorced. She had two boys with her, the eldest just approaching adolescence. Although I hesitated for some time, I eventually decided to live with her. I shall never forget the day I moved out, leaving Phyllis sobbing on the floor of our apartment and, as the years pass, I accuse myself more and more.

I had now inherited a family to care for, and it was not easy for any of us as we struggled to redefine our lives. I suffered terrible feelings of guilt for several years until I eventually learned that Phyllis had gone to live with (and later marry) Tom Mallinson, the chairman of our department. I have never completely overcome the guilty feelings about deserting Phyllis toward the end of her career as a singer, while my career was opening up as a composer. I remember how supportive she was during our first years together and how much she taught me about the voice. Of course I had learned a lot about singing techniques – phrasing and breathing – from my days as a choir boy in Grace Church; but listening to a professional singer warming up and practising Bach, Schumann or Mahler taught me how a text was set to music

Jean Elliot.

by great composers and brought to life by a professional singer. How does one sing diphthongs and nasals? Which vowels are best for a melisma and in what tessitura of the voice will they be most effective?

Twentieth-century music introduced a lot of new problems for the singer: more jumping from one register to another – from chest tone to high tessitura. Of course I was tempted by these new fashions also, but I was always able to discuss the practical limits of what was effective before pushing the vocal line into absurd registers that had nothing to do with the phonetics or meaning of the text and were unflattering or gave little pleasure to the singer. Phyllis's voice continued to haunt me for many years. Many vocal works, written for other singers, were memories of her voice, and it is not surprising that later when I met Eleanor James the works I wrote for her bore a strong similarity to those early works – but that is another story.

IN OCTOBER 1971 I went to Moscow as a member of the delegation of the Canadian Music Council to attend the meeting of the International Music Council of UNESCO. It was an exhausting trip from Vancouver to Toronto to London to Moscow. The first things I noticed on my arrival in Moscow were that (1) all Russian women looked like bags of dirty laundry, (2) in the shops they were still using the abacus, with great speed and nimbleness, (3) there was a strong smell of garlic wherever people gathered, and (4) getting service in restaurants was impossible. The waiters would lounge around the doorways but one would literally have to go and take the menu out of their hands. Then they would come and grab it back without taking your order.

But you could always get vodka. One night I was sharing a table with two men who were drinking vodka into which they were shaking pepper. 'Pepper in vodka?' I inquired of the one who spoke a little English. 'Eet ees very angry,' he replied.

Whenever I left my room I was required to leave my bag with a concierge, who sat at a little table next to the elevator. I assumed they searched one's luggage while we were out. Downstairs the officious guides would say: 'Wait here!' 'Sit down!' 'Come with me!' and we would be led out to a bus that would take us to the conference hall.

I gave a lecture but I can't remember what it was about. During my last night in Moscow I had a very strange experience. I had not

At work in the electronic music studio at Simon Fraser University.
The studio would later become an international centre for soundscape research.

adjusted to Moscow time, the difference between Moscow and Vancouver being eleven hours, so I went to bed early. Sometime in the night my telephone rang and a man's voice said: 'Mr Schafer, would you like to go to Leningrad?' I replied that I would love to go to Leningrad but unfortunately I had to return to Vancouver. 'At what time, please?' 'Early, at seven o'clock.' He: 'That is too bad. Are you sure you would not like to go to Leningrad?' 'Yes, I am sure. Now I would like to go to sleep. Goodnight.' I was dozing off to sleep when the telephone rang again. Same voice: 'I have two questions for you.' I (very sleepily): 'Yes?' 'The first is – who is singing for you now?' I jumped awake. My God, I thought, they know about my separation from Phyllis. I said, 'What do you mean?' Long pause. Then the voice said in French: 'Qui chante pour vous? Quelqu'un chante pour vous. Someone is burning for you.' I didn't say a word. Long pause. Then the voice said 'Do you mind me calling you up?' 'Yes,' I replied. 'I'm sleepy. I'm leaving Moscow in the morning. Goodnight!' The phone rang once more but I didn't answer it.

I've often wondered what was the intention of those calls. The only thing that suggested itself was that since I was listed as a professor of communication studies on the conference program someone in the secret police was making a proposal to try to get some useful information from me. This was only a month or two after the defection of Burgess and McLean, two British security officers who had been persuaded to remain in Russia by Russian secret service officers posing as homosexuals. Perhaps a similar proposal was being offered to me.

NOW THAT THE Centre for Communication and the Arts had been moved out of the Faculty of Education, there was great pressure to find a new home. My colleagues in the arts saw this as an opportunity to set up a centre for the arts or even an arts faculty. The other possibility was to link up with the Behavioral Science Department. This was the preference of our chairman, Tom Mallinson, who was a social psychologist. I was afraid that an arts school would remain weak. There were already two other universities in British Columbia with arts faculties and they would undoubtedly argue with the provincial government that a third school was unnecessary.

Other developments were occurring at the same time. I was

beginning to research a new subject which I called the *soundscape*. The sounds of the environment were changing rapidly and it seemed that no one was documenting the changes. Where were the museums for disappearing sounds? What was the effect of new sounds on human behaviour and health? So many questions could be asked for which there were no answers in 1970.

I raised the questions in an article 'The Music of the Environment' that I wrote for UNESCO in 1973. The international response to it surprised me. I applied to UNESCO for a grant to research the changing soundscape and received it. At the same time, I approached the Donner Foundation, hoping to win a large grant that would allow me to hire research assistants and seriously begin the study of the changing soundscape.†

I remember meeting the chairman of the Donner Foundation in one of the high bank towers in Toronto. He listened patiently to my proposal and then asked me to write him a one-page letter outlining what I wanted to do. I did so and received a grant of forty thousand dollars.

In 1972 I established the World Soundscape Project at Simon Fraser University and began to look for research assistants. I wanted to bring together an interdisciplinary team but I found that difficult, either because the money I was offering was not tempting enough, or the applicants didn't know what the soundscape was supposed to be. Finally I put together a team consisting of Hildegard Westerkamp, Bruce Davis and Peter Huse, all of whom were composers, and Howard Broomfield, whose background was in sociology. Barry Truax was to join us a year or so later. Several other young people assisted in researching the seventy (!) projects I had identified for investigation. These included establishing an archive of disappearing sounds, a glossary of all unusual sounds encountered in world literature, documenting urban sounds such as car horns, sirens, factory whistles, and studying their morphology over time, interviewing elderly people about

---

† It has been suggested that I borrowed the term *soundscape* from the geographer Michael Southworth, who used it in his article 'The Sonic Environment of Cities', *Environment and Behaviour I*, 49–70. This is entirely possible; I read the article. At any rate, it was the research I was beginning to develop that defined the term and brought it to international attention.

sounds of the past, and collecting noise bylaws in Canada to compare them with those in other cities around the world.

We used to meet on Friday afternoons and each team would bring us up to date on what had been accomplished. There was a lot of laughter particularly when researchers described the reactions they were getting from some people.

We did outrageous things like organizing a conference on aircraft noise to which we invited the President of Canadian Pacific Airlines, and interrupted his talk by playing recordings of jets as they would be heard by people living next to Vancouver Airport. The president of the airline wasn't happy and complained to the university president. A few days later, I received a memorandum from the academic vice president requesting that I furnish him with more information about the anti-noise workshops we were giving. We put together this reply.

To: Dr I. Mugridge, Assistant, Vice-President, Academic
Subject: Noise Workshop

From: Professor R. Murray Schafer, Communication Studies
Date: November 16, 1973

In reply to your request for further information on our Noise Workshops, the study program will proceed as follows: We have broken the subject into three categories:

a) The Public and Noise
b) Acoustical Terminology
c) Psychological response to noise.

Section (a) will discuss the following subjects:
1. Frequency attenuation in crowd noise – positive or negative in its effects?
2. The usefulness of acoustical ecology as a measure of public dissatisfaction. Is it extensive enough in its scope or is more precise vocabulary required?
3. Hearing loss in urban environments – its relation to heightened visual perceptions.

Section (b) will discuss the following more technical issues:
1. Noise baffling in the public sector – a boon to efficiency or a technical problem?

2. Decibels as expressed in dBA, dBC, or dBS. Should we budget for a Hertz system?
3. Binary and vertical parabolic effects in studio line readouts. Imaginary or real?

Section (c) will discuss psychological problems:
1. Dynamic range in mylar tape systems and its correspondence to thresholds of aural perceptions. (This would involve a subsidiary discussion of the relative merits of size differentials in so-called 'reel-to-reel' direct-flow and recall situations.)
2. Signal to noise ratio in functional clearance.
3. Mumble-sequences in steady-state noise contexts. Does octave band analysis and rejection mitigate any of the impulses that arise as a result? Should questions influenced by information of MS (mumble-sequence) and BS (S-weighted decibels) be ignored?
4. Side-band analysis and Sine-wave extrapolations as a counter-baffle to cybernetic interference from sources extraneous to the study itself.

R. Murray Schafer

We received no reply to this letter and continued with our research. The first important document produced by the World Soundscape Project was *The Vancouver Soundscape,* which consisted of a book and two LP records. The book contained some earwitness accounts of early inhabitants, beginning with the Coast Salish First Nation and continuing with accounts by the first European emigrants. We then discussed how the change of materials from wooden planks to cement transformed the soundscape. Electricity was another transformative. Foghorns and factory horns were important signals in the early days of the growing city, to which train whistles were later added. The city soon acquired other soundmarks, for instance, the nine o'clock gun which was added in 1900 and is still sounded today. We discussed the rise of the ambient sound level as the city grew, and we conducted surveys among the inhabitants to check their reaction to these changes. Vancouver is a new city and the evolution of the soundscape can be more dramatically presented than in older cities.

The book was complemented with recordings, giving the listener a quite vivid impression of the dramatic evolution. I remember a listener from UNESCO in Paris writing to tell me that for the first time in his life he had learned about a city from its sounds rather than from photographs and words.

The recording of horns and whistles from the Vancouver Soundscape document began to be played on radio, first in Germany and then elsewhere, as if it was a musical composition – an extension of the *musique concrète* of Pierre Schaeffer and his fellow composers in Paris. This was certainly not our intention, but the notion has flourished to a point where we are now swamped by the discharges of anyone and everyone who knows how to operate a recording device.

How often have I listened to 'soundscapes' of frogs or insects dashed together by would-be composers. 'What kind of frogs are they?' I ask. 'Don't know.' 'But you have an obligation to know that just as Bach or Scarlatti knew the difference between a cembalo and a clavichord.' Technology annuls perception as much as it reveals information.

Following the Vancouver Soundscape I decided that we should make our researches more public. I approached the CBC to determine whether they would be interested in a series of broadcasts that I was proposing to call 'Soundscapes of Canada'. I posted the following memorandum on the door of the Sonic Research Studio on October 26, 1973.

Subject: Six Months That Shook the World

> I have decided that after Xmas we are going to make a series of radio programs incorporating all our researches to date. This will be the major project we will be concerned with between January and the summer. I want you, therefore, to begin considering ways to make our work the subject of household conversations across the country. These programs must be radically inventive – unlike anything you have ever heard from a tweeter before. They must be rich, informative, shocking, bold, sweet, sad, urgent.... Make them the thoughts for your midnight blackboard.
>
> Orson Welles

(Orson Welles was the writer and producer of a famous radio drama, *The War of the Worlds,* in the form of a simulated news broadcast reporting an attack on New Jersey by invaders from Mars which thousands of listeners took to be real, and panicked.)

The CBC program *Ideas* agreed to commission ten one-hour programs to be called *Soundscapes of Canada*. The programs were titled: 'Six Themes of the Soundscape', 'Listening and Games', 'Signals, Keynotes and Soundmarks', 'Soundmarks of Canada', 'Summer Solstice', 'Directions', 'Dawn Chorus', 'A Maritime Diary and Soundscape Design', 'A Radio Program about Radio', and 'Soundscape Study: The Bells of Percé'.

To gather material for the series I sent two researchers, Bruce Davis and Peter Huse, on a tour across Canada in a Volkswagen van. One of the programs they produced ('Directions') consisted entirely of asking locals for directions to their next destination. The program consists exclusively of their replies in local dialects all the way from Newfoundland back to Vancouver.

The program 'Games' was a montage of several games, both interior and exterior, from sandlot baseball games to pin-ball machines – games that are now almost extinct in Canada.

'Summer Solstice' was prepared from a twenty-four-hour recording we made near a monastery in Mission, B.C. Each hour was identified by the recordist on duty: 'It is 2 a.m.'; 'It is 3 a.m.'; etc. Otherwise the only sounds to be heard were those of nature and occasionally the monastery bells. Two minutes were taken from each hour to produce a forty-eight-minute montage showing the circadian rhythm of the rural soundscape.

'Soundmarks of Canada' consisted of horns, whistles, bells, sirens, etc., which occur in many towns and cities across Canada. Many of these have now vanished. The question of vanishing sounds is interesting. Only a few years after we had recorded them we began to get requests from factories, churches and town halls for copies of our recordings. The original signals having been silenced, people wanted the recordings for their archives and museums.

IN 1975 I WAS TO GO on a lecture tour in Europe. I decided to take some members of the Soundscape team with me. My hope was to document the soundscapes of five villages, one in each of the countries I would be visiting: Sweden, Germany, Italy, France and Britain. We would spend a week or more in each village recording, interviewing, studying and measuring the sounds at each site in order to produce a portrait of *Five Village Soundscapes*. In each village, we would require a native speaker who understood the local language and dialect. These were often teachers or students at my lectures given at universities or conservatories in Stockholm, Stuttgart, Merano, Paris and London.

When we returned to Canada we produced a document that was to have an important impact on future soundscape research, for we were able to show how the soundscape morphology of each village was unique and how it shaped the life of each village. Although we were only able to stay in each village for a week or ten days, we were an experienced team of five researchers and in each village we also had an interpreter to help us in understanding local inhabitants. We gathered an enormous amount of information, enough at least to demonstrate the uniqueness of each village soundscape, and in one case, we were able to save a village from destruction. Lesconil in Brittany was a fishing village. Our research showed how the changing tides and winds affected the daily fishing patterns. Shortly after we left, the French government announced plans to build a highway just north of the village. We contacted the press and informed them that a highway would destroy the subtle patterns of the *vents solaires* (solar winds) from which the fishermen took their cues. Radio France produced an award-winning documentary, *Questions pour Lesconil* which attracted so much attention that the highway was rerouted.

For the first time in history we had gathered a range of sounds both interior and exterior from five different environments that could be compared with later recordings. This was really the beginning of the acoustic ecology movement.

Twenty-five years after our research, a team from the Finnish Soundscape Association[†] revisited the same villages we had studied

---

† *Acoustic environments in change,* TAMK University of Applied Sciences, Tampere, 2009. This study also includes a reprinting of our original *Five Village Soundscapes* book and recordings.

and documented the enormous changes the soundscapes of each village had undergone. This was the first critical study showing how changes of the acoustic environment transform the social life of communities.

Returning to the university in April 1974 I discovered that the administration was still chasing me about the 1973 anti-noise workshop. They wanted a report. This is what we sent.

> To: Mrs Kay Pearson, Division of Continuing Education
> Subject: Noise Workshop
>
> From: R. Murray Schafer, Communication Centre
> Date: April 11, 1974
>
> In reply to your memo of April 2, my staff has been able to assemble the following particulars:
>
> a) The total enrolment for the course or workshop.
> – Do you wish us to include the two-headed and four-legged creatures who also attended?
> b) The breakdown of students in terms of those who were regular SFU students versus those who came from the community at large.
> – Numerous broken-down students, both regulars and irregulars, attended.
> c) The fees charged (if any) and total revenue obtained from the course.
> – No fees were charged but a lot of money was collected for the Howard Broomfield Florida Retirement Fund.
> d) The total expenditures made for the course.
> – Millions. Six labs were also wrecked by the crowds.
> e) Comments regarding any special operational problems such as space, staffing, equipment, etc.
> – The only special operational problem I experienced was the opacity of the mind of Dr Ian Mugridge and the nuisance created by peep-o people.
> f) Advertising of the course; how, when, what type, etc.
> – Four announcements were superimposed over one another

in coloured chalk on the blackboard of CC6203. *Time Magazine* picked it up from there.

g) Feedback

– Seventeen vice-presidents from *Canadian Pacific Airlines* attended. All of them agreed they did not like our attitude. As for our own students, they did not like the polysyllabic words we used and said that if we offered the workshop again, they would like to be given lollipops at the door.

R. Murray Schafer

Clearly there was more administrative interference in our work than in the early years of the university. I was finding this very frustrating. The freedom we once had to create our own curriculum was drawing to a close; nor was there as much money for equipment and other expenses. In November 1974 I submitted my letter of resignation.

November 18, 1974

Dr Pauline Jewett
President, Simon Fraser University

Dear Dr Jewett:

With this letter I wish to resign my position as Professor of Communication Studies, effective August 31, 1975.

Having taught at Simon Fraser since its opening in 1965, it is with many regrets that I have taken this decision. I am grateful to the University for many things. First of all, for having enough faith to hire me without academic qualifications (a risk which, if taken more frequently, could, in my opinion, benefit university life considerably). I am grateful, too, for all the assistance I have received, particularly towards the establishment of the Sonic Research Studio. In terms of its versatility in sound generation and analysis, it is one of the best on the Continent. I am also grateful for the freedom, particularly during the early years, to teach the subjects of my choice in the manner in which I felt comfortable.

As the University has developed many changes have taken place. I do not know whether they are for the general good or not, but their cumulative effect has been to alienate me. Money and space are both in shorter supply than formerly and the continual scramble one must indulge in to obtain minimal facilities is tedious and wasteful of energy for everyone.

The innovative Centre for Communications and the Arts, which I came to join in 1965, has become (for me) a more conventional American-styled Communications Department, with its customary quota of 'heavies'. All my old colleagues in the arts have either fled or have had their contracts terminated. The perennial promise of a department in the Fine and Performing Arts remains an administrator's paper skirmish while departments in Computing Science and Criminology are approved and set up, even before office space is available for them.

Much of my early work at the University was in music education and I developed here what is now considered by many to be a valuable new approach to that subject. My books on music education are having a considerable influence in many countries of the world. It is a deep personal regret that my work in this field has been completely ignored by our own Faculty of Education.

In recent years my work in the Communications Department has been concerned with the development of aural perception and the analysis of the acoustic environment – to which I have given the name 'soundscape'. Since the establishment of *The World Soundscape Project* in 1972, numerous documents have been published and we have been successful in applications for some large research grants. Recently, as you may know, we have received $67,000 from the Canada Council to extend our work.

I have often wondered how long it would be possible for me to combine an active career as a composer with teaching responsibilities and research work. I have always known that, of the many kinds of work in which I am engaged, musical composition is the most important. When it becomes threatened, I suffer. Therefore I recently bought a farm in Ontario and it is my plan to make that the centre of my future life.

In closing, I wish the University and my colleagues well and (in so far as one is entitled to have such a wish) I hope that my successors will be musicians of talent and Canadian citizens.†

Yours sincerely,
R. Murray Schafer

---

† At that time Canadian universities were desperate for teachers and most of them came from the United States.

PART TWO

THE MUSIC OF THE ENVIRONMENT

MONTEAGLE VALLEY

IN THE LATE SPRING OF 1975 Jean Elliott and I moved to our future home: a farm between Bancroft and Maynooth about 270 kilometres north of Toronto. I use the word 'farm' rather loosely. It had once been a farm, although the fields were growing in and the outbuildings were collapsing. The house was a log cabin covered with face boards and had been heated by a stove in the kitchen, though all that remained of that was a hole in the ceiling where the stovepipe had once been.

What a change this was to be from teaching at Simon Fraser University! We got busy at once, marking out the floor with tape to show the prospective carpenter where we wanted rooms. 'What's that tape for?' asked Dalton Welsh, who lived up the road and came over to get acquainted. 'That's where the toilet is going to be,' I replied. 'You mean you're going to piss, fart and shit right in the centre of the house!?' Like most of my neighbours, Dalton used an outhouse. Later he was to come and build one for me, 'just in case the water might freeze up', which it did once in the middle of winter; and he showed me how to hold an oil lamp between my legs and drape my coat over it so as not to freeze my butt when the temperature was minus 25 degrees Celsius, as it frequently was in winter.

The first task was to find a carpenter who could make the house habitable before winter arrived. Eventually, we found one in Maynooth, but when he came to look at the job, he was not eager to take it on. I had wanted to exchange the front door with the front window. Henry Neiman, for that was his name, stared at me in disbelief. 'Why?' Weeks later when he was actually doing the job, he sang to himself: 'Where there's a door, now there's a window, and where there's a window, now there's a door.'

As in most building projects, there were delays and mistakes and mounting costs. Twice I had to revise my estimate of how much time the reconstruction would take. During this time I was deprived of *all* intellectual pursuits (reading, writing, answering letters). We were living in a little one-room trailer all summer and fall, and did not move into the house until early December. We still spent about eight hours each day painting, tiling the bathroom floor and stumbling around.

The Monteagle Valley house (before).

I know that one should feel a certain pride in the things one accomplishes, but I got no satisfaction or joy out of carpentry and painting. During this time my father was diagnosed with pancreatic cancer and underwent an operation. I spoke with him on the telephone and then went back to my painting, weeping. I had so much hoped to invite my parents to come and see the finished job.

Finally, it *was* finished and I was able to unpack my books and papers. In the kitchen I could hear Mouche preparing a simple dinner which we would eat in the living room by the fire. Mouche was the name I had given to Jean. I realized it wasn't very flattering but she didn't seem to mind. It was the name Heinrich Heine had given to the French girl who looked after him on his death-bed. But with us life was finally returning and I often heard Jean singing as she made curtains for the windows.

I needed a piano. Someone told me about an old, square-grand piano that was about to be turned into a liquor cabinet. I went to see it. It was an 1840 Irmler from Leipzig that some immigrant had brought over many years ago. I offered the owner two hundred dollars for it and brought it home. At least the notes were all in working order.

I had been offered a commission by the CBC to write a piece for the celebrated Canadian contralto, Maureen Forrester. (This had been instigated by John Roberts, of course.) By coincidence, Maureen was

The Monteagle Valley house (after).

touring in Ontario and was able to adjust her schedule to visit us. I mentioned the idea I had for the commission, which was to set portions of Clara Schumann's diary, particularly those in which she described Robert's breakdown and final days in the mental asylum. I would work a lot of Schumann's songs and piano pieces into the orchestral accompaniment. Maureen was pleased with the idea and I began the work of composing *Adieu, Robert Schumann* on a piano that had been manufactured in Schumann's home town the year he and Clara had been married! Maureen performed *Adieu, Robert Schumann* with the National Arts Centre Orchestra in the spring of 1978, and my father was able to come and hear it shortly before his death.

Later, while making a few corrections to the parts of the score, I came across comments scribbled by some of the performers. One had changed my name to 'Murray Charlatan Schafer', and another had written 'Der Musiker und der Abfallmann' (The Musician and the Garbage Man). Such comments from orchestral musicians were quite frequent in those days.

The work that followed *Adieu, Robert Schumann* was *Hymn to Night*. The text was from Novalis, one of my favourite German authors. The poem begins with a paean to light before turning to the 'holy, ineffable night' and the eternal sleep that accompanies it. A recording of an Aeolian harp was added to the chamber orchestra accompaniment. The eerie wail of the wind harp, very popular among the Romantics, gave the work a special mood.† I remember the night I began work on *Hymn to Night*. I couldn't sleep and got up to read something. Novalis's poem was close at hand and even before I had finished reading the poem the whole work had taken shape in my mind. *Hymn to Night* is one of my favourite pieces from that period of my life though it is very rarely performed.

I must remind the reader of how different life in our renovated farmhouse was from the activities of my neighbours. They were friendly enough and were always eager to help us out even though they couldn't understand why we had come to live there.

Dalton Welsh gave me a rifle to shoot the groundhogs who invaded our vegetable garden. I killed a groundhog with the first shot I ever fired, but after that I missed every time. Elijah MacDonald offered to help me build a fence around the vegetables. When we hit a boulder he called it a 'Chinaman's head' and speculated on how much digging we'd have to do to get to China. He confessed that one sound he never liked was splitting a cow's skull with an axe. 'You could hear it clear across the valley.'

I was amazed at the way these men could spot things in the environment that totally escaped my attention. One day Elijah said, 'Go and fetch that stone over there.' 'What stone?' I asked. 'I don't see a stone.' 'Ten feet in front of you,' he replied. I took ten paces and found the stone in the high grass. He had known it was there by the bending of the grass around it.

The postman used to sound his horn when he arrived each morning with the mail. I would go down to the road to fetch it and he would report on all the happenings up and down the line. 'Willie Jones' wife died last night.' I said I was sorry to hear that. 'Yes, yes. He invited me in to view the carcass.'

When I went up to the General Store at Maple Leaf to buy stamps for Christmas cards, Gladys, the postmistress, said: 'I'll sell them to you but I ain't lickin' them. I licked Mr Nelson's last night and I ain't lickin' anyone else's.'

---

† I was to use a recording of the Aeolian harp again in the last movement of my *Eleventh String Quartet*.

Dalton Welsh told me the story of how when he was a boy there was a hunting accident on our farm. A man had been shot and was brought back to our living room until the doctor arrived. Unfortunately, the doctor arrived too late. The man died. A makeshift coffin was nailed together and rested on two stools. It was Dalton's job to empty the pans of blood that were dripping out of the corpse until the grave could be dug. Another story was of a wake at which, after the final prayers for the old man had been said, the coffin was taken outside and planted upright in a snowbank by the window so that the dead man could watch the dancing that followed.

About this time I decided to get a driver's licence. I had been driving the country roads without one but Jean had to do all the driving when we went on trips. So I went to Bancroft to take a driver's test. The examiner got in the car with me and instructed me to head downtown, that is, to the main street of Bancroft. I carefully stopped at the railroad crossing that had not seen a train in two years and started down the main drag.

'I'd like to see you parallel park,' said the inspector. Of course this was something I had never done before on country roads. But there was only one vehicle parked on the street, inside which was a man eating an ice-cream cone. I carefully pulled up beside him and then began to back up, but I hit the curb. 'Give 'er another try,' said the inspector. So I tried and hit the curb again while the ice-cream-eating man eyed me suspiciously. Two boys were also watching me from the other side of the street. 'Hey, mister,' one of them called out. 'Are you trying to park? You don't have to park there. You can park anywhere on the street!' Now the driver in front of me turned on his ignition and drove off. 'We'll call that a pass,' said the inspector, 'but give the parallel parking a little more practice.'

February of 1976 was quite significant for two reasons. 1) I began to write *Credo,* which was later to become the second part of *Apocalypsis,* and 2) we decided to start going to church. Up the road a few kilometres, near the village of Maynooth, was a Lutheran church. The reason for deciding to go to church was not so much religious faith as it was the fear of becoming 'bushed', the local slang for people who end up talking to themselves for want of company: a rather common problem at the edge of civilization where one could be forgotten unless one made at least occasional public appearances.

At first, I resisted telling my neighbours I was a musician, fearing that I might be dragged into local undertakings for which I had neither inclination nor aptitude. For country people, a musician is a limitless resource, able to repair a trombone, tune a piano, play a fiddle at a wedding or a Hammond organ at church. And sure enough, when the pastor learned that I was a musician, he immediately asked me if I would spend a little time improving the singing in church. A choir practice was announced. I recall the first night vividly. Six people showed up. The youngest was a girl of six or seven, the oldest was a woman of sixty. There were two men. I asked them how many could read music. One woman raised her hand. Later I learned she was lying.

We began with the known. We sang through trusty hymns and I confined myself to getting them to start together and not to drag the beat. The practice was evidently enjoyable for after a few weeks the choir had grown to about fifteen people. I was ruthless about regular rehearsal attendance, and had to be since attendance at first was very inconsistent. Some seasonal activities, like haying, interfered predictably, but there was also the case of the choir member who started out for rehearsal, met someone on the road, and went fishing instead. I announced that anyone missing three rehearsals without a valid excuse would be bounced, and I did bounce one man. Little by little, the message sank in.

By now, we were singing in parts. For the non-readers, I recorded the alto, tenor and bass lines on a cassette recorder for them to take home and practise singing their parts. Near Christmas, there was an ecumenical service in Maynooth. The Lutheran choir sang 'Silent Night' in four parts in German. After the concert, the girls from the Catholic Church rushed up to me and asked if they could join our choir. I told them I didn't think that would be possible, but perhaps I could help them. I would discuss the matter with Father Casertelli, the Catholic priest. He confessed a love for plainsong masses in Latin and sang some fragments from his days in the seminary. I proposed that if the choirs rehearsed together, we might spend half the time on the Lutheran music and half the time on the Catholic music, promising that I would teach them a plainsong mass in Latin.

I remember the first rehearsal. When the Catholic girls entered the Lutheran church, the Lutherans all hunkered down over their hymn books. But as soon as we began singing hymns together, the faces all brightened with the improved sound. A little gimmick I introduced was to have half the sopranos sing the tenor line while half the tenors sang the soprano line and have half the altos sing the bass line while half the basses sang the alto line – a device that enriched the sound substantially. When the bishop visited Maynooth we sang the whole of a Gregorian mass in Latin to his astonishment; and he would have been more amazed if he had known that half the choir were Lutherans.

I wanted to get more young people in the choir so I went around knocking on the doors of farms in the neighbourhood. I found a few people that way. Among them were two little girls, six or seven years old. They were sisters and they lived in a small house up Musclow Road. I never met the mother but it was rumoured that she 'entertained men'. The little girls never missed a rehearsal and I've retained a strong vision of them standing at the end of their lane surrounded by snowdrifts, clutching their hymn books and waiting for the choirmaster. They spoke very little but one spring day they asked me if I'd like to see their doll's house. So we walked to an abandoned barn and I saw the little house they had made in the straw for their dolls.

AFTER ABOUT THREE YEARS, the choir had close to thirty members. We decided to change the name to the Maynooth Community Choir so that we could perform some non-religious music. I wanted to do something more ambitious, perhaps create a music-drama based on a biblical story. The result was *Jonah*.† The story is clear and dramatic. Jonah refuses to do what God commands him to do and tries to escape on a ship with some sailors. There is a storm at sea; the ship capsizes and Jonah is swallowed by a whale. Only after he agrees to do what he is told to do does the whale vomit him up on the shore. The choir takes the role of the voice of God, and for the sailors I had a schoolteacher, a mechanic, a farmer and a hippie. We improvised the scene and this is how it came out. I wish I could give you the flavour of the country voices speaking these lines:

---

† See the article 'Jonah and the Maynooth Community Choir' in my book *The Thinking Ear*, Arcana Editions, 1986.

Jonah: Hey! Hey, you fellow! Do you own that boat over there?
The sailors ignore him.
Jonah: Hey! Do you guys own that boat?
The sailors look up slowly, suspiciously.
First Sailor: Say somethin', stranger?
Jonah: Yeh, do you own that boat over there?
Second Sailor: Maybe we do … maybe we don't.
Third Sailor: And who's askin'?
Jonah: My name's J-Jonah.
Second Sailor: What sort of name is J-Jonah?
Jonah: It's a Hebrew name.
Fourth Sailor: Well, we can't all be perfect.
Jonah: Is that boat going out? I'd like to go for a ride.
Third Sailor: He wants to sail!?
Fourth Sailor: Where ya goin'?
Jonah: Where are you fellows going?
The first sailor stands up slowly.
First Sailor: Straight to hell, boy, wanna come?
Second Sailor: You ever been to sea before, landlubber? Do you even know where Tarshish is?
Jonah: No, but it doesn't matter. I'll help work if you want me to.
Second Sailor: Is he joking?
Fourth Sailor: Our boat's small. We don't have room.
First Sailor: Yeh, it costs money to travel.
Second Sailor: You have no food. Four weeks is a long time.
Jonah: I have silver. I'll pay you ten silver pieces.
Third Sailor: Ten pieces!
Scornful laughter
First Sailor: For one of his kind?
Second Sailor: He wants to sail to Tarshish for ten silver pieces!
Fourth Sailor: We want at least fifty!
Third Sailor: Don't forget we have to feed you, ya know.
Jonah: O.K. I'll give you thirty pieces of silver. Maybe we could fish for food on the way.
Third Sailor: Maybe we'll use him for bait.
Jonah: Come on. Let's go now.

We got into trouble when Jonah shouted at God from the whale's belly.

'Gawd! Where are you Gawd!' Just at this moment the church elders decided to pay us a visit and witnessed Jonah in the darkened church screaming those lines. The elders called the pastor and a meeting was hastily organized in the church basement while the actors and the choir waited nervously in the sanctuary. I was summoned below to explain the blasphemy. I pointed out that the Bible says Jonah was 'angry unto death' with God (Jonah 4:9) and the pastor allowed us to continue the rehearsal. Another unusual scene was Jonah's encounter with the King of Nineveh. We had run out of male performers and had not yet cast the King of Nineveh so I decided we would have a child king. The role fell to Tony Fitzgerald, a twelve-year-old chorister whose singing voice was beginning to break.

Tony lived a couple of miles up the road from me. He was a gifted lad, one of a large Catholic family in which there was much musical talent. I knew he would accept the challenge of playing the King and decided that he should write his own part. So one day we read the rather brief dialogue between Jonah and the King in the Bible, and I then asked him to write down the story of that conversation in his own words.

> Jonah: Halt! Repent! God gives you forty days before he will send his anger upon you sinners.
>
> The King: Begone, thou art a farmer not a prophet. Return to your hovel and attend your animals. That's where thou shouldst be.
>
> Jonah: No! This city will be completely destroyed if its wickedness prevails.
>
> The King: Thou art a fool! Thou art ignorant of what thou sayest.
>
> Jonah: I have been sent from God to tell you this. The Lord commands it.
>
> The King: Thou art saying blasphemies against our gods. There is not one sole God.
>
> Jonah: But there is. I am the prophet Jonah. I am to bear this proclamation to the city: 'Repent! God gives you forty days before he will destroy Nineveh!'
>
> The King: But how did you find out thereof? You, a mere peasant?
>
> Jonah: God told me in a dream …

I had also asked Tony to write the text for his procession through the streets of Nineveh on a litter while other children threw flowers and sang his praise. I suggested it might begin like this:

> The King of Nineveh is great,
> he is a mighty king.
> he rules o'er land and sea and sky,
> he rules o'er everything.

Tony continued:

> The King is loved and worshipped well,
> he comes with trumpet blasts.
> His reign is just and glorious,
> his subjects hope it lasts!

Jonah has been performed several times in churches across Canada. The nice thing about it is that it brings children and adults together. There is even an important role for very young children, four or five years old. When the ship capsizes in the storm all the lights are suddenly extinguished and the pitch-black church is filled with phosphorescent fish swimming up and down the aisles.

Another piece that has travelled far from Maynooth is *Gamelan,* a little vocal exercise I wrote for six or eight of my best singers, based on the Indonesian pentatonic scale: dong deng ding dang dung. I have seen programs from all over the world for this little piece stating that it is Balinese folk music. It could have been but actually it came into existence on a snowy day in Monteagle Valley, Ontario.

A more authentic and original work was *Snowforms,* which was derived from a series of drawings of snowdrifts seen out my window on a winter day. I drew the shapes of the snowdrifts in white over a pale blue background, then spread the pentagram over the snowdrifts so that the singers 'drift' from note to note softly singing Inuit words for snow. I have heard performances of Snowforms given by many choirs, but one of the most memorable was in Mendoza, Argentina. The work was beautifully performed but with almost full-voice singing. Afterwards the choir gathered around to hear my comments. 'Beautiful,' I said, 'but it was rather loud. Snow is very soft.'

'We don't know,' explained the director, 'we have no snow.' But one thing we did agree on was the wonderful Mendoza wine after the concert.

YEARS BEFORE I began to write *Credo* (in the winter of 1976), I had a dream in which I was standing on a stepladder putting the final touches to an enormous choral piece. *Credo* must have been that work. The text was a description of the universe by Giordano Bruno, the sixteenth-century philosopher and astronomer. My musical inspiration was Thomas Tallis's forty-eight-part motet *Spem in alium*, a copy of which I had in hand; but *Credo* would be a much longer work, consisting of twelve Invocations proclaiming 'Lord God is Universe' together with twelve responses defining the states and elements of the universe. There were to be twelve choirs, corresponding to the twelve gates of the Holy City, each of which was inlaid with a precious stone. The choirs were to be in a circle totally surrounding the audience, and they were to be accompanied by a track of cathedral bells, collected on our European soundscape tour, filtered at first, then ringing in all their glory at the conclusion of the forty-five-minute work. Working out all the details of the forty-eight-part composition made me dizzy. From my diary:

> The feeling is by no means unpleasant, rather like a slightly drunk sensation in which the eyes won't come into focus on anything but look straight into the distance ... At the beginning the nude white page dances before the thought and away from it. At the end it leaves the fingers all pale and scratched, as if I had been struggling with some archangel; yet this twisted wreckage gives me a certain satisfaction, really the only satisfaction in this unsatisfactory world, in which we can only brandish the scars of impossible hopes.

Credo received a performance by the Mendelssohn Choir before the staged production of *Apocalypsis*. This was to be a CBC broadcast, without audience. In retrospect, it was a very funny event, though it didn't seem so at the time. For whatever reason, the producer, Clark Kent, failed to tell me when the taping was to take place. When I

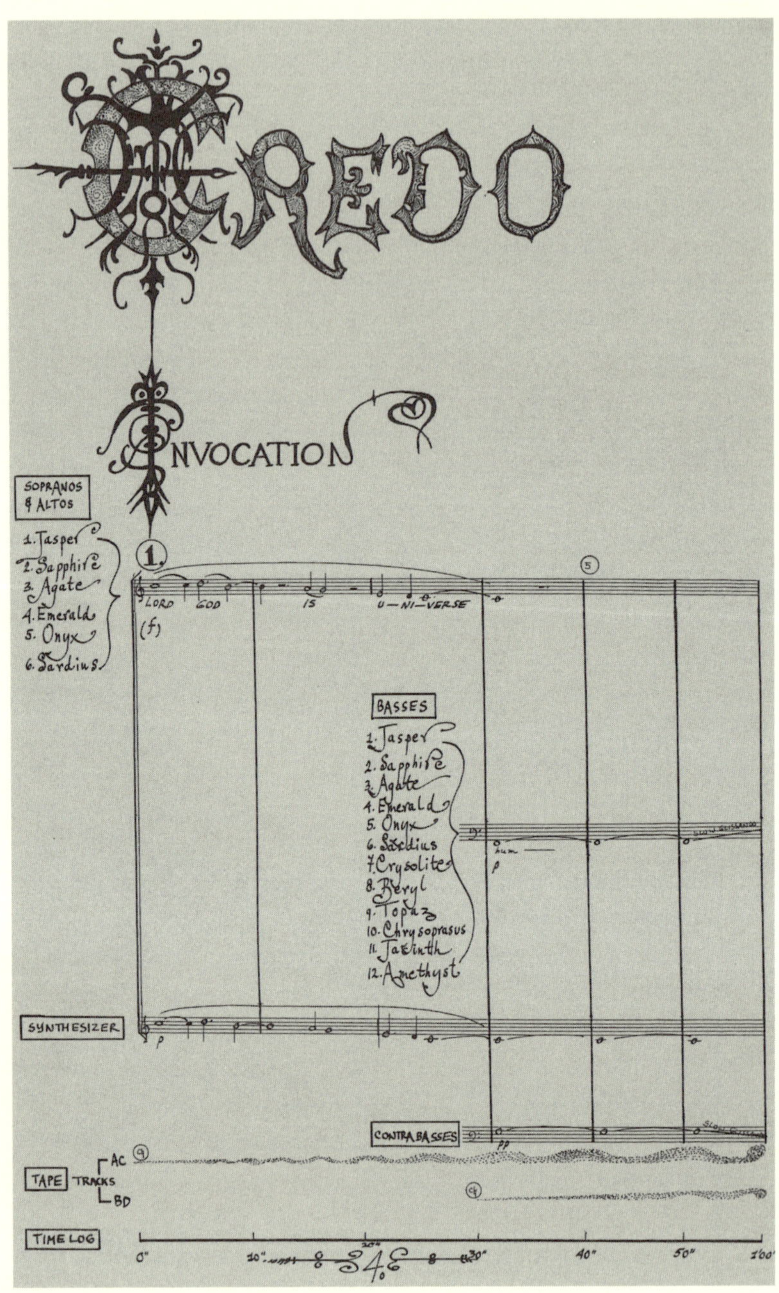

The opening page of *Credo*, the second part of *Apocalypsis*.

called him he hummed and hawed and finally said it would be best if I didn't attend. I hit the roof and demanded to be there. I suspected that the conductor, Elmer Iseler, preferring dead composers, had asked for me to be locked out. Anyway, I was allowed to attend provided I sat quietly and promised that I would in no way interfere with the proceedings. They had decided to record the work in short sections, leaving the tape of bells to be mixed in later. To help Elmer keep to the timing, a lighted stop clock had been rigged up, but he ignored it. Elmer came into the recording booth after each take and announced whether it was good or not, looking out of the corner of his eye to detect whether I agreed; but when I once said I thought it could be improved, he ignored me and went on to the next section.

We ran out of time with three sections still to be recorded. Elmer came into the studio with the choir managers and said: 'Go and tell the choir that the conductor is prepared to continue but only if every member agrees to stay.' While this was being done, his wife, Jessie, massaged his shoulders and someone brought him a bottle of pop. The managers returned delightedly and said that everyone would stay. Elmer, however, was not pleased. 'You used the word "demanded",' he said, 'I did not say *demanded*.' So they had to go out again and repeat the request in a mollified manner. Finally, after wasting half an hour we were able to continue, completing the taping at close to midnight.

I worked hard to edit in the bell track, which was almost impossible because Elmer's timings were totally askew. Strangely, *Credo* was never broadcast and I was never able to find out why.

Credo was the second part of what was to become *Apocalypsis*. I spent the rest of the winter working on the first part: 'John's Vision'. I knew the group of Toronto poets who called themselves the Four Horsemen and I had attended many of their performances. One could not call them readings, since they declaimed their texts contrapuntally with a great deal of body movement. I decided to cast bp Nichol as the apocalyptic John, Paul Dutton as the Angel Michael, and Steve McCaffrey as the Antichrist. Our first attempt to produce the work was in an abbreviated version at the Dayspring Festival, held in Metropolitan United Church (Toronto); the church was too small for the enormous scale of a full production. Both parts of *Apocalypsis* were staged in complete form in London (Ontario) in November 1980.

From *Apocalypsis*.

There were more than five hundred performers in the production which I directed myself. The memory of the production still remains in people's minds. Years later the poet and playwright James Reaney wrote a long article about it in *The London Free Press*:

> My strongest memory is of constant sound and motion all over the hall. The swirls and sworls of action still play in my mind. Along with hundreds of others, I was proud to be part of an epic that swept us away for two hours into a better, madder world where the end was a new beginning.

Other critics were equally generous in their praise of the work. The *Toronto Star* critic, William Littler, called *Apocalypsis* 'One of the most spectacular events in the history of Canadian music.' I was so excited by the reception that the work received that I had five hundred copies of the score printed. I still have four hundred and eighty-five of them in my basement. The work has never been performed since.

Apocalypsis was followed by a much more delicate work, *The*

Crown of Ariadne, which I wrote for the Toronto harpist Judy Loman. Judy wanted a piece that would show off all the new techniques possible on the harp. It was Toru Takemitsu who suggested the incorporation of percussion instruments. So Judy and I worked through the winter developing a whole realm of new effects resulting in a virtuoso piece that harpists the world over would later perform.

About the same time, I decided to build some sound sculptures from junk that had been left on the floors of my barn and drive shed. I was aware of the sound sculptures built by the Baschet brothers in Paris. In fact, during a visit to Paris, I had spent some time with François Baschet. François used to host a potluck lunch every day in his studio and it was open to everyone, provided they brought some food or wine. I liked the man, and since he liked everyone who visited him, we got on very well. Of course, the junk in my barn was very different from the expensive materials of the Baschet sculptures.

My neighbour, Elijah MacDonald, came down and identified each piece of junk: 'That's off a cream separator ... this here's a binder guard.... Look here! You've got a plate from a disc.' I picked up the pieces one after another and clinked them together. One piece suddenly rang with a clear, bell-like tone. Elijah caught the sound immediately. 'That's a horse-tooth rake. Lad could make a good dinner bell outer that.'

That year the young composer Murray Geddes was driving up from Toronto every couple of weeks for a composition lesson. The next time he came up I said, 'Let's build a sound sculpture.' Before long we had gathered a large variety of materials and began to consider how the whole thing should be powered. We decided to use a large rock as a pendulum. We tied it to a roof beam and ran guy wires from the pendulum rope to different parts of the sculpture. With a good push, the sculpture would continue to ring for up to ten minutes. The most beautiful sounds were those at the very end when they began to blend with the chattering of autumn leaves and flocks of migrating birds. But the winter was too violent for the sculpture and by spring it lay in ruins on the barn floor.

THAT SPRING, 1976, I had a letter from Yehudi Menuhin outlining a series of television programs he was planning with the CBC under the

With Yehudi Menuhin listening to the sound sculpture in my barn.

general title 'The Music of Man'. For years Yehudi had been a strong supporter of the soundscape research I had been conducting. One day, while he was on tour in Chicago, he saw an article about our work and he called me up immediately to encourage us. Yehudi realized that the soundscape work flipped the anti-noise theme into a positive modality by encouraging the public to participate creatively in the acoustic design of the community. He wanted to discuss this subject with me in one of the programs of his series.

The next day the producer called me. 'We don't want to film you and Mr Menuhin in two armchairs,' he said. 'No, not in a studio,' I replied. 'Why not on my farm where the hi-fi soundscape will tie in nicely with the discussion?'

'And what if it rains?'

'In my barn,' I said.

'Is it full of animals? Will they kick the cameraman? I don't think Yehudi ...'

'No animals, just a pile of junk.'

'We need a nice setting. Something that will look nice.'

'I'll rig up something, don't worry.'

As the nearest motel was fifty kilometres away, the Menuhins elected to stay with us. I remember them driving up in a long black limousine. As the white-gloved driver removed the luggage, Yehudi said, 'That was the roughest trip I've ever had in my life.' But things turned out fine. Jean made a very nice dinner for them and they bought one of her quilts.

The shoot was set for the next day and began with a walk through the forest while we discussed the sounds of nature. Then we entered the barn, which was a very big surprise for Yehudi. Together with Murray Geddes I had built a new and much larger sound sculpture out of saw-blades, sheets of roofing, steel pipes, scrapers and hammers of all kinds – even the guts of an old piano. The whole contraption was to be powered by a teeter-totter with Yehudi on one end and me on the other. Yehudi was delighted by all the commotion. After a few moments, we stopped to examine the mechanisms and talked about the relationship between music and noise. 'Let's make it go again,' said Yehudi, and we did. I suppose the program can still be seen somewhere even though the CBC has long since excluded serious culture from its programming.

Conducting *Music for Wilderness Lake* at dawn.

The French call a person who lives by recycling a *bricoleur*. Junk sound sculptures are then forms of *bricolage*. They breathe new life into old or dead objects. They prove that nothing in the world is dead or past usefulness if the imagination can bring it to life again.

Another film from around this same period was *Music for Wilderness Lake,* my first environmental composition. I had been canoeing around one of the many unpeopled lakes in the Madawaska area and had noticed how the sounds changed throughout the day and evening. I decided to write a work for the lake and take advantage of those changes. There would be two sections to be called 'Dawn' and 'Dusk', performed at the appropriate times. But what musicians could I lure into performing such a piece at such an inconvenient time and place? Just at this time I was approached by a group of twelve trombone players who wanted me to write a piece for them. I suggested my idea and they liked it. But who would come to such a performance? Perhaps we could attract a film company. CBC Television had had enough of Schafer but John Reeves of CBC Radio was interested in testing the new Kunstkopf microphone he had just acquired from Germany. I then approached three film students, Niv Fitchman, Barbara Sweete and Larry Weinstein and they were immediately captivated by the idea. Later they were to form Rhombus Media and devoted themselves to making many fine films about music and musicians. *Music for Wilderness Lake* was to be their opus one.

We rehearsed in my barn with the cameras running, then drove to the lake in the late afternoon and performed 'Dusk' in the evening. I conducted it with coloured flags from a raft in the centre of the lake, where the CBC was also recording it. The flags were necessary because of the distance between the players and the conductor (five hundred metres or more), but actually the score is written in such a way that the players can take cues from each other aurally most of the time.

The next morning I drove back to the lake at 4:30 a.m. The performers were just up and were slapping themselves to keep warm. The boatmen were ready to ferry them to their positions with the first glimmer of dawn. The recordists took up their positions in canoes, looking fantastically surreal with their wind-socked microphones rising above the gunwales as they paddled silently in the misty water. The whole experience was very beautiful and very strange with the mist drifting across the water and the trombone chords slowly evaporating over the hills.

Since we were recording simultaneously from the raft and from canoes moving about the lake, we were able to mix the takes to zoom in on different soloists so that within a second or two we could hear them from the distance to close up or in reverse. I think this panning and zooming at such great distances must have been a first for sound recording but, of course, most of the effect was lost when it was all mixed onto the optical film track.

Though it has not been performed very frequently, some unusual performances of *Music for Wilderness Lake* have taken place: I once conducted it on a lake in the centre of an urban park in Wiesbaden (Germany) and once on the Amstel river in Amsterdam, with the audience standing on the bridges while I was on a tugboat in the centre of the river.

Several other new works followed over the next year, but the most significant, at least for me, was *The Garden of the Heart*. I had fallen for a blond singer at the University of Western Ontario while we were organizing the premiere of *Apocalypsis*, and I had not forgotten her when I returned home for the summer to write a new work for Maureen Forrester commissioned by the National Arts Centre Orchestra. Maureen was, by this time, past her prime, but would, I hoped, give the vocal line just the right touch of senescence suggested by the text – in the same way as the declining voice of Julius Patzak singing Mahler's *Das Lied von der Erde* resulted in a better recording of that decadent work than any other made since.

I first composed the vocal line from beginning to end. I intended the accompaniment to consist entirely of the same material with the instruments anticipating and recalling phrases sung by the singer, overlapping and underweaving like the arabesques of Persian art. I wanted the score to shimmer like a garden full of flowers, birds and fountains, surging forward to greet the singer then hesitating and falling back to make room for other voices. The orchestration of this piece is one of the most delicate and sensuous I ever achieved. The work was written over the summer of 1980 when the birds in Monteagle Valley were at their most joyful and the evening air was filled with the scent of the earth.

Many years later I wrote a novella about *The Garden of the Heart*, fictitiously situating the premiere of the work in Vienna and reintroducing my blond muse as a character together with Richard Strauss, whose sensuous orchestrations had influenced the colours and hues of my composition.

DURING THE 1970S AND 1980S I was doing a lot of travelling. I could not live from commissions and royalties alone. For a few years SOCAN, the Canadian performing rights society, had been paying some of its members advances against future earnings. I had been lucky enough to be included, but when the program was discontinued (at least for me) I was forced to accept more lecturing and teaching jobs which, fortunately, had increased following the publication of my music education booklets, and *The Tuning of the World* in 1977. I travelled to many colleges and universities across the USA and Canada and gave lectures and workshops in Germany, Austria, France, Spain, Portugal and, later on, in Sweden, Finland and Japan.

In those days I was so full of soundscape ideas and information that I lectured impromptu. The same was true for music education classes because I always wanted to keep the door open to creativity. One day in December 1977 I was to meet a group of Portuguese music teachers in the Gulbenkian Museum in Lisbon. I was ushered into a large auditorium. The Portuguese radio had set up microphones to record the event. The theme of the lecture was to be 'Creativity', but I couldn't imagine how a hundred people stuffed into plush seats with microphone wires all over the little stage could be creative. I was genuinely scared and stood there for ten minutes without saying anything while the radio people were frantically gesturing and pointing at their watches. Finally I said: 'If anyone wishes to teach, go ahead and teach.' Then someone rose up and said, 'Let's teach Mr Schafer some Portuguese folksongs.' So they did that and then we went on to other exercises which various people conducted. The ice was broken.

One thing I have learned in my career as a teacher: if you want a creative response from others, learn to keep quiet yourself. The moment you say 'I don't know', someone else will come forward with an answer. Then you can become a learner again. But it is a hard lesson to learn. I won't go on about the many things we did that week

In Paris during a lecture tour in Europe.

because I have described them elsewhere but it was one of the most enjoyable weeks of my life.[†]

Many teachers feel that if they don't maintain total control, the class will degenerate into chaos. Of course there is always a risk of that, but it is more likely that the class will reorganize itself with some new ideas that are worth developing. It is a heuristic approach that I have adopted and I have never been disappointed because there are always new ideas to be investigated. Even if many of them lead nowhere there will always be a chance of discovering a path that leads us into the undiscovered future. That is what happened in Lisbon. There was much laughter over our failures and pride in our discoveries.

I remember one day giving the Lisbon teachers a homework assignment of taking a tone I had given them home and trying to remember it until the following day. I also tried to do it. I hummed it all the way back to my hotel, but lost it over a splendid dinner. The next day when I returned to class I asked everyone to hum the 'sacred' tone. Total cacophony! What did it prove? That nothing is sacred, everything is subject to change. We laughed our heads off and then went back to other exercises.

A very different but equally memorable experience occurred in October 1978. I had been teaching a short course in Madison, Wisconsin, when I received a call asking me if could come to Eau Claire the next evening to give a lecture to students in the music department. Where was Eau Claire? 'Only about seventy miles west of Madison.' There was a bus that left at 5:30 p.m. and arrived at 7:30. There wouldn't be enough time for dinner but the caller said he would meet the bus with a hamburger and a Coke and take me directly to the hall, then he would bring me back to catch the 10:30 bus to Madison. It was absurd and I said no. 'Oh, please, Dr Schafer! Our students have been studying your work and would be so honoured to meet you.' I suppose vanity can be aroused by curiosity and the next night I found myself on the bus. It was raining and the windshield wipers were slapping back and forth.

[†] See 'Letter to the Portuguese', in *The Thinking Ear*, Arcana Editions, 1986, pp. 318–326.

At Eau Claire I met the music professor with a cold hamburger and a warm Coke in his hand. He drove me to the school. There were a lot of people there. 'Oh, they're performing *Guys and Dolls* tonight,' said my guide. 'We go this way.' He led me into a large and empty lecture hall. 'Our students are always late,' he said. 'You unpack your notes and I'll go round them up.' A few moments later he returned with an elderly woman on his arm. 'Mr Schafer, I'd like you to meet my mother,' he said. 'I'm almost blind,' said the mother, 'but I have very good ears, and I'll be concentrating on everything you're saying.' 'It's just the way I like it,' I replied and began to lecture vigorously to cover my dispiritedness. Two other faculty members turned up late. The lecture over, I was driven back to the bus. It was still raining.

One more strange lecture – or rather, the prelude to a lecture – took place in Seattle a few years later. I had been taken out to dinner by a charming woman who was somehow involved in architecture. The title of my lecture was 'Walls and Soundwalls' and I was hoping to make my audience more aware of the ways in which architecture could respond to the changes in the contemporary soundscape.

It was pouring rain as we drove to the campus. A quite large audience was waiting patiently, for we were a little late. I thought I should visit a washroom before a lengthy lecture and asked where it was. 'Down one flight of stairs on your right,' the organizer replied rather impatiently. I ran downstairs, turned right and opened a heavy metal door, thinking that this was a strange door for a washroom. The door shut behind me. I was in the basement and the door was locked. I ran around looking for an exit or someone to talk to. No one. Only a few parked cars. Eventually, I found the exit. It was still pouring rain. A huge complex of buildings met my eyes. From which building had I come? Two students were crossing the campus with newspapers over their heads. I ran up to them and asked which was the architecture building. 'Don't know. Chinese visitors.' I ran behind a bush and peed in the rain. Then I ran to the nearest building. Not this one. Ran to another. Not that one either. Finally, someone identified the building for me and I ran towards it, slipped in the mud and fell, but eventually got back wet and fifteen minutes late to speak to an audience that was not amused.

It was always a joy to return to the farm after a lengthy lecture tour. But the farm had its problems too, particularly during winter storms or during the May-June blackfly season. Jean was especially bothered by blackflies, tiny flies that swarm around naked skin sucking blood. While they bothered me less, they still swarmed over every inch of exposed skin. Jean's temperament, usually at peace with nature, could also be wounded by the hostility of nature and the failure of civilization to subdue it. We were living at the edge of civilization, where nature disintegrates into chaos, where roads end up as dirt paths leading to abandoned farmhouses and broken-down barns. The futility of it was almost more than her spirits could bear and her depressions were wretched to observe.

Looking through my 1979 diary I came across this short entry:

> Two hands, both reaching for the same doorknob, momentarily
> close over one another. Surprise in the eyes, then both hands
> are withdrawn quickly. Smiles. The door remains closed.

I remember the moment well. The door was that of the Maynooth Lutheran Church. The hand was that of a young woman in the choir. We had arrived early for a choir practice.

ON JULY 9, 1979, the Maynooth Community Choir gave its first concert. The audience was surprised by the quality of the performance and the choir received a standing ovation from the full house of approximately two hundred people – which immediately raised the Maynooth per capita commitment to culture miles above the national average. *Gamelan* and *Hear Me Out* received the strongest ovations. *Hear Me Out* consists of nothing but aural metaphors for sound. 'Stop blowing your own horn,' 'Give him an earful,' 'You had to hear it to believe it,' 'Put a bug in his ear,' and so forth, spoken and sung contrapuntally by four performers.

The summer of 1979 marked the beginning of what would eventually become the *Patria* cycle of music-dramas. Several short pieces that would eventually be incorporated into *Patria 3: The Greatest Show* were conceived at that time. *Hear Me Out* was one of them. The other *Patria* work that had begun to take shape in my mind was the Prologue to the cycle: *The Princess of the Stars*. At least the theme of the libretto was beginning to become clear. Like *Music for Wilderness Lake, The Princess of the Stars* was to take place on and around a lake.

At this time, I also began to think about publishing my own books and music. My Canadian publisher, Berandol Music, made a decision to discontinue publishing 'serious music', and Universal Edition, whose editors had once taken an interest in me, was now only interested in publishing works that had proven themselves with a dozen or more performances. McLelland & Stewart decided to remainder *The Tuning of the World* after only a few months in print, which made me particularly angry because I had insisted on holding the Canadian territory for a Canadian publisher. Knopf had wanted world rights.

Jean and I discussed a name for the company and eventually settled on Arcana Editions because Schafer's work was always so *arcane!* We printed a thousand brochures and sent them out to all the university music schools in North America and also to all the harpists in the American Harp Society since Judy Loman thought that *The Crown of Ariadne* might attract some attention. We spent hours licking stamps and envelopes.

Replies? Only one, from a man who was outraged because we had addressed his wife as Ms, rather than Mrs. Any regrets? None at all. When I inaugurated Arcana Editions in 1979 I became my own publisher, editor, manager, publicist and salesman. I alone am responsible for copying, printing and promoting my own music. Most of the income earned by the company is invested in the printing of new works. My basement is full of boxes of scores and books I have published over the years. I could never live on the sales of this material, but at least I can see where my books are being used in classrooms and where my music is being performed. Arcana now has over 150 printed books and scores in stock, with recordings of many of the works available for curious performers or listeners, and I intend to keep them available as long as possible.

IN THE SPRING OF 1980 I was invited to go to Basel by the Swiss section of the International Society for Contemporary Music. I was to be there for about ten days. On the last day, I would play some of the soundscape recordings we had made in Canada, but as a prelude I was to plan some soundwalks and other activities exploring the soundscape of the inner city of Basel. For this I would need some help, and it was promised. I still don't know whether it was the audacity of what I wished to do or the incoherence of my explanation that got me off to a slow start with the Baselers. The organizing committee seemed totally indifferent to the success or failure of the project. Balz Trümpy, the person designated to help me, turned up fairly regularly but only to complain that the project was ridiculous. 'Was hat dass mit Muzik zu tun?'

I have described the exercises in *A Sound Education.* They were aural games and were intended for the general public (including children) to acquaint them with the sounds of the city. Sometimes they were given a list of sounds to be found in a particular area; sometimes they were to find a path through the city by listening to sounds in sequence.

For the Sound Treasure Hunt people were asked to locate about a dozen different sounds made by ordinary people moving about in a designated area on a Saturday afternoon. The sounds were quite ordinary – a boy with a cap pistol, a girl with a flapper on the wheel of her bicycle, two women speaking English, etc. When they located a sound, they were given a coloured card. The first person to collect all ten cards was declared the winner. Children loved the game but adults were rather reluctant to play. They thought it might make them look ridiculous.

I had asked for half a dozen students to help me organize the events, but none of the students helped me consistently. On Monday, I'd have three students. I'd set them tasks for Tuesday. On Tuesday only one student would return, and he could only stay an hour. And so it went. Nevertheless we got several events ready for Saturday, and about thirty people attended the events. Saturday night I delivered my lecture in an art gallery to about thirty (different) people, and the soundscape tapes were played in three different rooms so that the audience could move around and sample them. After three hours the only people still there were the organizers who were standing in the lobby thumbing art books. Jean and I collected the tapes and carried the heavy box to the streetcar while the Swiss organizers watched us. They say Switzerland has never been conquered. Well, *I* never conquered it.

June 2. RETURN HOME! Breakfast in Paris, lunch on the plane to Montreal, dinner at Jim's Restaurant in Renfrew and to bed in Monteagle Valley. Amen.

A few nights later, while I was scoring *The Garden of the Heart,* I heard a howling pack of wolves. First the leader would start, then the others would join in, howling first then ending with a kind of tense whimper. They sounded very close, certainly on my property (an odd way to express it) and stopped as suddenly as they had begun. Then the following afternoon they began again, more or less in the same position, and continued to howl for ten minutes, then fell suddenly silent.

What I loved about living close to the wilderness was that I was sharing the same territory with living creatures other than humans. One winter we heard a lynx – or at least assumed it to be a lynx from descriptions of locals who also heard it. It sounded almost like a woman panting. My neighbours in the wilderness were, in many ways, as strange as the animals. They didn't speak much but they knew their way in the forest.

The winter of 1980–81 was particularly cold. There were nights when the temperature would drop to minus 35 degrees Celsius. I remember going out on the porch in the mornings to listen to the crackling of the trees. Sharp explosions like gunfire were followed by a sizzling noise as if the trunks and branches were shivering in the cold. Even walking across the veranda made a ferocious noise as the floorboards creaked and shuddered with the frost. Then Jean would start knocking down the icicles, her sparkling laughter mixing with the frost and ice, and we would go back inside for breakfast by the stove.

PATRIA

FOLLOWING THE SUCCESS of *Music for Wilderness Lake,* I began to think of a larger, more theatrical work in which the action would take place on a lake with the musicians situated around the shores. This was to be *The Princess of the Stars,* the Prologue to the *Patria* cycle which has occupied my attention for over forty years. I have already mentioned *Patria 2: Requiems for the Party Girl,* which was composed in Vancouver and performed at the Stratford Festival in 1972. *Patria 1: Wolfman* had also been composed in Vancouver though it would not be performed until 1987.

I suggested to my friend Bob Aitken, who ran New Music Concerts in Toronto, that he might give the premiere of *The Princess of the Stars.* He agreed to consider it if the funding and a suitable lake could be found. Finding the lake proved to be as difficult as finding the funding. Eventually, we chose Hart Lake, near Brampton. The size and configuration of the lake were satisfactory; the only problem would be Toronto Airport, but we hoped to avoid most of the noise because the performance would be over at 7 a.m. Bob was afraid the audience wouldn't be able to find the lake, but there was a surprisingly large turnout.

In order to realize the work I needed to find a costume designer and lots of paddlers for the canoes. I approached the painter Harold Town first, but he was too busy. Then I approached the sculptor Sorel Etrog. He was interested, but quoted a fee that we could never afford. Finally, a young man whose name was Jerrard Smith approached me. 'I *really* want to design this work for you,' he said, looking straight into my eyes and I knew I had found the right person. Jerrard has designed all the *Patria* productions since then and his wife, Diana, has designed the costumes.

Jerrard came up to Monteagle Valley in the late spring and worked in the yard just outside my window while I was drafting the final version of *The Princess of the Stars.* Because the figures would be seen at a substantial distance they had to be very large constructions. The actors would be inside them and would be able to coordinate some moving parts of the costume with their chanting.

In order to model Wolf, the hero of the work, Jerrard went to the

Rehearsing for the premiere of *The Princess of the Stars* at Hart Lake, 1981.

drugstore in Bancroft and borrowed the stuffed wolf that stood on a shelf above the cash register and duplicated him about six times life size. And so, as the score neared completion, the yard was filled with huge animals, birds and a sun-disc that glittered in the sun.

For the actors I again chose the Four Horsemen, with bp Nichol as the Presenter, who moves close to the audience and narrates the story as the others move around the lake chanting strange animal languages. Paul Dutton was Wolf, Steve McCaffrey was the Three-Horned Enemy, and Raphael Barreto-Rivera was the Sun Disc. In the summer of 1981 the Four Horsemen drove up to Monteagle Valley several times to rehearse their parts. The soprano Kathy Terrell sang the part of the Princess, unseen on the far side of the lake. I have already extensively written about the productions in *Patria: The Complete Cycle,*† and I will only comment on *The Princess of the Stars* briefly here. What made it unique was the enormous spaciousness of the set. And, of course, the set was nature itself, not an attempt to imitate nature, or to avoid it as the sets of drama or opera productions do.

The work begins in darkness before dawn with the aria of the Princess floating across the lake. The singer is a kilometre or more away from us. Later she is joined by other singers in different places around the lake, echoing the phrases of her song. As the dawn light unfolds we see an old man slowly paddling down the lake towards us. This is the Presenter who will tell us the story of *The Princess of the Stars*. We learn that the Princess was listening to the mournful howling of Wolf from the forest below, but she leaned over too far and fell to earth where Wolf, frightened by the brilliant light, lashed out at her. Wounded, she ran bleeding into the forest leaving dew wherever she went. Eventually she arrived at a lake and slipped into the water to bathe her wounds; but she was dragged to the bottom by the Three-Horned Enemy.

All this has happened during the night so that when we arrive we hear the echoes of the Princess's voice still reverberating across the lake. Now Wolf arrives, searching in vain for the Princess in order to apologize to her. Wolf calls on the Dawn Birds to help him find the Princess. As the real birds begin to awaken the singers around the lake

---

† Coach House Books, Toronto, 2002.

stimulate them by echoing their calls and from the far side of the lake dancers in canoes move across the water, dipping their wings, in search of the Princess.

Suddenly the search is interrupted by the arrival of the Three-Horned Enemy, the hideous creature in a war canoe. Wolf and the Three-Horned Enemy engage in battle on the lake accompanied by vigorous drumming. Then the combatants part to reveal the Sun Disc slowly moving down the lake surrounded by the Dawn Birds, who have gone to seek him in order to restore order on earth. The entry of the Sun Disc is coordinated with the official time of sunrise. The singers perform a hymn of praise to the sun and the Sun Disc predicts the future for Wolf, the Princess and the Three-Horned Enemy, a forecast that will be realized in the eleven works of the *Patria* cycle to follow.

It is obvious that one must make some effort to attend a production of *The Princess of the Stars*. To get to the site one may have to stay up all night or travel a considerable distance. The weather may be uncooperative – though we have never cancelled a production. With this work we reintroduce the notion of pilgrimage into art. It is not new, but it is alien to societies trained to believe that great art can be revealed with the flick of a switch.

Another work dating from 1981 experimented with moving sound around in an interior space. This was my *Third String Quartet,* which is still one of the most frequently performed. It was written for the Orford String Quartet, the leader of which, Andrew Dawes, became one of my best friends. Andy and his wife Karen came up to the farm several times so I was able to discuss the work with him in considerable detail. The work begins with only the cello on stage; then, one after another, the other players enter from various places in the hall and backstage. In the second movement, the players vocalize with shouts and screams that never fail to shock and amuse the audience. The third movement is a meditation with a lot of quarter-tone playing and, at the end of it, the first violinist stands up and slowly moves off stage, repeating a simple three-note theme until the sound gradually drifts away to a point where the audience cannot determine whether the sound is still there or is only a memory trace in the mind. This is a similar effect to the final phrase of the Princess's voice as she disappears at the end of *The Princess of the Stars,* and it occurs again at the conclusion of the Epilogue of the *Patria* cycle, *And Wolf Shall*

Inherit the Moon. When the Princess returns to the stars, the singer sings the same aria that opens the cycle, this time while being paddled down Wildcat Lake in total darkness under the canopy of moon and stars, until we cannot be sure we are still hearing her or are only hearing her in our imagination. This ceremony has been performed for over twenty years and I have witnessed this aria slowly vanish from an audience that remains in hushed silence and darkness for many minutes before rising and dispersing into the night, speechless.

During the 1980s the soundscape movement was growing rapidly. *The Tuning of the World* had been translated into German, French, Italian and Japanese. It had also appeared in paperback in the United States. I was receiving many invitations to give workshops and lectures in Europe as well as the USA. One day, while lecturing in Calgary, I received a request from the archives librarian to come and help sort out some manuscripts of mine which Phyllis Mailing had sold or given to the university. I went to the library where I was met by two mother-bird librarians who brought out the manuscripts one by one, all nicely wrapped in non-acidic paper. I saw many things I had totally forgotten about but was prevented from getting too nostalgic by the librarians who had a wide range of questions to ask. I made up a few dates for them. At one point, I came across a scrap of paper on which I had scribbled a short list of things to do, ending with instructions to reach someone's house: 'turn left at the gas station, go over the bridge ...', etc. 'That has nothing to do with music,' I said, and was about to crumple it up, but the librarians both rushed forward and said they would keep it anyway. How flattering all this attention was – but how petrifying also.

IN JUNE 1981 I had some trouble with the government. The census officer arrived and left a form to be filled out. 'You're lucky,' she said, 'you get the long form.' I glanced at it and immediately got angry at the kind of questions asked as well as the form of the questionnaire, which had obviously been designed by people who believed that humans ought to be treated like electric circuits.

When the lady came back the next day I was painting the roof of my house. I told her I didn't understand the form. She began asking

At the University of Southern California, January 1980.

questions: age, occupation, etc. When she asked how most of my time was spent in my occupation, I said, 'Thinking.' She hesitated. I spelled the word for her. When she asked what ethnic background I came from I asked her what were the options. She read off a string of tribal names. I said, 'Chinese.' She left. The next day a different lady came along and asked a series of financial questions such as: How much do you make? How much money do you spend on electricity? How old is your furnace? What was the date of your first marriage? And a lot of other silly things that I would prefer not to remember at all.

The next day two men came and spelled out the penalties for non-compliance with the law. I then decided to write to Jean-Jacques Blais, Minister Responsible for Statistics Canada.

> Dear Monsieur Blais:
> … the matter is very simple. You evidently believe that valid decisions can be made on the evidence of statistical findings and I don't. I admit that you will have plenty of clients for the decimalization of humanity which your statisticians will produce – big business, big government and big users of information of any kind, including academics; but I do not accept that 'free, democratic society' depends on it. I should have thought that this depended more on the individual and the idiosyncratic than on the statistical heap – or at least, let us say, that this is what brought it into existence and continues to keep it from being ground into the powder that statisticians and bureaucrats would find easier to sift.
>
> What I resent is that governments increasingly (under the influence of the users of statistics) feel it necessary to threaten individuals with the power of this form of assessment. For some time we have witnessed the way the infatuation with numbers has overtaken other modes of evaluation, so that today, it has even replaced money as the value-tab for reality. Even money has become a wild number, shifting as if by legerdemain, from one column to another in invisible institutional hands.
>
> Anything can be reduced to numbers, programmed and played with in a variety of ways. Even organic creatures like humans can be torn into fragments in this way. But this is not

how 'free, democratic society' works, and you ought to know that. It works through the dialectic of exchanging points of view and is best defended by individuals speaking out unyieldingly whenever their determination to remain individual is threatened.

Democracy was not shaped by the decimal point. It was shaped by people: whole people, unique people, and 'difficult' people. Therefore I say, count the bags of nuts or the pails of bolts if you think this will give you some key to the historical process, but leave individuals out of your equations. You will only be deceived.

R. Murray Schafer

THE YEAR 1982 was devoted almost entirely to the writing of *Patria 6: Ra*. Right from the beginning I decided that the work would last eleven hours, all night from sunset to sunrise. As source material I used ancient texts describing how the Sun-God Ra passes the night travelling from west to east through the Netherworld – a dangerous time for him and full of encounters with his strongest enemies. The myth solves the cosmological problem of how the sun, dying each day in the west, can rise up the next morning in the eastern sky. In the Netherworld, Ra encounters Osiris, or rather *becomes* Osiris, and by means of this metempsychosical exchange is able to rise up again new-born. Thus the theme of the work is that everything runs to its extreme in death, then turns back on itself and returns to life. The Egyptians detected this transformation in the cosmos and it was celebrated by priests who performed the necessary rituals each night to ensure the return of the sun god and the continuation of life and light on earth.

My helper in selecting the texts to demonstrate this hierophany was Don Redford of the Department of Egyptology at the University of Toronto. Don helped me choose the appropriate texts and transcribed them into the original language in which they were chanted.

I proposed a theatre piece based on the story of Ra to Comus Music Theatre in Toronto, a company that had been founded by Maureen Forrester, Michael Bawtree and Gabriel Charpentier, all of whom had been involved with productions of my work. Although new personalities were now running Comus, the magnitude and novelty of an eleven-hour production excited them and I began to look for a suitable site. We would need the Temple of Amun-Re at Karnak to present *Ra* properly.

The Ontario Science Centre, a new building at the time, possessed a certain grandeur. Some of the exhibit areas were still empty. There were long corridors and cellars and high-walled exterior pavilions that could be sites for rituals. We approached the Science Centre board and a meeting was arranged. I don't recall much of it except that the then director said to me: 'Young man, don't you realize that what you are proposing kept science back two thousand years?' He then went to sleep in his chair and two hours later we seemed to have convinced his colleagues that, subject to certain restrictions, the Science Centre might be made available to us.

By the time we had approached the Science Centre I had written the libretto and much of the music, so the next thing was to try to adapt the work to the site, scene by scene. To do this, I wanted to walk through the building in real time with the director, Thom Sokoloski, the designers, Jerrard and Diana Smith, and the choreographer, Sally Lyons, so we could determine how the text would fit the site. We were given permission to do this one night so that by dawn we had a map of the spaces we proposed to use.

The audience or, as we were to call them, the initiates, would be limited to seventy-five; each person would receive one of the seventy-five names of Ra. They would be robed in caftans and would wear a burnoose, thus masking their identity as individuals. During the early part of the night, they would go through a series of exercises designed to assist them when they descended into the underworld. They would learn to distinguish the gods by their appearance as well as by the sounds and perfumes associated with them; they would learn to chant in ancient Egyptian, and finally, each initiate would be given a secret name which would have to be repeated before the guardians of the Corridors of the Dead.†

---

† One of the underworld passages consisted of seventy-five mummies in a dimly lit room. Seventy-four of the mummies were constructed out of papier-maché, but one was alive and would move slightly from time to time to the terror of the initiates near it. We often had to take people to the Green Room who found some of the experiences in *Ra* overwhelming.

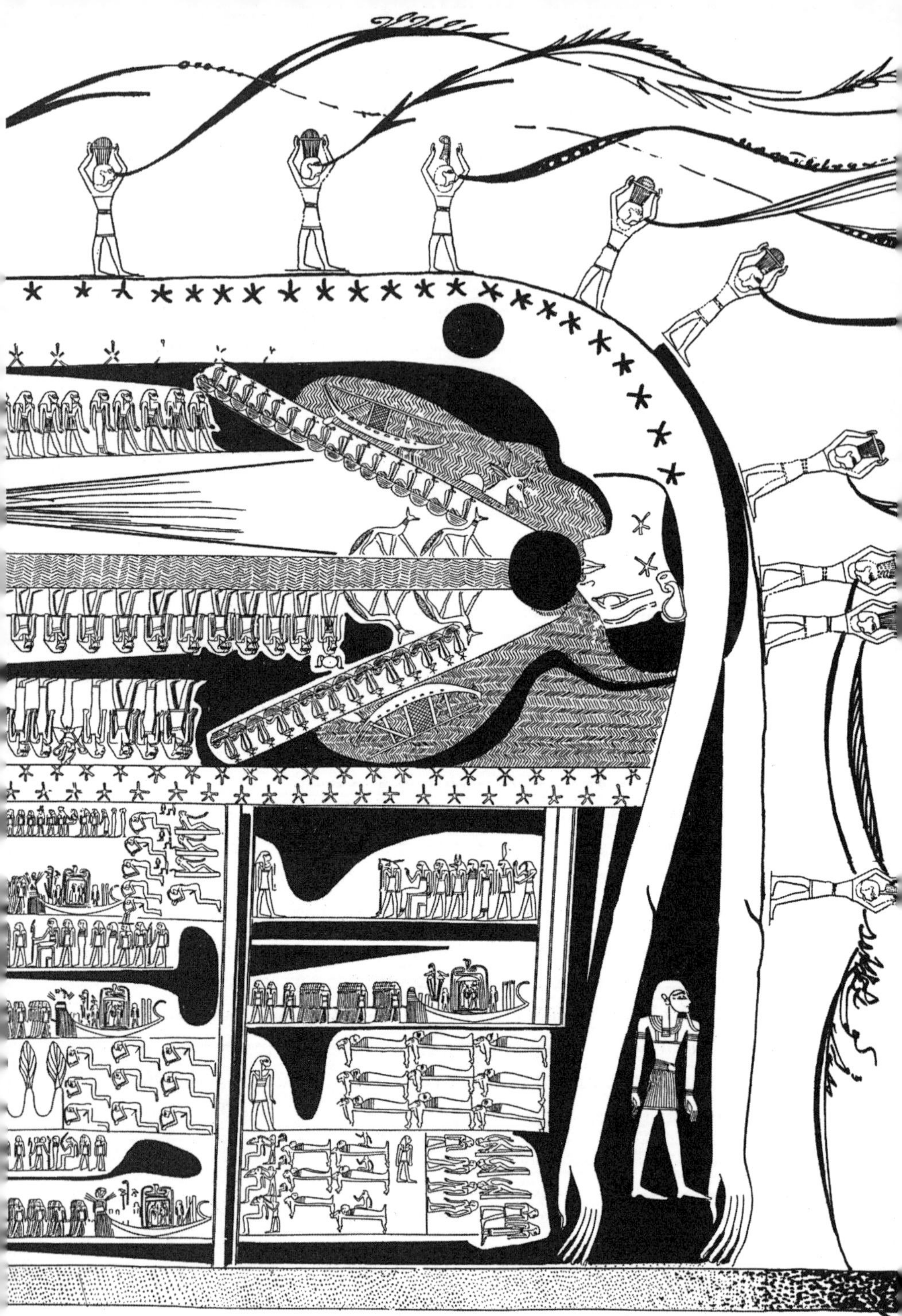

A page from *Ra*.

There are many spectacles in the netherworld but in the darkness the senses of touch, hearing and smell are especially important. The initiates would visit approximately thirty different sites inside and outside the building. In the middle of the night, they would be confronted by Ra's enemy, the dragon, Apophis. The initiates had been taught sacred chants to drive Apophis away and were also directly engaged in the battle.†

After the victory the initiates were provided with a magnificent dinner of Middle Eastern food followed by a quiet rest. Each person was given a mat to lie on in a large, dark space. From above, Maureen Forrester sang the aria 'Amente Nufe' accompanied by John Wyre playing gongs and bells. After the rest, a hierodule bearing a candle approached each initiate and whispered: 'Are you ready to be reborn?' Then each person singly would go through a cleansing ceremony to the accompaniment of soft choral music. I remember seeing people actually weeping as the hierodules bathed the face of each initiate with scented water. The celebrated 'Weighing of the Heart against the Feather of Truth' brought all the gods together for a final ceremony which is almost operatic in character. After their departure, Thoth gives each of the initiates a hug saying, 'You have passed through' and the initiate exits into the sunrise of a new day.

Ra was produced at the Ontario Science Centre in May 1983. The production provoked a lot of commentary and attracted a large assortment of people, some of whom regarded it as a kind of opera and others who were inspired by its religiosity. I remember one woman with flaming red hair who went through the whole performance clutching a knife, which she held vertically, blade up. Another woman, a Christian, wrote me a very disturbed letter criticizing my evocation of mystery cults. Her letter bothered me a lot and I felt the need of replying to her. Unfortunately, I can't find her original letter though my reply gives some idea of its contents.

---

† One night the head of the fire-breathing dragon blew up adding a real touch of terror to an already exciting encounter. From that night on Apophis was headless.

Images of masks from *Ra*.

December 13, 1983

Dear —,

I received your letter of October 28 a few weeks ago when I returned home but didn't reply immediately because I wanted to think about it first. Now I have just returned from another trip and want to try to take up the task.

First of all, you must realize that we are living and working in different worlds, yours of Christianity, and mine of Art (I capitalize it not in order to make the two states equivalent but in order to give mine the dignity it deserves.) Although I was brought up a Christian and, at various points in my life have been a practising Christian, I have never succeeded in entering the blessed state in which you find yourself. I envy you because I know how hard it is. I am reminded here of Kierkegaard, who always said he was not a Christian but was only *becoming* one. He also said that Christianity does not negate art but merely dethrones it.

What prevents me from becoming a Christian is its exclusively humanistic bias. I am not a humanist either but closer to something like pantheism. The elevation of man to the position of primary and some would believe exclusive importance in the universe has led us into a lot of problems, the magnitude of which we are only now beginning to realize. This humanistic arrogance, which seems to place the whole world of nature at man's exclusive disposal, irritates me. If Christianity had emphasized more the Holy Spirit and less the idea of God made Man (and exclusively *man*), perhaps I could accept it more effortlessly – but then it wouldn't be Christianity.

When I moved to the country eight years ago and began to share the same territory with the animals and the birds and the trees and the snow, I began to feel a great recrudescence of a faith in all nature and my own (in)significant place in it that seemed to me to come from a very ancient and wonderful time. In searching for a means to describe my faith that deity is manifested in all things, I eventually came on the ancient text of *Ra*, among other things. What seems to me to be the strong point in Egyptian religion is the acknowledgement that everything has its place and time of ascent and descent – that one moment after midday midnight begins, that death leads to life as surely as life leads to death and that these alterations form a kind of circle of transformation. Within this circle there are no improvements or declines but rather merely changes in the life-line under the protective instruction of the god or gods. (It seems to me of little importance whether God is singular or plural just as it is of little importance whether God is masculine or feminine, black or white.) The Egyptian Ennead was a marvellously balanced creation myth embracing both the masculine and feminine principles as well as all the elements: earth, sky, moisture, life, death and light, which was Ra's particular gift. You must admit that this is a magnificent paradigm for a naturalist.

I would not say that this is all there is or needs to be in a religion and, in fact, in *Ra* I indulged in a lot of psychologizing to make the initiates aware that this was not necessarily the end of the subject but rather the beginning. Of course, Christianity triumphed and the Egyptian religion fell into decay; but this was perhaps a historical necessity, just as in a minutely similar way, I see my own inclination back to a worship of the elements as a historical need.

One day perhaps you will experience *Ra* and then you can judge for yourself whether it is Satanic. Dark it certainly is, probing to the roots of the unconscious, but Satanic it would only be for those who feared coming to terms with the dark side of themselves. The function of rituals and ceremonies is to give us a stylized presentation of the utter limits of human experience, to put them, as it were, into a form which we can handle. In this sense *Ra* is created because one cannot look at the sun directly. The ritual or the ceremony is the means of clarifying the experiences of life and showing us their purpose. I don't think of this exploration of consciousness through art as Satanic though I do admit that my insistence on creating a work of theatre, moves us closer to a position where some confusions could result between exhibitions of magic and faith in magic.

Incidentally, I have also written Christian works and written them with faith and zeal. One of these works, *Apocalypsis*, deals with John's vision of the Second Coming. I think I was inspired when I wrote it; but I'll let you be the judge since I am sending you, under separate cover, a copy of the score and a performance tape of the first part of this work. Part Two deals with the New Jerusalem and for it I've used in part a text by Giordano Bruno, which begins: 'Lord God is Universe ...' This I believe. Thank you again for your letter. As you may be able to tell, it affected me deeply.

Sincerely,
R. Murray Schafer

ABOUT THIS TIME I met Jim Henson, creator of the famous Muppet show on television. He was in Toronto with his team, some members of which had attended the production of *Ra* and concluded that I must be a person with a vivid imagination and might be of some use to them in the creation of a new television series they were contemplating on the theme of music. We had dinner a couple of times. I liked Jim a lot. He didn't correspond to my conception of a famous television figure. He was very polite in conversation and asked questions about my work, never boasting about his own accomplishments.

We came to an agreement that I should visit New York for a few days to discuss the proposed new series. A couple of days later I received a call from New York asking for the name of my manager to discuss financial matters. I told him I had no manager. No problem. How much did I want for a three-day introductory meeting with the team? I was rather nervous about committing myself to a project that I only had a very dim conception of, so I said that all I wished beyond the travel expenses was to have three tins of Barking Dog pipe tobacco on the table the first day of our meeting. 'I've seen a lot of strange contracts in my time but this beats them all,' he said, but he adhered to my request. The tobacco was on the table when we went to work the first day.

It was a very strange meeting. There was a small table in the centre of the room, Jim at the head of it. Around it were four or five

Eleanor James.

musicians in different fields of music, popular, classical and jazz. We were throwing around ideas as to how Muppet characters could introduce different forms of music to children 'world wide'! I stress that because it soon became clear that they were thinking *big!* Around us in a larger circle were ten or fifteen people who contributed information from time to time. 'It won't work in South America,' they might say, or 'We tried that in Japan and it flopped.' Clearly they were thinking world-wide. Jim never contradicted them and we would move off in another direction hopefully more rewarding.

The series was eventually produced in England under the title *The Ghost of Faffner Hall,* but I had little to do with it. I don't think it was very successful.

I HAVE NOTICED that whenever I undertook a large project I seemed to need a woman to play up to. Regardless of whether anything ever came of these relationships they nourished me and gave me the inspiration necessary to push the project to the limit.

This is how my relationship with Eleanor began, but soon I knew it was different. Eleanor had auditioned for the part of Hasroet, Goddess of the Necropolis, in the production of *Ra*. She fascinated me in a different way from other women and before long we were experiencing a passionate relationship which was, however, not consummated until after the *Ra* production was over. We did nevertheless, manage to escape down some of the dark unused corridors of the Science Centre for tender caresses. I called her 'Mignon' after the girl in Goethe's *Wilhelm Meister* – a sweet girl from the South who entertained the poet with her singing and dancing, inspiring some of the most beautiful poems in the German language.

On my return to the farm, Jean sensed at once that something had changed and quickly understood that another woman was involved. 'What did I do wrong?' Jean asked, looking up at me with what seemed to be more resignation than surprise. It was spring but neither of us wanted to put in a garden as we had always done. We talked a lot about the past, but somehow couldn't decide how to deal with the present. 'It has beaten us. Nature has beaten us,' Jean said. I just wanted to be with Eleanor, or at least to be free to see her. And eventually that is what happened. I went to Stratford and rented an apartment with a piano to try to do some composition.† Eleanor visited me frequently and by the end of the summer we were making plans to live together. We were both very tense and, although neither of us was really ready for it, we rented a house in Toronto in September. It lasted about three months and even that was amazing.

Like many middle-aged men, I wanted to have a younger woman as a partner; an intelligent, beautiful person, but also a person who was 'someone' and whose career would mesh with mine. For about a week, I imagined that Eleanor and I would be seen in all the best places in Toronto; at concerts, receptions, and of course, the opera, where Eleanor would sing leading roles and patrons would nod approvingly in my direction and explain to their friends that I was the dark companion of the beautiful singer and an internationally famous composer and author. Of course nothing like that happened. We rarely went out to anything social. I think I drank more during those three months than at any other time in my life. Also I had never enjoyed sex so much. But sex is not enough to hold people together.

I went home to the farm. Jean was by this time studying at the University of Ottawa. It was a very lonely time. Can a person love two people at once? States of mind I had always considered impossible had become the reality of my life. I recall driving along the country roads like a maniac, half hoping to kill myself. I cried to God to help me. I brooded, I swore, I wept.

THE FOLLOWING SPRING (1984) I was commissioned by the Kyoto Community Bank to compose an orchestral piece to celebrate the thousandth anniversary of the founding of the city of Kyoto. I was invited to spend ten days with my wife visiting the shrines and temples and then go home to compose the work and return a year later to hear it performed by the Kyoto Symphony, conducted by Seiji Ozawa. I went, with my wife, who later said I was gloomy the whole time. Perhaps I was, but I learned a great deal about Japanese culture and traditions that was to affect both my music and my philosophy from that time on.

---

† The work I wrote there was *Theseus*, for harp and string quartet, commissioned by Judy Loman, the harpist for whom I had written *The Crown of Ariadne*.

Toru Takemitsu had also been commissioned to write a piece for the orchestra and he and his wife travelled about the city with us, interpreting Japanese culture and traditions. There are 1,620 temples in Kyoto, each with abundant grounds, punctuating the busy city with quiet zones. Toru also explained the difference between the bells of Christian churches and those of the Buddhistic temple. 'Christian bells have a deliberate personality. They are given names and a distinctive character. Different bells are played at different times to bring news to the people, weddings, funerals ... They are struck, metal against metal. The Buddhist bell is struck with wood wrapped in cloth. They provide an atmosphere rather than information.'

We visited the Kiyomizu-dera (Clear Water Temple) where *gagaku* (court music) orchestras had once performed. Walking in the park beneath the *butai* platform, I understood how the music would have been heard from different angles and distances rather than from the cramped seats of Western churches and concert halls. I began to understand how oriental music encouraged diffusive listening, just as oriental art encouraged non-focused, diffusive looking.

The famous rock garden of the Ryoan-ji Temple imparts this message. Fifteen stones, in a field of raked gravel, imbue stillness in the landscape. The immobility of stone in space is matched by its immutability in time, uneffaced for centuries, yet changing moment by moment with the light that plays on it, slowing the minds of those who contemplate the still point at the centre of motion. These things I learned from Toru Takemitsu and they may be found at the centre of his music, and in certain reflective moments of mine as well.

In a little pavilion near the Ginkakuji Temple Jean and I attended the ceremony known as *ko wo kiku* ('listen to the incense'), which, like the much more famous tea ceremony, dates from the eighth century. Four different kinds of incense are used in the ceremony. The incenses are not identified by their real names but are given descriptive titles such as 'the view from the bridge', 'the mountain in the mist', 'gentle rain' ... Three of the incenses are identified and a fourth is known simply as 'the mystery incense'. The incenses are passed around the circle of kneeling participants in small cups. Each participant lifts the cup from the floor, turns it three times in the palm of the left hand, then inhales the fragrance, shading the cup with the right hand. After each inhalation, the cup is raised towards the left ear, then is placed on the ground before the next participant. After all the incenses have been identified, the game begins. The incenses are passed around in any order and each participant tries to identify them, writing the name down on a neatly folded piece of paper with a brush and ink. At the conclusion all the papers are handed in and the person with the most correct answers wins a prize, a large scroll on which a master calligrapher has been painting famous statements and poems about incense. Like the tea ceremony, the incense ceremony can last a few hours. The purpose of each of the ceremonies is the same: to teach us that less is more.

We returned to the hotel in the early evening and I was already imagining how I might create a piece for the Kyoto Orchestra that would somehow incorporate the 'listen to the incense' ceremony, even if I couldn't incorporate the actual incense. I wanted the piece at least to move with that mysterious slowness. But, in the end, I *did* manage to incorporate incense! The piece opens with the conductor slowly raising a bowl of incense, inhaling it, then ceremoniously passing the bowl to the first violinist, who does the same then passes the bowl to the second violinist, and so on throughout the whole orchestra. The performers begin to play only after they have inhaled the incense, which is intended to provide inspiration for their playing.

Each evening from the hotel balcony, I was enchanted by the beauty of the mountains surrounding Kyoto. I would watch them folding into shadow with the descent of the sun, the near ones still green, the more distant taking on blues and the far fading into pearls of grey. No city I had ever visited was as fortunate as Kyoto in being served by mountains on all sides. With a slight mist in the air they were especially lovely.

WHEN JEAN AND I returned to Canada I told her how I felt about Eleanor, and a few days later she left me, moving to Toronto where she took a secretarial job in a law firm. That was to be the end of our time in Monteagle Valley and with pain I put the farm up for sale and moved all my furniture, library and manuscripts into storage.

Meanwhile Eleanor had been contracted to join the opera company in Sankt Gallen, Switzerland, to begin in August (1984). Before she left Canada we rented a little cottage near Kirby (Ontario). She brought her son, Kingsley, who was about eight years old at the time, and we passed a couple of pleasant weeks before her departure.

In September Bob Aitken gave a superb performance of my *Flute Concerto*, written over this period of excitement and desperation which can clearly be heard in the music. I had rented a small apartment in Toronto where the only pleasure I received was a flood of letters, handwritten in all sorts of coloured inks, from someone who signed her name 'Mignon'.

I began to set *my* Mignon's letters to music. The texts were so varied that I was certain they would work as a song cycle. Many years later, back in Canada, Eleanor was to record *Letters from Mignon* for Atma Classique with the Esprit Orchestra conducted by our close friend, Alex Pauk. I still cherish this work, which was written partly in Canada in my miserable apartment, and partly in Sankt Gallen – for in February 1985 I moved there to be close to my love.

The year 1985 was to be one of my most significant. In May of that year we performed *Ra* at the Holland Festival in Leiden, and then went to Banff for a production of *The Princess of the Stars*. Jerrard and Diana Smith moved to Holland early that year to supervise the reconstruction of the sets and costumes of *Ra*. I had been in Holland the previous year to try to locate a suitable site with Willem de Ritter, the festival director. Eventually a complex of buildings was chosen including a museum which housed a real Egyptian temple.

To move the initiates from building to building we had them wear blindfolds. This slowed things down somewhat. At times, they would spontaneously begin to hum the three 'magic tones' that they had been given during the introductory ceremonies, which possessed apotropaic powers in times of peril. During the dress rehearsal I saw one group, without a hierodule to lead them, heading straight for a canal. I managed to take the hand of the first person and angle them to safety. I was especially glad to have saved them from drowning since I noticed near the front of the line the mayor of Leiden, who had been an enthusiastic supporter of presenting *Ra* in his city.

The reviews of *Ra* in the Dutch press were enthusiastic. Thom Sokoloski was favourably compared to Peter Brook. But I never pay much attention to reviews. More significantly, the production was successful with the audience and, despite the high price of the tickets, the production was sold out or nearly so each night. Years later,

The Presenter, bp nichol, in the Banff production of *The Princess of the Stars*.

during visits to Holland, I would meet people who still remembered the production favourably.

Almost immediately after the Dutch production of *Ra,* I moved to Banff, where the Banff School of the Arts was to produce *The Princess of the Stars*. Brian MacDonald and I were to co-direct and Micheal Century was to be the producer. Although Paul Fleck, the director of the Banff School, was enthusiastic about the project, not all the faculty shared his enthusiasm. The music department said that, due to other commitments, they would be unable to provide the dozen or so musicians required and the vocal department, run by a 'pommy' absolutely refused to allow vocal students to participate for fear that they might chill their voices. Eleanor sang the role of the Princess with warmth and beauty. The production was a spectacular success, attracting far more people than had been predicted (2,500 on the last of three performances) which was totally unexpected, since the production began at 5:30 in the morning and Banff is an isolated town in the Rocky Mountains. The cars were streaming off the Trans-Canada Highway at 5 a.m. and winding their way up to Two Jack Lake where they were parked and the occupants were guided down the hill towards the lake to be seated on the ground in total silence to await the beginning of what would more accurately be described as a ritual than a show.

I remember one man getting out of his car and when the usher approached and told him she would seat him he replied, 'Seat me? Why? I'm just trying to get to Vancouver!' He thought the traffic was being detoured from the highway. I also remember two fishermen arriving after the show had begun and the Dawn Birds were moving down the lake in canoes. 'Look at the f—g reflections in the water,' one fisherman whispered to the other.

There is no doubt that of all my works *The Princess of the Stars* has the most immediate appeal for Canadian audiences, or at least, for those who have had some experiences or background in the Canadian wilderness. Four successful productions of the work have been given to date, and a very good recording was made by David Jaeger for CBC Radio of the Wildcat Lake production in 1997. Other *Patria* works such as *The Enchanted Forest* and *The Spirit Garden* also evoke Canadian geography but *Princess* is the most unequivocally Canadian because of its wilderness setting and connection with native folklore.

FOLLOWING THE PRODUCTION of *Princess* in 1985, I moved to Switzerland to be with Eleanor. My life in Switzerland was to last nearly two years with frequent returns to Canada. Eleanor was much happier with a steady job singing opera. When she was free we would take long walks in the country and eat delicious meals together in the charming apartment she had rented on the outskirts of Sankt Gallen.

I was getting some work in Europe, lectures and workshops, but there were few performances of my music there. While Universal Edition had published a lot of my earlier work, they were reluctant to publish more until there were signs of increasing performances. Anyway, I was now publishing my own work with my own company, Arcana Editions. The main problem was: who would look after it when I was not in Canada? There were scarcely enough orders even to pay a part-time employee, but when orders come in customers naturally expect immediate action. Some orders – for instance, the rental of orchestral material – require a person who knows all the instruments of the orchestra and how to read the orchestra librarian's code, viz: 2222/4221/Str 8,7,6,5,4/timp, perc.[†] Aside from this, I needed someone who was honest about billing and banking, and checking to see that all rental material was correctly returned.

I employed a young woman part-time but as she did not read music there were frequent problems that had to be sorted out by transatlantic phone calls and frequent visits to Toronto. Eventually, I decided to rent a coach house, which was large enough to house the Arcana material and where I could compose when I was in Toronto. The coach house was in an area known as Lower Forest Hill. My mother called it 'a very good address'. So I spent much of my time in Canada. Eleanor returned to Canada when she was able. But her time-table was complex and, in fact, she would soon be moving to Germany to sing at the Munich opera.

[†] The code deciphered means: two flutes, the second doubling on piccolo, two oboes, the second doubling on English horn, two clarinets, two bassoons, four horns, two trumpets, two trombones, one tuba, eight first violins, seven second violins, six violas, five cellos, four contrabasses, timpani and percussion.

In the spring of 1986 I taught a semester at San Diego State University. I was assigned a very spacious apartment in a complex surrounding a large swimming pool which was constantly occupied by blond co-eds with brightly painted toenails reading books on psychology through dark glasses. The day I arrived, I went looking for a restaurant, having decided that a restaurant with a tablecloth ought to be capable of producing a nutritious dinner. I walked for miles down a brightly lit boulevard without finding one.

My students at the university all had beautiful suntans but they seemed to be only half present in class. They say the Arabs were prevented from conquering Europe by the forests. I believe I was prevented from conquering San Diego by the sun and ocean. I had a dark little room on campus where I went to compose after my classes were over. I was working on a harp concerto for Judy Loman and was having problems. My diary says:

> After devoting every available hour to the concerto, I am now in possession of forty pages of trash which is supposed to be the first movement. Its triviality astounds me. Is it because I have grown tired of this instrument that I am so bereft of ideas? Additionally, it must be confessed that a work whose only purpose is the inflation of a solo performer's vanity disgusts me. Nor is the harp particularly suited to this kind of boastful display. It seems an effrontery to place before the orchestra an instrument whose role has traditionally been little more than providing the occasional sonorous gush. Even half the orchestra going about their normal business is enough to drown this little water baby. An amplified harp is an obscenity but . . .

Actually, the Harp Concerto turned out to be quite successful. And I did amplify the harp, but only at the end of the piece where the 'water baby', in a great tidal rush, drowns out the entire orchestra.

One day while working at the San Diego State University I received a phone call informing me that I had won the Glenn Gould Prize for Music and Communication, worth fifty thousand dollars. I jubilantly rushed out of my room and grasped the first colleague in the music department that I encountered. 'I've just won the Glenn Gould

Award worth fifty thousand dollars!' I said. 'Canadian dollars?' he sniffed.

But the prize meant a lot to me. I had certainly not expected it, even though Yehudi Menuhin had been the chairman of the jury. Later there was a hundred-and-fifty-dollar-per-plate dinner to celebrate the awarding of the prize. I sat next to the Governor General, Jeanne Sauvé, with whom I argued about free trade with the USA, she being in favour of it. 'You've got to grow if you are going to survive,' she said, 'otherwise you're nothing.' I annoyed her with my 'small is beautiful' arguments, so that when the time came to present me with the cheque and the silver bowl, she simply handed it over and declined to speak into the microphone, though everyone was expecting her to say something.

On April 9, 1986, Eleanor premiered the *Letters from Mignon* with the Calgary Philharmonic Orchestra. Unfortunately, the work served as a prelude to Andrew Lloyd Webber's *Requiem*, a piece of trivia. But her singing was beautiful and was a public endorsement of our love. The audience, however, seemed bewildered. I felt I had to disguise the origin of the texts so I explained that they were letters written by Mignon to Goethe. It worked and one or two people said how beautiful the poems were without commenting on the music. We laughed a lot at dinner – at the parodies of musical styles disguising events that only we could identify.

INDIAN RIVER

IN 1986 I BOUGHT A FARM at Indian River, near Peterborough; Eleanor was able to spend some time with me towards Christmas of that year. She had coached the singers for the first production of *Patria 3: The Greatest Show* that summer, but with her busy schedule in Europe, she had to return before the premiere. It seemed I was destined to live alone on the farm over the winter and spring while I reworked *The Greatest Show* which I intended to remount in the summer of 1987. Thom Sokoloski was to be the director and Jerrard and Diana Smith were to be the set and costume designers.

The Greatest Show was modelled on the travelling carnivals I remember having seen as a child. Aside from the rides on Ferris wheels and in go-carts, there were lots of sideshows: from haunted houses to freak shows, magicians, dancing bears and trapeze artists. I decided that *The Greatest Show* was to comprise a hundred events of this sort. It would happen at night and, despite its comical flavour, it would have a sinister theme. At the beginning, the showman, Sam Galuppi, calls the audience to the main Odditorium, an open stage at one end of the fairgrounds. He declares that in order for *The Greatest Show* to function, a hero and heroine will have to be found. He requests volunteers from the audience. Of course the hero and heroine he chooses are plants and part of the production. They are invited to the Odditorium Stage and asked their names. 'Ariadne,' says the woman. 'Wolfie,' replies the man. The showman, Sam Galuppi, puts Ariadne in a coffin with her head and feet projecting. He then orders the Black and White Magicians to saw it up. Next he conducts Wolfie to an animal cage. The White Magician fires his pistol at it and the cage is empty.

'Vanished! Cut to pieces!' says Sam Galuppi. 'And they were going to be the heroes of our show! What a spectacular beginning! And so much more to come! … Let the Greatest Show begin!' The showman blows his whistle and suddenly all the sideshows spring to life. As the audience moves around visiting them the man, Wolfie, is occasionally seen running past followed by the police. Presumably, he is a wanted criminal. He also makes cameo appearances in some of the

The disc jockey Eddie le Chasseur in *Patria 1: Wolfman*, Canadian Opera Company production, Toronto 1987.

sideshows. Also in some of the sideshows parts of the sliced-up woman make an appearance: her clothing, her feet and, in one of the most celebrated cameos, her head, which has been snatched by an accordionist and made to sing to a malicious accompaniment.† There is a text explaining it all and videos were made of parts of the show though, being a linear medium, a video fails to communicate the multi-sensory all-at-onceness of the live show.

The Greatest Show was to be repeated and enlarged in 1988. Meanwhile, in November 1987, *The Characteristics Man* (later titled *Wolfman*) was produced by the Canadian Opera Company. Right from the beginning, it was a doomed show. The subject was a 'displaced person' or, to give him his pejorative title, DP, which is the title all refugees to Canada bore when I was young. At the time I wrote *Wolfman* 38 per cent of the population of Toronto were immigrants who were not born in Canada. It is now over 50 per cent. Of course, to write a work in which an immigrant was to be laughed at and persecuted was to raise a lot of questions. People talked about the immigrant 'problem' and laughed at immigrant jokes, but not in public. The story is based on an actual event: a Yugoslav immigrant in Vancouver, unable to integrate into Canadian society, grabbed a little girl and held her at knifepoint while he hurled abuse at the public and reporters exclaiming how Canada had failed him, then, letting the girl go, he stabbed himself to death.

For this dreadful story the COC hired, as director, Christopher Newton, an expert in Shavian farces. I guess they must have felt that he would keep the show distanced from the grim theme that Canada has never solved: how to make a nation out of immigrants. My treatment of the theme was to try to evoke sympathy for the poor, misplaced fellow. To do this I turned to Expressionism, the artistic movement in which forms and colours are distorted or exaggerated. Often there would be violent contradictions between the sound and the lighting. I introduced a whole arsenal of noise weaponry to the percussion department and added recordings of aircraft and jackhammers

---

† That she appears to have no body is, of course, a magician's trick, accomplished by mirrors. As a solo piece, *La Testa d'Adriana* (The head of Ariadne) has proved to be a favourite of accordionists in many countries.

from the soundscape project. To this Christopher Newton added the pommy accents and elegant postures of his Shaw Festival actors in a messy merger that neither the critics nor the public could figure out. *Wolfman* has never been performed again. *Basta!*

During the spring of 1987 I occasionally saw Jean. She was having some problems with her sight, but the lawyer she worked for refused to give her time off to see an eye doctor, so she impulsively resigned. Now what would she do? Eleanor was back in Sankt Gallen and I felt sorry for Jean. I suggested she might come to the farm until she could find a new job. She was to remain for several years. When Eleanor called me in January of 1987, I broke the news to her that Jean had moved back in with me. This was a traumatic event for both of us. Eleanor was devastated, but we began to live our lives anew, apart from one another. Eleanor had already been cast in the role of Melusina for the 1989 production of *Patria 4: The Black Theatre of Hermes Trismegistos* at the Festival de Liège in Belgium, so I knew I would see her again.

I went to Liège in 1988 to choose a suitable site for *The Black Theatre*. I didn't want the production to take place in a theatre, rather in an unusual environment, preferably a site that would be completely unknown to the audience. The presentation would begin at midnight. After seeing several sites, I selected an abandoned *cirque d'hiver* in a remote area of town.

At that point Claude Micheroux, director of the festival, suggested we take a day off and visit Waterloo, site of the famous battle, which was relatively close to Liège. I had read with enthusiasm both Hugo's description in *Les Misérables* and Thackeray's in *Vanity Fair*. I wanted to see the place where so much vainglorious passion had produced so much bloodshed. The size of the battlefield was most impressive – much larger than the Plains of Abraham, or any other site of combat I had ever visited. By luck we were in time to hear a local band playing various fanfares, marches and retreats of the various armies, particularly Napoleon's. I had always known that armies had musical codes for directing their troop movements, as clear yet varied as the codes of the *cors de chasse* or of the post office postilion communicating ahead to the changing stations. There must have been musical codes to give directions to the troops, yet in the 360-degree mural of the battle I could only see one lonely trumpeter amidst ten thousand or more soldiers on horseback or on foot.

We had an interesting discussion about who won the battle. Of course, as British subjects, we were taught that Wellington won the battle. But a German who was listening to our discussion could not resist pointing out that the battle was actually won by Blücher because he arrived with the Prussian troops just in time to save the English from defeat. Then Micheroux pointed out that Napoleon actually won it because he was fighting for a united Europe against the dying aristocracies – exactly what was emerging with the European Common Market. Napoleon was just a hundred and fifty years before his time.

Returning to Liège we had lunch with the Belgian composer Henri Pousseur. Micheroux animatedly explained the *Black Theatre* project to him, anxious to secure his support. Pousseur, blue eyes flashing alternately at Micheroux and at me, his smile rarely departing from his face, looked young to me for a man of sixty. As an *enfant terrible* who had been somewhat abandoned by fashion, he seemed both proud and frightened. Although his countenance was friendly he was quick to put down other composers and even his own students who had deserted him.

Someone spoke of Kafka's *Castle*. I mentioned the descriptions of the telephone system. His eyes lit up suddenly. 'Like the *Gesang der Jünglinge*,'[†] he said. When we said we would be returning next March he said, 'Good. Then you'll be able to come to the premiere of my new composition in honour of the French revolution.' His body grew visibly straighter over the plates of rather Germanic stew we had been eating. Micheroux smiled broadly: I had not yet been designated an enemy.

Leaving Belgium until the following year, I took a night train to

---

[†] An early electronic composition by Stockhausen, which consisted of a lot of buzzing and humming voices. The telephone sound from Kafka's *The Castle* is as follows: 'The receiver gave out a buzz of a kind that K. had never before heard on a telephone. It was like the hum of countless children's voices – but yet not a hum, the echo rather of voices singing at an infinite distance – blended by sheer impossibility into one high but resonant sound which vibrated in the ear as if it were trying to penetrate beyond mere hearing.' (*The Castle*, Secker and Warburg, London, 1965, p.33)

Rabindranath Le Meul (centre) delivers a monologue on the lost gods and heroes, accompanying himself with a razzle-dazzle of instrumental effects.

The Three-Horned Enemy destroys the fairground. (Both images are from *Patria* 3: *The Greatest Show*, Peterborough Festival production, 1988.)

Italy. I was to give a lecture in Umberto Eco's department at the University of Bologna. When I arrived the room was packed with maybe 150 students, all waving copies of *The Tuning of the World*, which had just been translated into Italian. My diary says that I lectured for four hours, which seems an exaggeration but, of course, that included the translation and Italian always seems to require more verbosity than English.

When I concluded it was about five in the afternoon. 'So that's it,' I said, or something like that and sat down. The dismayed organizer approached me and said, 'You wanta pausa?' 'Dieci minuta pausa!' he announced, during which I signed about fifty books, and the lecture continued. It must have been eight o'clock when we finished. 'Now we go to dinner,' said my host. And we did, all fifteen or twenty of us. I'll leave the reader to imagine what it is like seated at the head of a long table populated by fifteen or twenty eager Italian students, each with twenty questions to be compacted into an English vocabulary of twenty words or so.

I got into bed at 2 a.m. and was up at eight to be interviewed by two lady journalists. I couldn't understand most of their questions, which were buried under a superabundance of giggles and smiles. Then I was driven back to the university to meet a smaller group of fifteen or twenty students who had returned to ask more questions about the soundscape. Afterwards we went to a small apartment where five students cooked a magnificent dinner, then took me to the station to catch the night train northward.

I RETURNED TO INDIAN RIVER in early June. There was still time to put in a garden, so I planted tomatoes, cucumbers and zucchini.

Following the semi-production of *Patria* 3*: The Greatest Show* in 1987, we were now determined to present a full production in 1988. Excitement among the actors and musicians was very high as we began rehearsals, but the weather was not cooperating and on dress rehearsal night and opening night it rained heavily, saturating the ground so thoroughly that we dared not turn on the lighting with some of the cables under water. A few actors lit lamps and candles in their tents and I realized that we should have used lamps for many of the mysterious activities in the small tents inhabited by palmists and

Murray dressed as Wagner, creator of *The Greatest Show*.

fortune-tellers. Never underestimate the role of shadows in revelation.

Finally, by the third night, the show was running smoothly, but we never got a large enough audience to give it the frenzied excitement it needed. As a result, we lost a lot of money. I never received a fee for all the work I put into *The Greatest Show* over the two years that it ran and I contributed $30,000 to help pay the debt. We managed to get most of the one hundred events or scenes running. After the introduction the audience was free to wander the grounds and experience as many activities as they wished. When they paid their entrance fee at the box office, they were given a strip of ten coupons. Attendance at each event would require one coupon. More could be purchased if one wanted to see other events. But there was no entry to the Rose Theatre, the Blue Theatre and the Purple Theatre by coupons. One had to win one's way into these tents. There were various ways to do this. One could play 'ring the bottle' by throwing quoits over coloured bottles. Ring the blue bottle and you would win a ticket to the Blue Theatre, etc. But there were other more unusual ways. For instance, one could be shackled to the Jingling Fakir, a dark-skinned, half-naked mendicant who was looking for blonde wives. If a blonde agreed to shackle herself to him, he would take her directly to one of the restricted theatres. I remember witnessing a memorable spectacle of four or five blonde women chained together on their way to the Rose Theatre. And what was there? A soprano and a string quartet performing my work, *Beauty and the Beast,* the singer singing all the parts behind hand-held masks of the characters in the well-known fairytale. And small boys would be seen sneaking in under the flaps of the tent to hear the performance. Can you imagine that? The same piece on a program of contemporary music would be lucky to attract twenty customers, while we were attracting six times as many every night, thanks to our strategies of enticement.

Dressed as Wagner I gave a lecture in the University Theatre, a tiny cubicle with seating for three or four people only. Nevertheless, the newspaper critics would come and sit there for fifteen or twenty minutes, hoping to learn something about the show's purpose and plot; but when they realized that my lecture was about the decipherment of the Ectocretan language and had nothing whatever to do with the activities that were spinning about them, they left in dismay.

The Greatest Show is a multicultural event in which we laugh at ourselves and each other.

But the highlight of the night came when the Showman summoned everyone to the Mighty Finale on the Odditorium Stage. This began like a Broadway musical but gradually careened off into a Dadaist spectacle. Explosions began to be heard around the grounds as smoke filled the stage. 'It's all gone wrong,' screams the Showman. 'Cut the lights! Go home! Everyone go home! It's dangerous here!' And the cast would push the customers out of the smoking fairgrounds and lock the gate. Then, looking back at the dying embers of *The Greatest Show,* the audience would see the Three-Horned Enemy, an enormous puppet, prowling about the deserted grounds. Such was the end of *The Greatest Show,* a masterpiece of creation, deception and destruction.

The production left me totally exhausted. I couldn't even muster the strength to appear at the closing night party. From my diary (September 8, 1988):

> For several nights (ever since the show) I have been having restless dreams and nightmares. Often the characters in the dreams are from the show. They seldom speak; rather they leer or laugh at me. The night before last I dreamed about being attacked at home. I was working alone at night when there was a pounding at the door. As I went to answer it I suddenly went blind and had to grope my way towards it. When I opened it a whole stream of unpleasant characters pushed past me. I could feel them and smell their mephitic breath. This morning I got up exhausted from having wrestled with myself all night. I am in a state of nervous exhaustion ... and I feel like a dried-up stamp pad.

Rhombus Media made a film of the second production or, to be precise, they shot a lot of footage and tried to arrange what they had shot into a film. But you can't film *The Greatest Show* because a film is linear and *The Greatest Show* explodes in all directions simultaneously. There is no way to rearrange this all-at-once-ness in a linear form. When they showed the CBC what they had filmed they were told that what was missing was the hero and heroine of the story.

Precisely! Because each of the customers was the hero or heroine of their own experience of the show. However, for the work to be accepted for broadcast on CBC-TV, there would have to be a hero and heroine; so Rhombus Media scripted and shot scenes with a hero and heroine, placing them in the foreground of the other material they had shot. I refused to allow them to call their film *The Greatest Show* so they gave it the title *Carnival of Shadows*.

IN NOVEMBER I went to Bonn to hear the German premiere of *Adieu, Robert Schumann*, sung by Hanna Schwarz. It was in Bonn that Schumann had spent his last days, in the Endenich asylum, now a museum of Schumann letters and memorabilia. The asylum archivist showed me Robert's letters to Clara and a lot of pictures of the couple as young lovers. With the help of the asylum archivist and Hanna Schwarz I was able to restore the text of *Adieu, Robert Schumann* to German. I had written the text originally in English.

From Bonn I went to the Huddersfield Festival, where Bob Aitken was to give the British premiere of the *Flute Concerto*. As I carried my bag down the four centuries of British hotel corridor to what I had been promised would be a quiet room, I kept my eyes open for the WC and the communal bath since I had been told that my room had neither. I found four bathrooms but never found a toilet so I was forced to use the sink in my room, which is what I can only assume countless other bewildered guests must also have done. The television set faced away from the bed so that one had almost to sit on the windowsill to look at it. The switch to turn it on was under the desk so that one had to crawl on the floor to get it operational. The switch was identified by a small red sticker that read 'Fire Escape'.

Turning on the TV I watched a passionate defence of one of those late-fifties pieces of urban architecture, which in Britain always seem so much more drab and grimy than elsewhere, by an architecture critic who claimed that the building in question was Bruno Mendelssohn's masterpiece. It was the triumph of his career, and even more important than his Watford Junction shoe factory. The building in question seemed to me to be utterly irredeemable, but we were given many angle shots of it, and the apologist appeared in the corner of each shot waving his hands excitedly about how Mendelssohn had combined British brick with universal glass to produce one of the architectural astonishments of the age.

The window of my room groaned every time a car passed down the busy street. Unlike windows in other hotels it was not double-glazed nor did it close properly. I tried stuffing paper in it to stop the vibration but without success.

Bob gave an excellent performance of the *Flute Concerto* and the audience received it enthusiastically. I was reminded of his last performance of the work at the National Arts Centre in Ottawa at which a patron complained in a letter to the director general that I was improperly dressed to appear on the stage at the end of the performance. 'If the other musicians can dress up properly for a concert, he should be able to do so too.' He complained also that my hair was rumpled and my shoes were scuffed.

What amazed me was that the director general of NAC, Donald McSween, wrote the man a three-page reply, apologizing and explaining that perhaps my hair was rumpled because I had been anxious about the performance and had sat backstage nervously running my hand through it. As for my dress, it was true that my boots were scuffed, but for his part, he considered my Uruguayan peasant jacket rather *sportif* and the turtleneck sweater was definitely chic. I was sent copies of both letters.

At least I was spared letters of complaint about my clothing at Huddersfield, where everyone looked as if they were coming home from a coal mine. Bob and I then went to a restaurant for something to eat, which the menu identified as 'battered blood sausage' – it was surprisingly good.

THE PRODUCTION of *Le Théâtre Noir* was to take place in Liège in March 1989 and on February 25 I flew via Sabina, Flight 568, to Brussels. My mind was in turmoil because I would be seeing Eleanor again. *The Black Theatre* was to be staged in the abandoned *cirque d'hiver* that I had discovered on my previous trip. Circuses had once been performed, but it had not been used for this purpose for seventy-five years and now served, intermittently, as a parking garage. The lower area was quite dingy but the upper area was topped by a large dome with resonant acoustics. Although the dome was conspicuous on the

A page from the score of *The Black Theatre of Hermes Trismegistos.*

skyline, scarcely anyone knew anything about the history of the building, which worked to our advantage in shrouding the production in mystery, just as alchemy was shrouded in mystery in the days of Hermes Trismegistos.

The audience would assemble at midnight at a designated place near the building, and would be led to the site where, in the lower area, the alchemists were waiting to introduce them to the various metals. This was conducted in the semi-darkness of candlelight. Then they were taken upstairs to the dome where the story of the alchemical wedding was revealed, culminating in the birth of the Divine Child, who appeared and sang from high above in the cupola.

The production received a lot of attention in the press, both before and after the presentation. I have on file seventeen articles and reviews from Liège, Brussels and Paris newspapers. In many ways the later Canadian production in Union Station was technically better; the site wasn't as dirty. But the premiere in Liège was delivered with great dedication by a young cast and I have not forgotten it.

Eleanor had been contracted to perform the role of Melusina in the production. After she arrived, I took her to see the riverboat where Thom Sokoloski, the Smiths and I were living. We were alone there and fell into each other's arms. It would be a long time before we were able to live together but I believe we both felt that this would one day happen.

AFTER THE PRODUCTION of *The Black Theatre* I returned to Canada. The next production would be very different: a week-long event in the wilderness, to be known as *And Wolf Shall Inherit the Moon,* was to be the Epilogue to the *Patria* cycle. I had begun to imagine as far back as 1983 how this might develop. First of all, we would abandon the separation between performers and audience. Everyone would, at one time or another, have a role to play as a performer. Then we would cancel the convention of the theatre as the performance venue and situate the work outdoors in a wilderness environment. And thirdly, we would encourage all members of the project to participate in the creation of the work; this would include music, text and action.

I prepared a little ad inviting people to join with me in the creation of this new work and inserted it in the *'Patriotic News Chronicle'*, the program newspaper for *The Greatest Show*. Eleanor was the first to volunteer, but her job in Europe prevented her from participating in the initial development. Five other people responded and we met for a couple of days on my farm to discuss how we might develop such a work. The next year we camped together at Gun Lake Provincial Park. There were sixteen participants that summer and we began developing an outline for the project. For instance, it was then that we established the *aubade* and *nocturne* rituals that would frame each day. Our signal to rise in the morning would be an *aubade*, played or sung across a lake. There would be no talking as we arose and prepared ourselves for the day. After we had washed and dressed we would meet and form a circle at the campfire site to greet the sun, the four directions and the new day with invocations. A similar ritual closed activities each night. The evenings would be spent around the campfire telling stories and chanting songs, mostly of our own creation. Then, when the campfire was dying, the *nocturne* would be played or sung across the water. That was the signal for silence in the camp; no more talking. One could remain at the campfire, but only as a listener to the dying music and the night songs of the forest.

The *nocturne* ritual came about in a strange way. On the first night out, some people wanted to sit up around the campfire and drink beer while others wanted to go to sleep. A discussion the next morning led to a trial of the silent closure and it has been like that at all four campsites ever since. Actually, I shouldn't have said 'silent' closure for life is never silent in the forest. There are always animals howling in the distance or scurrying around one's tent. The wind swirls and the rain speaks a thousand different languages. Sometimes lying in my tent and listening to the *nocturne* being played or sung across the lake, I have the distinct impression that the *nocturne* I am hearing was not written by a human but belongs to the forest. We have released it from the trees and the stars and the water … and at its conclusion it will be absorbed again by the environment.

The main theme that runs through all the *Patria* works is Wolf's search for the Princess of the Stars in order to seek forgiveness for his accidental wounding of her in the Prologue to the cycle. In the Epilogue Wolf will be pardoned and redeemed and will ascend with the Princess into the night sky where the Princess will reclaim her crown, the seven-star diadem known as the Corona Borealis,[†] while Wolf ascends to the moon.

The next year we had the good luck to be able to move the Wolf Project (as we call it for short) to Haliburton Forest and Wildlife Reserve, a sixty-thousand-acre tract of land owned by Peter Schleifenbaum, an ecological forester who has won much recognition for his work in restoring the forest rather than ripping it down. I went to see Peter and described my vision to have sixty-four camper-participants divided into eight clans[‡] at four different campsites. Each clan would prepare a part of the ritual performance that would be given on the final day of our sojourn. Peter sensed that my proposal – though crazy – was sincere and to my astonishment we were soon looking at a map and Peter was pointing out various lakes where we might set up campsites. Doug Brown, an expert woodsman and wilderness camper, accompanied me in the exploration of the various proposed sites and, eventually, as membership in the project increased, we were able to set up four sites on three lakes. My original outline for *And Wolf Shall Inherit the Moon* called for eight clans of eight adult members each, making a total membership of sixty-four campers. We have not yet quite reached that number, but now, after twenty years, we have well over fifty members, many of whom have been in the project for up to twenty years.

The first thing that distinguishes the Wolf Project is that all participants are equal. It doesn't matter whether you are a trail-maker, a cook, a builder or a musician, no one is encouraged to think that his or her contribution is more important than that of others. Another matter that makes our project unique is that we do not apply for or receive funding from any outside source. All costs for food, equipment, tools and materials are divided equally among the members as are all tasks: preparing meals, clearing trails, fetching and purifying water, etc.

There are Eight Clans in the Wolf Project. Each clan is named after an animal native to the Ontario wilderness: Turtle, Deer, Squirrel, Beaver, Bear, Crow, Fox and Loon. There are two clans at each of

---

† The ancient Greeks called the Corona Borealis the Crown of Ariadne.

‡ The eight clans were to be Crow, Bear, Turtle, Deer, Beaver, Squirrel, Loon and Fox.

the four campsites. The campsites are situated a mile or so away from each other. The only time we may hear sounds from other campsites might be while one of the groups performs the Wolf Chant at the close of the evening. Sometimes it is answered by real wolves.

There is no speaking while people get up in the morning. When they are ready they gather around the firepit to greet the rising sun and then to greet each other. After breakfast we visit the Wheel of Life. Each campsite has a Wheel of Life, a large circle in the forest marked by stones, trees or stumps with an entrance and an exit. Each person has his or her own place in the Wheel of Life, which may be decorated with ferns, flowers or personal objects. We touch the ground as we enter the Wheel of Life and quietly say *Ho-ma-ta-qui-a-sin* (meaning, 'all my ancestors'). This is a meditation period which may last as long as each individual wishes. We leave the Wheel silently, touching the ground again as we exit.

This is followed by a vocal warmup and a rehearsal of the songs we will be singing on Great Wheel Day – the final day when all clans come together. But before Great Wheel Day each clan will visit the other campsites to experience what we call Forest Encounters, opportunities for each clan to demonstrate its uniqueness in a short theatrical or musical creation. The Forest Encounters are usually different each year and are the result of the special talents of the clan members. Some are humorous. Some are serious. All are unique.

On the final day all members come together to reenact the finale of *And Wolf Shall Inherit the Moon*. This takes place in an enlarged Wheel of Life in a broad meadow. What a spectacle it is to witness fifty or more people, each in costume in the colour of their clan, gathered together to perform the ritual of Great Wheel Day. This is the only time during the week that all the clans come together. In the meadow beyond Moose Rock an enlarged Wheel of Life has been constructed, decorated with the colours and emblems of all the clans. On Moose Rock we encounter Tapio, Protector of the Forest, to whom each clan offers a gift in order to gain entry into the Great Wheel of Life. Each clan has its own special place in the Wheel of Life where an elaborate ritual is enacted uniting Wolf and the Princess of the Stars. At the close of this ritual which lasts several hours and is performed no matter whether it is sunny or raining, Wolf and the Princess, hand in hand, lead us to the lake from which they will take their departure for the heavens.

A handsomely decorated canoe awaits their arrival. They enter it, and as Wolf slowly paddles down the lake, music is performed by wind and brass players echoing from the hills above. No, it is not the end, for the stars are not yet shining. We move to the kitchen to eat a celebratory dinner, and then gather around a campfire to tell stories and sing songs until it is totally dark. The Fire Bird, an eight-star float, burns silently on the water as Wolf, now totally unseen, slowly resumes his paddling down the lake while the Princess sings her aria from *The Princess of the Stars*, which opened the entire *Patria* cycle. The Princess's voice grows fainter and fainter as it echoes into the distance until we do not know whether we are still hearing her or only the memory of her song; and when we look up we see the seven-star necklace of the Corona Borealis from which she, as the eighth star, fell to earth at the beginning of the *Patria* cycle. Silently we return to the campfire and extinguish it. Tomorrow we will leave the site for another year.

It may seem strange to readers that the ceremony of Great Wheel Day has never been filmed or photographed. In fact cameras have never been permitted in the Wolf Project. The reason? When you shoot a picture you are not *in* the picture. By banishing recording equipment of all kinds we have united ourselves more closely with the environment and with each other. It is the memories we share, just as it was with the native people who used to live in the Ontario forests long before us and whose lifestyle we are imitating. There is no doubt in my mind that we feel more closely dependent on each other than with any other group of people performing a play or an opera together. Productions can be intense but rituals are unforgettable, especially when they are performed by a dedicated team of volunteers. I know of nothing in Canada that can compare with the Wolf Project.

UNLIKE MOST OF MY COLLEAGUES who had comfortable jobs at universities, I had opted in 1975 to be a freelance composer, which meant that I would have to seek work more vigorously. I would have to accept more lecturing engagements and hope that I might be offered commissions for orchestra pieces. These had always been the largest commissions, except for operas, and I have never been offered a commission for an opera. A work dating from this period is *The Darkly*

Splendid Earth: The Lonely Traveller. The work is scored for violin and orchestra but it is certainly not a concerto. Although I have written several concertos for different instruments, I have always been suspicious of the medium, which tempts the composer into flashiness and the soloist into meretriciousness while the orchestra is reduced to applauding everything the soloist utters.

I wanted to write a piece that would challenge these habits, so I decided to let the orchestra and the soloist each go more or less their own way. The result would be a dual rhapsody in which the orchestra and soloist would never be controlled or influenced by one another's activities. I avoided galvanic rhythms, rhetorical arguments and somnambulistic duets. The soloist and the orchestra would each play their own material. Only at the close would a solo horn distantly echo a few phrases pronounced earlier by the violinist. A friend...? Too late. The soloist moves off into the twilight. Of course these techniques are totally different from those of a concerto; but I have finally, nearly twenty years after the work was written, heard a performance that captures the proper relationship between the orchestra and the soloist: Noémi Racine Gaudreault was the soloist with the Orchestre Métropolitain de Montréal, conducted by Yannick Nézet-Séguin.

Another work I wrote at this time was a cycle of songs on texts by Tagore for Donna Brown and the National Arts Centre Orchestra, which was scheduled to be performed in 1992. I first met Donna at the Canadian Cultural Centre in Paris where I was autographing copies of *Le Paysage sonore*, the French translation of *The Tuning of the World*. Donna was just about to begin her career as a singer; but to help pay for singing lessons she had taken a part-time job at the Canadian Cultural Centre. I probably would not have kept in touch with her had it not been for my friend Bob Walshe, who was also at the 'ceremony' and responded more quickly than I did to pretty faces.

When Donna gave the premiere of *Gitanjali* she was at the peak of her career and the National Arts Centre welcomed her back to her old hometown by commissioning a new work for her to sing with the excellent Arts Centre orchestra. But, unfortunately, the orchestra was to be conducted by my old friend Franz Paul Decker, who wasted no time in insulting both Donna and me. First he recalled *Son of Heldenleben*: 'Let me see ... ven vas dat? I did it in Montreal and in Rotterdam. It had a disgraceful reception. Zay didn't like it at all.' He then picked out some passages in the *Gitanjali* score that he said should have been notated differently. He tore into Donna when she hummed a wrong note. 'Do you have perfect pitch? No! Shall ve ask ze composer what he wants? He ought to know.' In case there are some skeptics who might think I am making up these conversations between conductors and composers, I assure them that I am not. You must remember that the conductors of most of our major orchestras in Canada were not Canadians. Canada provided an opportunity for them to learn the Classical and Romantic European repertoire so that when (if) they were eventually called back to Europe to conduct a major European orchestra they would know what to do. There was no significant interest in Canadian music in Europe so why bother to learn it? Unfortunately, many of them never got the call back to Europe and we've been stuck with them. It is only recently that conductors have begun to perform some Canadian works abroad.

In 1989 my performing rights income was cut in half, despite an increase in performances of my music in Canada and abroad. The pop music boys had taken over the performing rights society. 'They're out to kill us,' said John Weinzweig, who had just returned from a board meeting. The new society (SOCAN) would have a board of directors elected by members in which all votes would be weighted by earnings, guaranteeing that the biggest money-makers would run the society! Money music! The only kind for a capitalist society. And just as capitalism defines poverty, the triangulation of pop music, promoters and media in search of wealth turns anyone not searching for wealth into a disenfranchised beggar. Ironically, when copyright laws were first introduced, in the eighteenth century, it was the pop music of the streets that was considered too trivial to be eligible for copyright. The street musicians were the beggars. Only the composers of operas and symphonies enjoyed copyright protection.

In Canada it has never been possible for a composer of serious music to live on commissions and performances alone. Most of my colleagues who consider themselves serious composers have teaching jobs in music schools and universities, so they don't have to worry too much about royalties. I was a freelancer and royalty cuts, while performances were increasing, affected both my pocketbook and my *amour propre*.

In some Scandinavian countries, there are government programs available to assist composers by offering them lifetime pensions that allow them to continue to create music. These are recovered if and when their music begins to be performed more frequently and yields royalties. They are thus assured that they don't have to seek other work but may devote themselves to composing music. Although attempts have been made to introduce such a program in Canada, it has never succeeded in attracting much attention.

Copyright laws stimulated the growth of large publishing houses in Europe; but Canada has never had any publishing houses devoted to 'serious' music. The potential profits are not tempting enough. The job of promoting contemporary Canadian composers has been relegated to the Canadian Music Centre, whose duty it is to assist in the printing and circulation of music by anyone of talent. Needless to say, they are not given enough money to respond to all requests for assistance.

I SHALL NEVER FORGET my first visit to Brazil in February 1990. Although I was glad to leave Canada for a warm climate, I was not quite prepared for such large classes of eager students and teachers. I spent an exhausting week in São Paulo with 140 music teachers from all over Brazil, organized by Marisa Fonterrada. Despite the long hours (six hours a day) plus interviews with reporters almost every day, it was one of the best courses I have ever participated in due to the incredible enthusiasm of the Brazilians. Never had I found teachers so ready to seize my ideas and transform then in such unexpectedly interesting ways. The exercises I gave them were mostly heuristic and allowed for unlimited solutions; for instance, 'bring an interesting sound to class'. The next day there would be an enormous pile of fascinating sound-makers on the floor. This was our orchestra for countless exercises in listening and sound-making. By the end of the week, I would be sitting at the side of the room listening to the fascinating activities resulting from my suggestions or requests, for instance: create a piece in blue or a piece in red, or a piece using bells only, or bamboo only, or create a piece in rondo form – and off they would go in groups to work out their improvisations. In North America such requests were usually met with bewildered stares. Creativity is seldom encouraged in our schools. It is crippled by the neat rows of violins or trombones hanging on the walls of the music room together with the piles of printed band and orchestral repertoire on the music stands.

At the end of the course, the Brazilians formed a huge circle around me and, clapping and chanting, they danced forward, one after another, embracing me or caressing my ears and mouth with their fingers as if they were eating me. Marisa explained that they wanted my spirit to remain with them and that the ritual was very ancient.

I will not say I was forced to go to Brazil or to other countries to make money but, for a teacher in his prime, I was not being offered many opportunities to teach in Canada – certainly not at any schools in Peterborough or at Trent University, which is just up the road. I have always enjoyed teaching because I learn so much from the students. When I was younger, I often considered setting up a music school of my own where the emphasis would be on creativity but I knew that what parents and school boards wanted was a program that would look smart on stage as they sang and played recognizable tunes from American musicals, and so I reserved most of my music education work for other countries.

During the years I was living with Jean on the farm at Indian River, Eleanor was also living with someone in Munich where she was singing in the opera house at the Staatstheater am Gärtnerplatz. Somehow we contrived to see each other for a day or two whenever I visited Europe. These experiences, though brief, were more intense and passionate than anything experienced before or since. Of course a slowdown of activity would have increased the richness of these experiences, but there was no time for that. There was no time to reflect, no time to argue or blame, no time to plan for the future except to search our timetables for the next possible encounter, perhaps in Munich or Karlsruhe or Mannheim.

In the decade of the 1990s it was not uncommon for me to make quick trips of four or five days to Europe. Flights were cheap and often there were empty seats so that one could stretch out. Typical was a five-day trip to Munich and Paris in November 1991. In Munich (aside from personal matters) I was to speak on acoustic design at a large conference of engineers and designers. Acoustic and soundscape design was really a new theme for a design conference at that time, and to a great extent, it still is. My lecture was coupled with one by Max

Neuhaus who was attempting to design a fire engine siren that would signal alarm without destroying pedestrians' hearing. As usual, the technicians were surprised at the simplicity of my technical requirements. Besides a short tape of Vancouver soundmarks I had brought a couple of very simple Japanese sound sculptures that were intended to sound intermittently (not continuously) in rooms or restaurants, more or less like a little breeze that may bring some pleasure on a hot or busy day. Each room in a house or office would have its own sound just as it would have its own colour or décor. The sounds were not at all disturbing.

I am not sure whether the Europeans were quite ready to comprehend the simplicity of these little soundmarks any more than the technicians who were dismayed when I said I would address the assembly without a microphone. It has taken a long time for people in the mechanical world to understand that, in acoustics as in architecture, 'less is more'.

The end of that typical five-day trip to Europe was a stop in Paris to see my friend Bob Walshe, who made us a wonderful dinner. Then I flew home. My travels at that time totally contradicted my argument for a simple life.

ONE DAY, back on the farm, I found myself contemplating the patterns of yellow and brown bricks in the wall of my house, which was said to be one of the oldest in the area, dating from 1860. The patterns were simple but quite attractive at the corners and around the windows. I could almost hear the masons chatting as they went about their work, then breaking for lunch under the willow tree that still stands at the side of the house.

How different were the machine-made walls of my neighbour's pre-fabricated house that arrived on a truck and was ready for habitation within three days of its arrival. There were no accidents during the construction of my neighbour's house, but no laughter either, no good stories, and no pauses to drink a long draught of cool water. His house has neither character nor history; and this is what we are creating today: flat, uniform houses for a one-dimensional history-less civilization. How can we restore values of the past that have been lost? Can it be done at all?

Marisa Fonterrada's Brazilian translation of *The Thinking Ear.*

In 1991 I gave a week of classes at the University of Arizona in Phoenix. I had wanted to visit Paolo Soleri's Arcosanti, a large habitation that was being constructed in the desert by voluntary students following the rules of 'arcology', Soleri's word for the combination of architecture and ecology. So I rented a car and drove north to Scottsdale, where the experiment was taking place.

I appreciated the difficulties of an individual trying to create a community without corporate assistance, but the run-down appearance of Arcosanti was an immediate disappointment. A hideous yellow plastic fence screened off the parking area before any architecture could be seen. Fifty people lived there, most of them unpaid architecture students. A few buildings had been erected but the larger building projects seemed to be stalled. There was a lot of debris around the place: crumbling cement, faded murals, cracked panelling. Soleri was there only three days a week. Efforts to make the enterprise self-sufficient either in food, energy or culture had failed. Culture consisted of twelve concerts a year, arranged by a musical director who lived in New York City! There were a few fruit trees on the property but, according to our guide, 'no one, *at the moment,* wants to look after them.' It was a great disappointment to me, but it reinforced Schumacher's credo that 'small is beautiful', and I was glad to return to my small, beautiful farm.

I welcomed an opportunity to return to Brazil in March of 1992 where I was to give workshops to music teachers and students in Rio de Janeiro, São Paulo, Londrina and Porto Alegre. My book, *The Thinking Ear* had been translated by Marisa Fonterrada into Portuguese as *Oouvido Pensante* and that was a great help to me in assigning exercises and saving myself from lecturing and explaining everything. Leave-taking from the students was always a tearful experience. Whenever I left a class students would kiss me vigorously on both cheeks and then burst into tears. Marisa says it is common in schools, where children clutch at the teachers and beg them not to leave. Such emotional spontaneity is the basis of music-making here. At home I had to try to release students' emotions. Here one has to channel or control them, otherwise everything ends in a samba. The classes here were large. In São Paulo I had eighty-five students each morning for three hours and eighty-five more each evening. Jean accompanied me on this trip, which made things a lot easier. At least I had someone to talk to at dinner.

After Brazil we went on to Argentina where I was to give similar courses in Buenos Aires, Mendoza – where the University of Cuyo was to give me an honorary doctorate – and Tucumán, a city in the Andes.

Perhaps it was the remoteness of Tucumán that accounted for its abundance of ceremonies, which began at the airport where a young woman marched out onto the tarmac holding a diminutive Canadian flag. As the door of the plane was opened the stewardess asked the occupants to remain in their seats while the distinguished professor from Canada and his wife deplaned. We were then driven to the office of the airport director who offered us a drink, then ushered us back to the limousine which took us to our hotel.

There I was told that the governor's wife wished to meet me. Back into the limousine and I was driven to a large, monumental building where I was ushered up two flights of stone steps and was told to wait in front of an ornately carved doorway for what must have been at least fifteen minutes. Then, from nowhere, a bouquet of roses was thrust into my arms. I was told to present them to the governor's wife. A door suddenly opened and I was literally pushed into a large room where three women stood in a row before me. One was a heavy-set elderly woman in a dark dress wearing an enormous silver cross. Beside her stood a middle-aged peroxide blonde smothered in pearls and wearing a startlingly short skirt. Next to her stood a tall woman in a long, seemingly fashionable French dress with a high coiffure and large pendulous earrings. Which one? I advanced cautiously, smiled, advanced again ... then I suddenly remembered I'd been told that the governor's wife was a soap-opera actress. I extended the roses to the peroxide blonde. She smiled but said nothing. We were then joined by several other people who were overdressed and underdressed. We sat down around a table. The governor's wife sat at one end and I was ushered to the seat next to her. An elderly man, who had been introduced as an ecologist, launched into a long monologue in which he acknowledged the presence of everyone and then mentioned the pope. Everyone crossed themselves. We talked of music and noise. Someone said that young people today didn't know the difference between them. The governor's wife, whose husband was a former pop musician, smiled but said nothing. The ecologist mentioned the pope three more times in his next delivery and while the woman wearing the cross (perhaps she was a nun) excitedly crossed herself, the others gradually gave up the exercise. When I was asked to speak, I introduced the subject of acoustic ecology, while the traffic roared away outside the ornately stuccoed room that could have used a paint job and some new curtains. I found it hard to stay awake, but everyone around the table had to be given an opportunity to express an opinion – all except the governor's wife, who just smiled and barely turned her head to acknowledge the different speakers. At length, we were told to rise as we now had a meeting with the minister of education.

On the way downstairs, I was told that the governor's wife had once been asked by a TV interviewer whether she helped her husband to become such an excellent golf player. Innocently she replied, 'I kiss his balls before every game.'

The Tucumán course went very well despite the large number of people crowded into two smallish rooms. There were over one hundred participants. Young people dominated the class, which allowed me to move more quickly, without interruptions and pontificating. With older teachers, there are always those who are seeking a moment to deliver a message to the assembly about how their work and theories synchronize with what we are doing. They mean well, but they slow things down. I always want to place the experience first and decide afterwards whether it was worth doing. I keep telling them, 'Don't talk about it, just do it! We'll talk about it afterwards.' Occasionally, a professor will get his toe in, and the students, in deference, fall silent. But here in Tucumán there were surprisingly few interruptions. At one point, I had them singing long notes of their own choice as they gradually moved closer together until their bodies touched. I then told them to sing into each other's bodies. The power of this exercise almost frightened me. They became totally united, swaying as they chanted, eyes closed, hypnotized by the transmission of sound and touch. They *were* the sound. I allowed this to go on for fifteen minutes or so. Then I slowly peeled them away from each other and had them lie on the floor, which they did, eyes closed and still singing but slowly fading to silence. I had done this exercise before but never had it sustained itself for so long as in Tucumán.

From Argentina I went to Uruguay. By this time I had been travelling and teaching for nine weeks and was feeling quite exhausted. I was to give a three-day course in Montevideo, six hours each day. I didn't know until my arrival that 170 music students and teachers had registered for the course. When I was shown the theatre where the course was to take place with fixed rows of seats and a small stage half-cluttered with sets from a play in production, I realized we were in trouble. Although I often talk about teaching on the verge of peril, meaning that we should always be open to surprises and should be ready to move with them, I had to admit that the program I had planned would be absolutely impossible to execute in this space, and I was scared. Suddenly I started to jabber and gesture in an unknown language. I have sometimes done this in a class to break down tension and encourage what could literally be called 'freedom of speech'. I gestured for a girl in the front row to join me in dialogue. Uninhibited, she came up and we jabbered away in invented languages, much to the amusement of the class. I pointed down at my shoe and, to my surprise, she bent down and tied my shoelaces together! Now what? I gestured to the class to join us and was amazed as, one after another, they rose and tied their shoelaces together. What could I do but shout 'Forward!' and I hopped off the stage and headed for the exit with a troop of people jumping along behind me. They began to sing a Uruguayan folk song as we left the hall and started down a long corridor towards a shopping mall. Dumbfounded observers gawked and applauded as we hobbled past them. I had to stop the procession when we came to an escalator. We untied our shoes and laughed our way back to the theatre. The ice was broken. I don't remember exactly what we did after that but I know we did exercises in listening and sound-making inside and outside the classroom.

If we open up music education to include the soundscape, a whole treasury of listening and sound-making becomes possible, as I've described in the little books *A Sound Education* and *HearSing*.

From my diary:

> The music room is neither the beginning nor the end of music. Music is the whole sounding universe. In this 'composition' we are simultaneously listeners, performers and composers. Is the soundscape a good composition? Can it be improved? How? If we begin to think in this way, then the task of the music educator is much more important than it has been up to now. The responsibility is enormous.

THE 1990S: CANADA AND THE WORLD

IN A DREAM in 1992 I was opposing a group of government bureaucrats who were planning to institute a job-retraining program in which every citizen would be given a computer and taught how to use it 'in order to make Canada more competitive in the modern world.' (We had been hearing a lot about such matters on the news at that time.) It seemed I was the sole opponent to the scheme. 'What do you propose then?' said a surly person sitting next to me. Without a flicker I answered: 'Teach them to carry water buckets on their heads.' On waking I was struck by the shrewdness of my reply; for I've often thought that the rage for technology needs to be resisted, but my conscious mind has never produced such a colourful reply. And yet it is all in line with my thinking that less is more, and that the watercarrier indeed has a more precious commodity in his or her custody than a slave with a laptop. I must be the only person I know who gets along without one.

One day I was working away proofreading my *Accordion Concerto* and was thinking about how hard I work and how little recognition it brings me. In the midst of my work, the radio announced that the Toronto Blue Jays had won the World Series and the hoopla in the media was really quite insufferable: all the school children for miles around Toronto were told to wear blue to school in their honour; the city gave them the biggest parade in its history, etc. Then the players stepped up to the microphone: 'It's true,' said their spokesman, 'we are all American and Latin American but we love playing ball in Canada.' And the 500,000 fans cheered deliriously just to hear the words from their pearly teeth. I hunch over my desperate work and conclude there is no culture in Canada. It's absurd, of course, to say that there is no culture, but it is equally absurd to think that its greatest achievements occur in a stadium or a gymnasium.

IN DECEMBER 1992 I was invited to a choral conference in Espoo, Finland. The Vancouver Chamber Choir was to give a concert of my music and I had been invited to attend, together with Jean. While there I also gave lectures on the soundscape at a couple of universities and, when those were over, Helmi Jaarviluoma suggested a little holiday in Lapland. Of course we said yes. Helmi's family had a small cottage north of Revaniemi, so one day we set out in Helmi's car and eventually arrived at the cottage, which consisted of a large kitchen, heated by a wood stove and a sauna. We were to sleep in bunks above the stove. Surprisingly, it was not very cold outside – just a few degrees below zero – but it was dark twenty hours a day. There was a glimmer of light in the southern sky at about eleven o'clock in the morning, but by two it was dark again. It reminded me of the conclusion of Ibsen's *Ghosts* when the sick boy, Oswald, cries to his mother, 'Give me the sun!'

We talked in hushed voices, almost whispering; we yawned a lot and slept or, at least, remained in bed about twelve hours a day. We spent an hour every day in the sauna, sweating in the almost unbearable heat, after which I would stand outside naked in the snow and drink a bottle of beer. Sometimes we would take a drive but there are not many places to go. So I began to spend much of my time writing, or rewriting, my novel *Wolf Tracks* – a very unusual work that can be read in two directions, beginning to end or end to beginning on opposite pages – as the two protagonists, a man and wolf pass one another on two tracks. In fact, the subject of the story is a train ride from the city to the wilderness and a return to the city after the destruction of the train. Of course, it should not be difficult to write such a story but to arrange it so that it can be read in both directions at once on facing pages is no easy task; so Lapland, where there are no interruptions, seemed like the perfect place to figure it all out and that is what I spent most of my time doing.

The story of *Wolf Tracks* begins in a second-hand bookshop, where the book falls into the hands of the prospective reader but is unrecognized by the owner of the bookshop as one of his books. To add to the puzzle, I had the published book deposited in second-hand bookshops across Canada by student volunteers, so that if anyone picked it up, the owner wouldn't recognize it, as is mentioned in the story. Of course, the book never sold and I have five hundred copies of it in my basement for anyone who might like to read it. There were, however, some funny stories reported by readers. One bookseller wouldn't sell it at all; since there was no price on it he considered it a collector's item. Another bookseller sold it for a dollar because he'd never heard of the author. One woman returned a torn and chewed up copy of *Wolf Tracks* explaining that her dog had been aroused by the smell of a wolf in the house and had attacked it.

Over the years I have written several similar books of fantasy and fiction: *The Sixteen Scribes, The Chaldean Inscription, Shadowgraphs and Legends, Dicamus et Labyrinthos, Ariadne* and, most recently, *The Garden of the Heart,* a novella to accompany the song cycle by the same name.

In the winter of 1993 Claude Schreyer asked me to compose a piece for four brass bands in Montreal. I was not too eager to accept the proposal because, although I had played in a Boy Scout brass band when I was young, I never cherished the sound of brass or the repertoire they played. But Claude was persistent and so I went to Montreal to discuss the matter. Together we walked through the snow-covered Park Lafontaine, which is about a kilometre square in downtown Montreal. I could imagine the bands breaking into groups and moving through the park. As the park was once a military drill ground, I did some research into military drill music from the seventeenth and eighteenth centuries and combined this with some Indian chants from Lescarbot's *Histoire de la Nouvelle France,* followed by phrases from 'O Canada', our national anthem, which was written by Calixa Lavallée shortly before he emigrated to the United States, never to return to Canada. Another work that I introduced was the Sanctus by Charles Ecuyer, who was the first composer actually born in Canada.

Try to imagine all these works being performed at different times and places in the park, but not separately, rather overlapping and integrating with each other like acoustic ghosts from times long past. Canada is a new country but resonates with histories that are being largely submerged and forgotten. A park is a fine place for recreation and reflection. *Musique pour le Parc Lafontaine* conveys history in a livelier and more intensive manner than any monument can. But the work has never been performed again as Canada's history is forgotten.

IN THE SPRING of 1993 Barry Karp gave a workshop of *Patria 9: The Enchanted Forest* at his high school. I was still writing the work but the lively workshop helped to stimulate the final version which we presented at Rob Winslow's farm near Millbrook in the summer of 1994, directed by Barry with costumes by George Fry. Maureen Forrester,

Eleanor James as Earth Mother in *Patria 9: The Enchanted Forest*.

the celebrated Canadian contralto, sang the role of Earth Mother.

We were sold out every evening, but not only because of the excellence of the work or the performers. Mickey Hart, drummer with the Grateful Dead rock group, had read and been very inspired by *The Tuning of the World*. In gratitude he sent me all the group's CDs. When I replied that I didn't have a CD player, Mickey sent me a player to complete the collection. Later I read somewhere that the Grateful Dead had set up a fund to help needy music organizations. I wrote a letter outlining our production of *The Enchanted Forest* and mentioning our budget problems. Within a couple of weeks, we received a cheque for thirteen thousand dollars. Not only that, but Mickey mentioned that their current tour took them to Albany, New York, and thought that they might drive up to see the show one night. They didn't make it but a lot of 'Deadheads', as their followers are called, bought tickets with the hope of seeing them.

The Enchanted Forest has been successfully produced twice since then, once on a private property near Pontypool, Ontario, and once at Haliburton Forest and Wildlife Reserve. On both these occasions the role of Earth Mother was performed by Eleanor James, who by then had returned to Canada and was living with me. When the audience arrives they first see Earth Mother in a field surrounded by Flower Spirit dancers folding their petals to sleep as the sun sets. Their evening reverie is interrupted by a group of Children, lamenting that one of their number, Ariadne, has been lost in the forest. Earth Mother asks the Flower Spirits to help the children find the lost girl and so, led by the Flower Spirits, the Children enter the darkening forest, followed by the audience. The Children will meet many creatures in the forest, some who are willing to help them and some who are not. They are informed that an evil creature, Murdeth, intends to cut down the forest and sell the lumber but is being resisted by Fenris the Wolf who protects the forest. Eventually they meet an old woman, Hatempka, who agrees to help them find Ariadne. With the help of Hatempka and Shapeshifter, a strange three-horned caterpillar who transforms herself into a beautiful moth, they manage to thwart Murdeth's plan. Fenris the Wolf also appears and chases Murdeth away but Ariadne has been transformed into a birch tree and no amount of magic can restore her. Earth Mother returns to inform us that we have left our soul in the forest and therefore the forest will never be destroyed.

Everyone knows that fairy tales have always been the receptacle for moral wisdom. *The Enchanted Forest* belongs to this genre and its message is ecological. It contradicts the notion that humans are God's supreme creatures and substitutes the idea that everything is equal, interdependent and in a constant state of transformation. The work ends with a candlelight procession back to the meadow where it began.

In January 1994 I went to Brandon University for a semester as the Stanley Knowles Visiting Professor in Public Policy. The title was not taken very seriously, I suppose. My arrival passed with little commotion. In fact, no one bothered to tell me that, although my contract stipulated that I was to be there by January 2, no classes were held that week, so, when I went to the appointed room to meet my class, no one was there but the janitor washing the floor. The students did turn up the next week and I proposed that some of them might like to accompany me to Costa Rica for a week later in the semester. I had been giving a one-week course in Costa Rica for several years. Five or six of the students accompanied me and that became the beginning of an annual student exchange program between the universities.

Re-experiencing Manitoba was important for me. Both my parents had grown up in Manitoba, my mother near Souris and my father near Hamiota; and they were married in Brandon. I heard many stories about life on the Prairies 'in the old days' from them and from my many relatives who still lived in Manitoba. I also read the novels of Frederick Philip Grove and drove to Rapid City where he taught school and where he is buried. I was fascinated by Grove's stories, particularly *Over Prairie Trails;* they were so similar to those my father used to tell.

Although he was an immigrant, Grove was one of our most authentic authors in depicting life in rural and urban Canada a hundred years ago. He wrote about Canada while other immigrant authors wrote about themselves or subjects of more international attraction. In a pathetic letter to W.J. Alexander, written on Christmas Day 1937, he writes, 'I applied for the position of "Book Advisor" at Simpson's [one of Canada's leading department stores at the time]. They asked me to come in for a personal interview, but the moment they saw I wasn't a young man, they expressed their regret....' He was over sixty at the time and probably one of the most-read Canadian authors, though he couldn't survive on royalties alone. Yet he never criticizes Canada for letting him down.

While in Brandon I met Mike Hotain, a Dakota native whom I interviewed and recorded. I also had him visit some of my classes. Mike worked as a composer of songs for different occasions, such as weddings and birthdays. People would come to him and commission a song. He would compose it and then sing it to them over and over until they had memorized it; then they would take it home with them and it would be their song to sing on all festive occasions throughout their lives. Mike also had songs to make horses dance and to make dogs lie down. His inspirations came from nature. He once told me that every time the dust would spin in a circle, he would stop and listen; it was the voice of his grandmother telling him something.

While at Brandon University I wrote a large orchestral piece entitled *Manitou*. Manitou is an Algonquin word meaning 'mysterious being'. He is unseen but is sometimes associated with the sun. Mike used to call him 'a monster'. Certainly he was a god of great power and strength.

Manitou was commissioned for the Tokyo Symphony Orchestra by Suntory Hall, Tokyo. It was one of a series of commissions arranged by Toru Takemitsu. The idea for the concert was unique and could be repeated elsewhere. The commissioned work was to be the centrepiece of the program; but the composer was to choose the whole program and it was to consist of a composition from the past that had influenced him and a work by a young composer of promise. For our program I had selected Nielson's *Inextinguishable Symphony* and a work by the young Canadian composer Chris Paul Harmon, who accompanied me to Tokyo.

My Japanese commissions have always been offered with respect and fulfilled with pleasure. But a reader of this chronicle, even one who has only flipped through it, will know that I have often had problems with orchestras and opera companies. Of course, the composer is blamed for being uncooperative whenever he refuses to accept the insults of the most generously funded artistic institutions in the country, which are usually managed or directed by foreigners.

In 1994 the Toronto Symphony Orchestra hired a rising Finnish conductor as its new music director. When the plan for the season was announced it contained my *Flute Concerto* which Bob Aitken had worked very hard to get on the program, but practically nothing else by Canadians. I was outraged and told the administrators I was withdrawing the work.† I was getting to be known as a firebrand because, unlike many of my colleagues, I refused to stand at the stage door with my manuscripts, hoping to intercept the foreign conductor on his way from the stage to his limousine. Bob, of course, was very disappointed to have been deprived of the opportunity to play a major work in his own home town, not to mention the eighteen-thousand-dollar contract he had been offered.‡ Nevertheless, we remained friends, and a year or two later he played the concerto with the Vienna Symphony.

Over the years, I have written six concertos and a couple of other works that could qualify as concertos, although they have different titles. So it may seem strange if I say that I have always felt the concerto medium to be solipsistic or at least egocentric. I have never liked parties in which one person does all the talking or flirts to attract attention to himself, or herself. I mentioned that *The Darkly Splendid Earth* was not really a concerto because the violin and the orchestra remain at a respectful distance from one another. But when the trumpeter Stuart Laughton approached me about writing a trumpet concerto I realized that the dazzling sound of the trumpet could never be tamed or muffled. For a number of years Stuart had been a member of the Wolf Project. I had written him several *aubades* and *nocturnes*. So when he asked for a concerto I had no difficulty in hearing it in my mind. Stuart is a falconer and knows all about these birds, so I decided to call the work *The Falcon's Trumpet*. In order to suggest the echoing resonance of music being performed across a lake, I placed several instruments in different places around the hall as well as offstage. I also added a soprano soloist who joins the trumpeter in the last few pages of the work.

I wrote most of the piece in Strasbourg, where I was teaching at the university. One day I found myself absentmindedly adding the

---

† The same year I refused to let the Montreal Symphony perform *Scorpius* because they had broken a contract to perform my *Guitar Concerto*.

‡ That year the TSO paid Peter Serkin $34,000 to perform a piano concerto and Yo-Yo Ma was paid $65,000 for a cello concerto. I was to be paid $400 for the rental of the music, so by cancelling the performance of my own concerto, I wasn't losing much.

sound of a telephone I had heard in a Strasbourg bank to the texture of birds around the Canadian lake, but it seemed inoffensive so I left it. Just for the curious, this was the Strasbourg telephone bird:

Working with French music students was not easy. There were two obstacles: first of all was my lousy French; and then there was the difficulty of getting the students to understand the relationship of music to the soundscape. I had proposed that the final project in Strasbourg would be an outdoor composition in the streets, buildings and gardens of the medieval town of Sélestat, where our music education course took place. The students had never experienced an outdoor concert before. To make the project even more difficult I proposed that the students should invite local residents to join them in the preparation and performance of the final concert.

Of course music in the streets was nothing new. There had always been marching bands and choral processions and the further we delve into past history, the more of these events and activities we find. The medieval town was alive with music and ceremonious sound. Not only were there fanfares from the towers and ambient music in the streets, but the very streets resonated with sonic occupations. In Sélestat there was the rue d'Étain (Tin or Pewter Street), rue de la Poterie (Pottery Street), rue de la Cuirasse (Armour Street), rue du Marteau (Hammer Street); then there was rue des Oies (Goose Street), rue des Veaux (Calf Street), and rue des Canards (Duck Street), all leading to the rue de la Grand Boucherie!

So we went into the streets and tried to enliven them with some of the sounds of the past both with instruments and with our voices, to the amusement of the citizens of Sélestat. In the end many of them joined in the performance. I will only mention one event which was typical of the interaction we attained in the final concert. Four students chose a large square surrounded by three- or four-storey apartment buildings. Each student took one side of the square and visited all the people in the apartment block asking them to participate in a mini-concert. Each occupant was asked to find four sounds they could perform at their apartment window: a metal pan and a beater, a radio, a vacuum cleaner and a sound of their choice. Each sound corresponded to a flag of a different colour which would be operated by a student in the square below. When the red flag went up, the metal pan would be beaten; when the blue flag went up, the radio would go on and then be turned off when it was lowered, and so forth. When the audience, which was moving through the streets from event to event, arrived in the square, the four flagmen raised and lowered their coloured flags in counterpoint resulting in a noise concert which delighted everyone, particularly children.

In fact, our little itinerant event was so successful that the Mayor of Sélestat invited me back to create a much-expanded millennium event entitled 'Deux Mille Sons pour l'An Deux Mille', which involved a great many groups from the town: church choirs, bands, blacksmiths, even street-sweepers who produced a wonderful concerto with brooms and shovels. The public response to the event was so strong that the mayor wrote us a letter of congratulation:

> Cher Monsieur,
>
> Au lendemain de la soirée *'2000 milles sons pour l'an 2000'* qui a connu un fabuleux succès à tous égards, je tenais à vous adresser mes plus vives félicitations et mes chaleureux remerciements.
>
> L'itinéraire sonore que vous avez tracé entre les quartiers de la vieille ville a fait que Sélestat a vécu, vendredi dernier, des moments exceptionnels autant sur le plan de la musique que de l'émotion.
>
> Espérons que nous pourrons reconduire ensemble une telle manifestation qui a séduit petits et grands, et toujours à votre disposition, je vous prie d'agréer, Cher Monsieur, l'expression de mes sentiments les meilleurs et les plus cordieux.
>
> Pierre Giersch

AFTER MY SOJOURN in France, I went on a whirlwind lecture tour in the winter of 1996. First, I visited Switzerland, where I presided over the foundation of the Swiss Soundscape Association, then Paris where I worked for two days with music therapists at l'Université de Paris Cinq, then for a day at the École de l'Architecture la Villette followed by a lecture at the Literaturhaus in Hamburg and a week-long atelier with film students in Hannover, then a soundscape lecture in Copenhagen, two lectures in Stockholm, a workshop on 'Music and the Bauhaus' at the University of Tampere, Finland, a couple of lectures at the University of Gothenburg, Sweden, and finally a visit to the West German Radio in Cologne to talk about future radio programs with Klaus Schöning. Then, after only five days at home in Canada, I went to Victoria for lectures in both the music and anthropology departments at the University of Victoria, followed by a lecture in the Canadian Studies Department at the University of British Columbia. The premiere of *Once on a Windy Night* was given by the Vancouver Chamber Choir before I returned to Toronto for a week, where I gave a lecture in the English department at York University and attended rehearsals for the performance of *The Falcon's Trumpet*.

I had only been at home a few days when the news came that the University of Strasbourg wished to give me an honorary doctorate. This gave me special pleasure since Goethe had earned his doctorate from the same institution. This was my acceptance speech.

> It is a great honour for me to receive a doctorate – *honoris causa* – from the University of Strasbourg. When I first visited Strasbourg many years ago, I noticed a statue of Goethe before this university. It was only later, when reading Goethe's autobiography, *Dichtung und Wahrheit*, that I learned he had received a doctorate in law from your school, now exactly 225 years ago.
>
> Goethe loved Strasbourg, as you no doubt know. He loved the Vosges; he loved the plains of Alsace, and he especially loved your beautiful cathedral. His love of the cathedral inspired an important essay which had a great influence on the Gothic revival throughout Europe. It was not merely the accomplishment that he admired, but rather that the builders 'dared to wish' that this seemingly impossible structure might be possible.
>
> It was while in Strasbourg that Goethe himself 'dared to

wish' that he might become a writer. It was then that he began to see his future clearly – and it was not as a lawyer. That Strasbourg and its university still 'dare to wish' to render the impossible possible is something I fervently hope. When I came here two years ago to teach for a short time, it was because I believed in the ideal embodied in one of your programs. This was the *Centre des musiciens intervenant à l'école* at Sélestat.

This program was not limited to the training of music teachers for school classrooms but was committed to the ideal that music has its place in all strata of the community in churches, in factories, in hospitals, among the unemployed, among refugees, and among the aged.

That music can hold a community together and can enliven the spirit of all citizens is a larger ideal than the more traditional notion that music education is only for children.

I hope you can understand that. In the traditional system, music disappears after graduation or degenerates into passive consumership.

A program such as that attempted by the CFMI in Sélestat 'dares to wish' that music making might be sustained throughout life and that, with the proper encouragement by animators dedicated to this ideal, it can be.

I enjoyed my time in Sélestat among your students and teachers, whom I now call my colleagues, pursuing an ideal I could believe in. It has been a privilege to be associated with such an outstanding institution as the University of Strasbourg. Thank you.

DURING THE YEARS 1995–96 I wrote several extended choral pieces: *Once on a Windy Night, A Medieval Bestiary, Vox Naturae* and *Seventeen Haiku*. I like to think that these pieces are among my best choral works though they are rarely performed. (*A Medieval Bestiary* is performed relatively frequently because it is a much easier work.)

Like many of my other choral pieces *Windy Night* is an evocation of nature. I had already written about the sun, the moon, fire, a garden, water, and now I wanted to write about the wind: no easy task. The wind is devious. The Greeks imagined their god of the wind, Typhoeus, as having a thousand heads, each with a different voice. I remember standing on a windy hill on my farm for hours trying to transcribe the shapes and intensities of the wind into a work for human voices. The final piece incorporates wailing and whistling noises along with more traditional vocal sounds. I regard it as one of the strongest choral pieces I have written although I have never heard a live performance of it. The first performance in the Hotel Vancouver was murdered by a pipe-fitter hammering somewhere overhead. I rushed out with the intention of killing him but never found him and totally missed the performance. The second time it was performed in Toronto, Jean and I drove down for the evening concert only to discover that the concert had taken place in the afternoon. And the third time, at the American Choral Society Conference where it received a standing ovation, I was somewhere else.

Vox Naturae was commissioned by the Tokyo Philharmonic Choir. Their conductor, Chifuru Matsubara, wanted something with a Latin text because Latin, like Japanese, consists of an even alternation of vowels and consonants without consonant clusters, diphthongs or nasals. I chose a text from Lucretius' *De rerum natura,* where he describes the acoustics of sound transmission. Lucretius believed in the atom theory of sound rather than the wave theory. He also believed that echoes were the work of satyrs who romp unseen in the woods and hurl back whatever sound is thrown at them in satiric mimicry. So I divided the choir into three groups: the narrative choir on the stage and an echoing choir at the back of the hall who later become the choir of satyrs backstage. The Tokyo Philharmonic Choir has performed *Vox Naturae* many times and has made a splendid recording of it.

Seventeen Haiku was written at the request of the Japanese choir, Utaoni, which had previously won an all-Japan choral contest singing my work *Magic Songs*. I thought it would be interesting to set some haiku poems to music and began to collect poems that made some reference to sound. For instance:

> The sound of an acorn
> rolling down a shingled roof.
> Cold of the night.
> (Kato Gyötai)

A Medieval Bestiary

FOR MIXED CHOIR (SATB)

R. Murray Schafer

Arcana Editions, R.R. 2, Indian River
Ontario, Canada K0L 2B0

A Medieval Bestiary.

Cricket!
Although it was next door you sang,
I heard you here.
(Kobayashi Issa)

It occurred to me to ask the choir members to help me find suitable haiku, and I asked them to write some of their own if they wished. I wanted to set the poems in Japanese, a language I do not speak; but my friend, the Japanese composer Komei Harasawa, very generously translated and recorded the texts for me and provided a word-for-word translation.

One of the most pleasant times of my life was attending the all-Japan choral contest where the Utaoni Choir won the grand prize for the second year in a row, this time performing *Seventeen Haiku*. They then invited me to Tsu City where they gave an entire concert of Schafer choral works to a large and appreciative audience.

I have always enjoyed my trips to Japan because they have taught me so much. Above all, they have taught me to respect simplicity. It is present there, in the brevity of haiku. It is present in the décor of the home. It is the secret of Japanese cuisine, where freshness is prized above complexity. It is celebrated in the incense and tea ceremonies.

I was once taken to the tea house of the Grand Tea Master of Kyoto and recall the experience vividly while many other dinners and drinking bouts have totally faded from memory.

We were met at the gate of the garden in which the tea house was situated by the Tea Master's assistant and were taken on a walk down paths strewn with falling petals, and across bridges over small ponds. Here and there a branching path was closed with a stone because the blossoms were not in bloom on its bushes or had already passed their prime. We paused frequently to admire the view, which sometimes included what the Japanese call *shakkei* – borrowed scenery. When the distant view of a mountain is attractive the gardener will arrange his plantings to include it, and in a similar manner, will exclude less attractive scenes by plantings of thick bushes and hedges.

Before entering the tea house we will wash our hands in a stone basin at the entrance. We pour a dipper of water over them and then listen to the water as it drops into a resonant jar below the surface stones. These 'water harps' are evidently as old as the tea ceremony itself, which goes back perhaps as far as the eighth century. We listen to the water as it drips into the jar below, lingering before we move to the tea house door. To enter the tea house we must bend over, humbling ourselves, a ceremony that goes back to ancient times and was observed even by the Emperor.

Inside we are seated by the Tea Master's assistant and we listen for some time to the sound of the tea kettle on the hearth before us.

> The kettle sings well, for pieces of iron are so arranged in the bottom as to produce a peculiar melody in which one may hear the echoes of a cataract muffled by clouds, of a distant sea breaking among the rocks, a rainstorm sweeping through a bamboo forest, or of the soughing of pines on some faraway hill.[†]

The Tea Master serves each guest individually by pouring water into a cup and whisking the powdered tea, then passing it to the 'most honoured guest', who turns the cup three times then drinks the tea with a deliberate slurping sound. The other guests will then follow in order from oldest to youngest. After we have all been served, we exit into an adjoining room, where the Tea Master or his assistant talks to us, explaining the ritual and its ancient background. The whole ceremony has lasted perhaps two hours. And what have we done? We have drunk a cup of tea, that is all.

No, that is not all! A whole world has been revealed to us – a world of harmony and simplicity rather than of extravagance and disorder. Do we need harmonies such as the tea ceremony in our lives today? More than ever! There are moments in the *Patria* Epilogue, *And Wolf Shall Inherit the Moon,* when we come close to what the tea ceremony and the incense ceremony have achieved, moments during or following the *aubades* and *nocturnes* and, on the last night, when the Princess of the Stars returns to the heavens, singing her aria as she is paddled down Wildcat Lake until we lose her voice in a canopy of stars. Simple ceremonies, but strong and never to be forgotten. 'Simplify, simplify, simplify,' said Thoreau, and yet it is the hardest thing for us to do today in a society captivated by noise and complexity.

---

† Okakura Kakuzo, *The Book of Tea,* Rutland, Vermont, 1956, p. 63.

IN FEBRUARY 1997 Claude Schreyer and I rented a car in Winnipeg and headed north to record material for *Winter Diary*, a program the West German Radio had commissioned about life in the Canadian northland. We did not reach the Arctic, nor did we need to, since the cold weather north of Dauphin gave us all the material we needed. As the program was for Germany, we wanted to communicate the theme without talking, with sounds alone. After a single day of travelling, I realized what the theme of our program would be: the comparison of cold vast exteriors with the warm, populated interiors. That is the essence of the northern winter. Marshall McLuhan stencilled the same theme in his aphorism that Canadians go out to be alone and come in to be in company – compared with Europeans who go out to be in company and come home to be alone. It is a theme we find in the novels of Sinclair Ross, Frederick Philip Grove, Margaret Laurence and a host of other writers as well as in the daily lives of Canadian farmers, cattlemen, loggers and trappers. That we had managed to communicate this message successfully was endorsed when *Winter Diary* was awarded the German Karl Sczuka Prize for Works of Radio Art in 1998. So far as I know, no North American had ever won this prize before, and no North American radio station has ever broadcast the program – not even the CBC. [Subsequently North American John Cage also won the Sczuka Prize.] I'm sorry if I sound disgusted with the Canadian broadcasting scene. I'm just describing the facts.

In the spring of 1997 I returned to Europe on another lecture and workshop tour on the theme of the soundscape and music education. I was in Lisbon for three days, Faro for two days, Cadiz for a week, and Madrid for a week. Twice during the tour, I was sick and had raging fever, once after eating Canadian caribou at a dinner hosted by the Canadian Embassy in Lisbon.

Returning to Canada, I rushed to Ottawa where a production of the Spring section of *Patria 10: The Spirit Garden* was already in rehearsal. It was to be performed on a vacant piece of land at Carleton University. Many Ottawa people helped to make it happen. The pleasure the production might have given me was almost totally destroyed by an opening day of rain which reduced the expected audience of 350 to a mere 80 people. The rain stopped just before show-time but too late to sell tickets. I kept calculating what it all meant in lost revenue (about $5000), and from where or whom it would come. My own investment in the production was already $20,000 – exceeding the grant from the Canada Council, while the Ontario Arts Council had turned us down completely. But the meagre audience seemed to enjoy themselves and planted their seeds enthusiastically. Patricia Green sang the role of the Spring Child splendidly. The production in Winnipeg a couple of years later was to be much better and gave me the inspiration to complete the Fall section of the work which was to end with a banquet of the food produced by the garden after we had performed a ritual of thanks and turned the garden over to the Winter and the Four Winds.

Beneath it all is a secret feeling that what has been accomplished in works like *The Enchanted Forest* and *The Spirit Garden* will one day be reevaluated and pronounced good while the rest of what presently attracts public attention will slip into oblivion.

IN 1998 my *Seventh Quartet* was written for the Molinari String Quartet of Montreal, led by the violinist Olga Ranzenhofer, and named after Guido Molinari, the Montreal artist. Several of my quartets have been written for this group, and this one was to include an obligato soprano. At first I thought of having the soprano sing a wordless melisma that would drift in and out of the instrumental texture like a dreamer's delirium, but the discovery of some texts by a twenty-one-year-old schizophrenic patient changed my mind, since they would give the singer a strong, if confused, identity, providing a context for the singer's irrational appearances and disappearances during the work.

I began to imagine a work in perpetual motion with the members of the quartet moving on and off stage and even throughout the concert hall. At one point, the four instrumentalists play a rapid unison scherzo from four corners of the hall producing a 'liquid' sound which I have never heard in music before. In order for the cellist to move while playing, a special harness had to be made. At one point, the cellist sits down facing the back of the stage. During a pause, the back of the cellist's head suddenly springs open to reveal another face staring at the audience. This spectacular effect was created by Jerrard Smith, whose genius is evident in so many of the *Patria* works. Guido Molinari was also involved in the work by designing costumes for the

Chatting with the painter Guido Molinari in his Montreal studio.

performers as well as props and a backdrop to what had become quite a production. The few times the Molinari Quartet have performed the *Seventh Quartet*, the audience has received the work with much enthusiasm but the preparation time and expense has militated against frequent presentations.

About this time several of my string quartets were performed at a chamber music festival in Vancouver. Eleanor accompanied me to Vancouver to hear them and, at one of the concerts, we encountered my first wife, Phyllis, who was now living with Tom Mallinson, my former colleague and chairman of the Communication Centre at SFU. It was a strange sensation to be introducing the two singers for whom I had written so many vocal works over the years. Tom kept patting the sleeve of my jacket the whole time we were together, as if seeking reconciliation – or perhaps, just recognition. I was to see Phyllis only once more, a few years later when she was fighting cancer, from which she eventually died. I don't think I ever got over my guilt for having abandoned her and her voice is still present in all the pieces I wrote for her, no matter who sings them.

In the spring of 1998 I was grappling with a work for the St. Lawrence String Quartet with orchestra, and I was also skirmishing with what would later become *Patria* 8: *The Palace of the Cinnabar Phoenix*. The quartet and orchestra piece was to be called *Four Forty*: 'Four' for the quartet and 'Forty' for the number of players in the chamber orchestra that would accompany them. Since A440 is the frequency at which contemporary orchestras perform, the note A was to become the anchor note of the entire composition, returning frequently, right to the end of the piece where it slowly evaporates into harmonics. Balancing a string quartet against the strings of an orchestra is no easy task so I resorted to a bit of theatricality by having the first violin emerge from the audience while the second violin jumps up from the back of the second violin section. The violist begins in the percussion section, first playing a drum, and then throwing the drumstick into the air and picking up the viola. The cellist sits snoozing on the stage and has to be wakened up to join the others. This was my way of giving the soloists an identity before performing as a quartet in the second and third movements of the piece; but while it amuses audiences, it is not always to everyone's taste and the criticisms are sometimes harsh. 'Schafer over the edge – again,' as one reviewer proclaimed.

The *Eighth Quartet* was written for the Molinari Quartet and was a private commission from Ellen Karp to celebrate the fiftieth wedding anniversary of her parents, Fred and May Karp. The work is in two movements. The first movement is lively; the second movement is quieter and more gentle but is based on the same material as the first. For the second movement I decided to double the quartet with prerecorded material to suggest memories of the past. Ellen also arranged for a wonderful anniversary dinner when the Molinari group gave the premiere in Montreal. It was like going back to the past when music was often commissioned or performed to celebrate a special occasion – an experience we have largely lost today.†

'Better to get drunk on ink than on alcohol,' said Flaubert. In my case, it was graphite. But suddenly, in the middle of all my years of composing, the company that manufactured Beryl Turquoise pencils

---

† The *Fifth Quartet* had also been commissioned by Stan Witkin as a surprise gift for his wife, Rosalind.

changed the consistency of the lead, making it more intractable and lighter in tone, or at least, shinier. No matter how hard I pressed, I couldn't get the dark, rich black of the older pencils. My forearm began to ache. What should I do? Go to a doctor? 'What's your problem?' he would ask. 'My forearm aches all the time.' 'What have you been doing?' 'Lifting pencils.' Later I discovered a good German pencil, Faber-Castell 2B, and was able to go on scribbling all day and sleeping at nights. But not every night. When I'm working intensively, I never sleep all night. A diary entry from March 1998 attempts to explain what it is like when there is no easy flow of ideas or inspirations.

> I've been coming at it head on, forcing myself to write music five or six hours each day, forcing myself to have inspirations, which don't come, so that each day ends with a headache. I know the value of coming at inspiration sideways, tangentially, without thinking consciously about the work that is giving me trouble, and yet, belligerently, I refuse to adopt this tactic, and go on gripping the subject by the teeth. I refuse to abandon my determination, refuse to forgo my frustrations, my eye aches, and my head aches, for fear that, without self-destruction, nothing will be accomplished; believing secretly that my death is the life of the work. No sutures are possible for the bloody mess of creativity, no balm for the agony of shrieking birth-pains.
>
> Then follows a day of utter collapse when I can't write a line, can't fill a bar. Everything fades away before it is thought. And I just lie on the couch, a total invalid. But I'm experienced enough to know this that incapacity has its own value as a means – perhaps the only means – of shaming the ego, of coaxing it to relinquish control over the imagination.
>
> There is nothing wrong with ego-music (history is full of it) but there are times when the ego simply gets in the way of life currents that are beyond it. Sometimes one has to be 'sick unto death' to sense these currents. If a piece of music is to move with these currents, a lot of it will have to be written lying down, dreaming or hallucinating.

Eleanor James.

IN 1999 Jean moved out and went to see a lawyer about a divorce. Actually, she already had a little apartment in Peterborough which she inhabited every time I went on tour.

I spent many lonely weeks on the farm. Eleanor had returned to Canada to be with her dying mother but I could not invite her to the farm with tokens of my life with Jean strewn everywhere in the house, so we arranged to meet other places as often as possible, considering the critical state of her mother's health. That was not all that was upsetting Eleanor. She did not wish to leave me but she still had performances as Carmen to fulfill in Munich as well as guest appearances in Wiesbaden and Würzburg. She also knew that her contract would be coming to an end by 2002. So there we were: three agitated people, each alone, without any idea of what the future would bring. Actually, Jean was the first to accept her fate. She filed for a divorce and bought a house of her own in Peterborough, close to her friends. Eleanor wanted to be with me but she also wished to continue her work in Europe, hoping to sustain her international operatic contacts and her career. While she put off her departure as long as possible, it was inevitable that, for the present she would return to Germany, and to Robert, her faithful companion of many years.

I was the one who was going to experience the greatest isolation, and it frightened me. There were several weeks when I wept almost every day. Then I began to ask myself who I was weeping for, and when the answer came back, 'myself', I decided to pull myself together and get on with my life. When the divorce from Jean was finally legal, we were able to communicate more easily. I would sometimes visit her and the relief I felt in observing her creating a new life for herself brought a certain calm to my life and allowed me to try to plan my activities without feeling guilty. Finally I was living a life free of lies and deceptions. *Four Forty* and *The Palace of the Cinnabar Phoenix*, works with a certain levity and even a sense of humour, came out of this *laissez-faire* attitude, a quite different quality from the panic of the *Flute Concerto* which was written during the days of my first break-up with Jean when she left me on the farm in Monteagle Valley. In fact, there is one screeching chord in that piece which accompanied her departure and still makes me shudder whenever I hear it.

The King's pagoda boat in *Patria* 10: *The Palace of the Cinnabar Phoenix.*

WRITTEN IN 1999–2000, *The Palace of the Cinnabar Phoenix* was first performed in 2001 on and around a small lake near Pontypool, Ontario. I had always wanted to have one of the *Patria* works originate in the Far East. As I have already written about it extensively in *Patria: The Complete Cycle,* I will not take the reader through it here except to say that I had conceived the work for outdoor performance by *bunraku*-sized puppets manipulated by operators dressed in black.†

Everyone liked the production and so did I, especially the serene ending with the Palace slowly rising out of the water accompanied by a girls' choir on the far side of the lake. There is something for everyone in this work: humour, philosophy, beautiful singing and excellent puppetry.‡

The attacks on the World Trade Center and its collapse occurred during this production. Other events, such as concerts and film festivals, were being cancelled because all flights had been stopped, and the stars and headliners couldn't travel. But our show went on under the quiet sky, and the philosophical tone of *The Cinnabar Phoenix* created a mood that was shared by everyone.

In 2007 we repeated the *Palace of the Cinnabar Phoenix* production at the edge of a larger lake in the Haliburton Forest and Wildlife Reserve. There were several beautiful moments in this production. First of all, four tai chi artists performed a portion of my *Sixth String Quartet*. We had placed them on a float that was flush with the water some distance out on the lake, dimly illuminated so that they appeared to be moving on the water itself. Later, when the Blue Man arrives, he literally walks across the lake as he sings his aria. He too is on a float at water level illuminated by blue light. And when Shen Nu is describing her journey under the ocean, the water suddenly parts to reveal a life-size puppet that appears to be singing and then plunges

† The idea had originated when Eleanor took me to the Munich *Puppen-Theater,* which specialized in full-length operas with marionettes. Eleanor said, 'Puppets! Why not in the *Cinnabar Phoenix*?'

‡ Children begged their parents to bring them back to see the puppet of 'the naked man'. This was the Philosopher of the Left who had to be naked to philosophize.

back under the water. Altogether it was a beautiful production, mysterious and eloquent.

The production went well though I had to turn over $30,000 to meet current expenses, some of which was eventually returned to me after all the bills had been paid. You've heard about anonymous benefactors, but anonymous author-benefactors…? Someone, arriving at the box office to buy a ticket asked, 'Is Murray here tonight?' The attendant replied: 'Murray who?'

A NEW MILLENNIUM

ARE DIARIES a thing of the past? Who keeps them today? Are they being replaced by the photo album? Or the blog? There was always an intimacy about a diary that cannot be replaced by any other medium. A diary is a record of solitude, of a life of introspection and self-communication. I have kept a diary from my early twenties – not consistently, but now amounting to a metre or so of shelf space. I have also found it interesting from time to time to read extensive passages from other diaries, especially those of great artists.

One day – it was February 2000 – I picked up Thomas Mann's *Diaries* and began to read. There is always an abyss between the work of an artist and his life, even when it is relentlessly documented, as Mann's was. The entries occurred almost daily, and they follow an unremitting routine, containing frequent references to the exact time of rising, whether he took a bath or not, the substance of his breakfast, the time he went to work, who came for lunch, the length of his walk, the state of his stomach, which always conditioned how much he ate and whether he enjoyed it, his inveterate insomnia and the pills he took to try to get to sleep (something called Phanodorm). He certainly was valetudinarian and made frequent references to unpleasant odours from his dentures, upset stomachs and symptoms of many mysterious ailments.

Here is an example of a diary entry written at a time when he was writing an essay on Schopenhauer (January 18, 1938): 'Up at 8. Foehn, warm, snowing heavily – Tired. The work on *Schopenhauer* toilsome. Washed my hair. Walked ...'

The pedestrian prose goes on and on. There is scarcely an idea here, scarcely a thought about anything. Then I turn to the Schopenhauer essay. First sentence: 'The pleasure we take in a metaphysical system, the gratification purveyed by the intellectual organization of the world into a closely reasoned, complete and balanced structure of thought is always of a preeminently aesthetic kind.' Could anything be more contradictory? The journal is like the monologue of an old woman, one might say, obsessed with her daily routines and especially with her ailments. The other is the monologue of a disciplined, ruminating and frequently original thinker. The real question is why would such a complex and original artist bother to keep a diary confined to such quotidian matters – why waste time on it? Stravinsky (likewise a slave to pill bottles and symptoms of incipient health problems) also kept a boring diary. And I remember reading Tolstoy's diaries, hoping to find the genesis of *War and Peace,* without finding anything of value. For such writers all phosphorescence of thought was thrown into the outer statement, the persona, including brilliant observations and great subtlety of psychological and intellectual discrimination; the diary was a mere accounting of how the body was functioning and of what diversions entered the household. It was as if these great writers felt themselves forever hovering near death.

It was totally different with my friend, the composer Harry Freedman. He had one of the most original and loudest laughs of anyone I ever met and the slightest attempt at a joke released it in full glory. I will never forget our last meeting when he and his wife, the singer Mary Morrison, came to the farm one September night for dinner. To celebrate their visit I had bought a bottle of good malt whisky and a bottle of Pouilly-Fuissé. There was no sadness in our reminiscences; nostalgia, yes, resentment, a little, but no regrets over what we had failed to achieve. We had a lot of shared memories since Mary and my first wife, Phyllis, used to sing operas and other productions together. Harry and I had initiated and produced Ten Centuries Concerts together for several years. We laughed a lot that night. As they had to drive back to Toronto, the evening ended too soon under a starlit sky with Arcturus bright on the northern horizon, flanked by Boötes. It was my last meeting with one of Canada's best composers and a champion of new music in all forms and styles.

A day or two after that occasion, I left for Manitoba where we were to perform the Harvest section of *The Spirit Garden* at the St. Norbert Arts Centre, just south of Winnipeg. We had planted the garden and performed the Spring section in June. It was a good crisp evening, dark by the time the ritual began, lit largely by torchlight. When, at the end, we turned the garden over to Winter and his Four Winds, we went indoors to the banquet of the food the garden had produced, served up by the gardeners who had grown it over the summer and had now prepared it for our consumption. It was a wonderful experience, uniting the gardeners, the performers and the hundred and fifty audience members who had braved the cold night to taste the reward.

I have planted a vegetable garden every year for over thirty-five years and I cannot exaggerate how strongly I feel about the spirituality of agriculture and what a tragedy it is that most of the population in well-off countries have been deprived of this sensation. Of course, going to a good restaurant and enjoying a good meal can make a strong impression, but it is totally different from eating a meal of fruit or vegetables that you have grown yourself and have freshly picked an hour or two before consumption. I remember how, when I was a child in Toronto, my parents used to revile immigrants who ploughed up perfectly good lawns to plant vegetable gardens. And yet my mother and father both came from farms where vegetable gardens produced most of the food that kept them alive through long winters. To them the garden had become a sign of poverty in just one generation. They now drove up to the supermarket in the car and shopped for a week there. Perhaps the tide is beginning to turn back today, but I doubt it, at least as far as urban dwellers are concerned. All I can say is that people who cultivate vegetable gardens are rarely overweight. The folklore of the world is rich in songs, incantations and rituals involving planting and harvesting. To celebrate the pattern of planting and harvesting keeps us aware of the earth cycles and prevents us from imagining that our mission is to conquer the earth rather than celebrating our gratitude for what the earth has provided for us.

DURING THESE YEARS (2002–03) Eleanor had been travelling back and forth between Europe and Canada. Finally, in June 2003, she returned to Canada permanently to live with me on the farm at Indian River. I had prepared a surprise for her and even gift-wrapped it: a new composition. Sometime before this the CBC had offered me a commission based on the success of Eleanor's performance of our *Letters from Mignon* a few seasons back. We had decided that the new piece would therefore be for Eleanor's voice accompanied by the Esprit Orchestra. We were hoping to persuade the CBC to do a CD with Eleanor and the Esprit. We already had *Letters from Mignon* and an orchestral version of the *Minnelieder* which I made several years before for her, and one new piece would fill the duration of the CD.

Eleanor has always been interested in religious literature and so

Photo of Eleanor and Murray featured on the *Letters from Mignon* disc.

have I. The text I chose for the new work was *Thunder: Perfect Mind,* one of the religious manuscripts found at Nag Hammadi, Egypt, in 1945. The voice is that of a female theurgist and the tone is forceful and full of antitheses and paradoxes, viz: 'I am the whore and the holy one, the wife and the virgin.' The text also contains exhortations to hear and reflect on the antitheses, revealing that the narrator believes herself to be, and wants us to believe her to be, a seer, intimate with all the incomprehensible forces of the cosmos. This seemed to be the perfect text for Eleanor's dramatic voice and I wrote the piece quickly, finishing it just before her return to Canada.

In October 2002 Eleanor sang *Letters from Mignon* with the Esprit Orchestra. She had also sung *Thunder: Perfect Mind* with the same orchestra. We were now in a position to record these works, together with the orchestral version of the *Minnelieder.* The only problem was that the CBC had decided to stop making CDs of 'classical' music, this after having promised that they would support the project fully. A few years later they decided to eliminate all (or almost all) contemporary and classical music from their programming.

What were we to do about the recording? The Esprit Orchestra had been booked and Eleanor had prepared three difficult works. Eventually we worked out a 'rescue plan'. The CBC would contribute the recording hall and the services of the producer and technician while I paid the conductor and the orchestra. I need hardly say which cost more. But with the talents of David Jaeger as producer and David 'Stretch' Quinny as recording engineer – both of whom we had worked with for many years – and of course, Alex Pauk and the Esprit Orchestra, who had performed so much of my work over the years, we produced the recording as a celebration of twenty-five years of Eleanor's and my love. It was released by ATMA Classique. The disc received many favourable reviews and was nominated for a Juno Award in 2008.

In the spring of 2003 I also wrote another work for Eleanor together with the harpist Judy Loman, for whom I had written *The Crown of Ariadne* and my harp concerto. The new piece, *Tanzlied,* is based on texts from Nietzsche's *Also Sprach Zarathustra,* which Eleanor had unearthed and suggested might be appropriate. The singer describes her dance with life, sometimes rushing forward, sometimes stumbling and retreating. There are many arresting lines in Nietzsche's text and one stands out as a maxim: 'Don't crack your whip so terribly: Noise kills thought!' To give the work an authentic flavour I also included fragments of Nietzsche's own music, inspired by his admiration for Wagner.

Sometime in 2002 I had been approached by Lawrence Cherney to write another large choral piece, this time for six professional choirs from various parts of Canada and the Toronto Children's Opera Chorus. This was no doubt stimulated by the success of the *Credo* performance and recording. The result was *The Fall into Light,* a syncretic work based on texts from a wide variety of sources – gnostic, hermetic and mystical for the most part, but some also from texts by Rilke and Nietzsche, and some personal reflections. The basic theme is Manichean, the fall of the soul from its heavenly home of light to the darkness of the earth and its attempt to escape from the *archons* who rule there and to pass through the *aeons* of space back into the *pleroma* of light. The direction of this passage may be up or down since the earth is surrounded by starry light, hence the title, which Eleanor serendipitously invented. Since the soul in Manichean thinking is also a drop of light, the whole work is a study of light within darkness as well as darkness within light.

The performance was to take place in the atrium of the CBC building in Toronto. There were wide corridors on every floor facing the central plaza, which suggested that space both vertically as well as horizontally could be a feature of the presentation. That is something that is missing in the presentation of music today: the vertical dimension – which is, after all, significant in the word 'fall'. For *The Fall into Light* I wanted the audience to lie on mats on the floor while the choirs sang from various balconies. On the ceiling of the atrium there would be a 'choreography' of lights reflecting the mood and action of the text. But my idea was vetoed by both the producer and the conductor, and the whole production was presented on the ground with a single exception: the children's choir was placed in one of the upper balconies. The audience, instead of lying down, was seated in narrow, upright chairs for a tourist-class flight across the empyrean.

The performance took place on February 29, 2004. I was surprised during rehearsals and the performance how often I had shivers up and down my spine. Of course, I had a cold and was somewhat feverish; but Eleanor said she had similar sensations, and perhaps others in the audience also did because there was great enthusiasm at the end of the performance. I was going to call the work 'The Fall from Light', but Eleanor suggested that a more appropriate title would be 'The Fall into Light' because it reminds us that we can fall upwards as easily as downwards in space and it is really as weightless souls that we return to the *pleroma* of light, wherever it may be.

IN MARCH OF 2003 I went to Australia to attend the World Forum for Acoustic Ecology meeting in Melbourne. The WFAE had come into existence in 1993 at Banff, Alberta, during a meeting of people interested in soundscape research. During the years I was at Simon Fraser University we had worked vigorously on a variety of projects relating to the soundscape, its evolution and the variations throughout the world. This work was attracting researchers in many disciplines in many countries, and the conference in Banff attracted a lot more people than were originally expected. Since that time there had been international meetings in several countries and we were meeting for the first time in the southern hemisphere. I had arrived a few days early in order to work with some student teachers and nine-year-old children doing 'ear cleaning' exercises, with the intention that at some point in the conference the children would then lead the delegates in the same exercises. To witness the children helping the experts to listen and to create little improvisations together was one of the highlights of the whole conference. What I remember most from our preliminary meetings was the little hand of a child in mine as I led the children on a blindfolded listening walk throughout the schoolyard: the excitement in the child's hand yet the trust that no deceptions or tricks would be introduced.

Although I love working with children, I have never wanted any children of my own. And neither have any of my three wives, Phyllis and Eleanor because of their careers – although Eleanor had a boy by a previous marriage before she went to Europe, and Jean because she already had two children by her first marriage.

Once, while I was teaching at Memorial University in Newfoundland, Phyllis and I visited Toronto to stay with Harry and Mary Freedman. Phyllis had been in pain during the long trip to Toronto, in those days by train, and so Mary had taken her to the hospital on our arrival.

Harry and I stayed at home and talked about the plight of music in Canada. Late at night, Mary returned and informed me that Phyllis had had a miscarriage. I have often thought of that. It was the only time in my life – so far as I know – that I could have been a father. How Phyllis bore this, I cannot say. We never talked about it, and five years later we were divorced.

IN THE FALL OF 2002, I was invited to Portugal by Carlos Alberto to discuss the possibility of creating an event to be called 'Coimbra Vibra', similar to 'Deux Mille Sons pour l'An Deux Mille', which I had organized in the Alsacian town of Sélestat. Carlos had attended a course I had given for music educators at the Gulbenkian Museum in Lisbon many years before.† In 2003 the medieval city of Coimbra was to be the cultural capital of Portugal and Carlos had been appointed director of all musical activities. So I visited Coimbra to determine what might be done. The winding streets, many wide enough only for pedestrian traffic, the balconies and the gardens, the churches and the cellars, seemed to me to constitute a perfect setting for an itinerant carnival in which the moving audience would be entertained by musicians, singers and actors performing their own repertoire but in unusual locations.

One of the things that is always taken for granted is that each type of music has its own performance location: sacred music in church, the orchestra in the concert hall, the brass band on the parade field and the pop group on the radio and in the pub. But what would happen if we shuffled these venues and put a pianist in the drugstore window, or an opera singer in the fruit market, and an orchestra on the roof of a bank? Perhaps such a reconfiguration would engender new audiences. Carlos loved the idea and we began auditioning interested soloists and groups of all kinds. I made it clear that no one who wished to participate would be turned down and, in the end, we had about a thousand participants signed up to perform.

When I returned in 2003, I listened to all the interested perform-

---

† I describe the course in 'Letter to the Portuguese'. See *The Thinking Ear*, Arcana Editions, 1988.

ers and then tried to find a special venue for each of them. It was not always easy to convince them to accept my suggestion. For instance, I wanted to place a church choir in a row of third-storey windows on a commercial street, with the choirmaster conducting from the rooftop opposite. They refused, but I succeeded in persuading them to give it a try and, when they did, people stopped on the street and applauded them. They were convinced. They even had cards printed advertising their next concert for distribution below.

I placed three girls playing flute trios in front of a pet shop and persuaded the owner to hang all his birdcages around them. 'They won't sing at night,' said the owner. But they did, stimulated by the fluttering flutes.

Another group of wind players, who were not very advanced technically, would have had trouble attracting and holding an audience; so I had the city place ten large (and clean) garbage cans in a row along a side street. Whenever people passed by, the group would spring up and play a piece, then pop down out of sight to vigorous applause.

I was insistent about one thing right from the beginning: there would be no amplified music in Coimbra Vibra. Hearing natural voices and instruments echoing in the streets of this medieval city was wonderful, and I was not going to allow it to be destroyed by anyone with a potentiometer on his tweeter.

The centre of the city had been closed to traffic. The audience was to arrive at seven o'clock at four checkpoints on the perimeter of the old city. There they were met by leaders who would take groups of about twenty-five people on a designated sound walk through the old city. Each group leader had a sound-maker, a drum or a triangle or a horn to keep the group together as they moved from place to place along a predetermined route.

Many groups of school children participated with their music teachers. All of them performed music *they* had created using their voices and sound-makers they made themselves. One school performed a very rhythmic shoe-concert so I placed them in front of the display window of a shoe shop.

While I was rehearsing with the schools, I had a call from the principal of a school for impaired children. Could they also participate in Coimbra Vibra? I was dubious, but visited the school and, after some time there, we concluded that perhaps each child could have some

Coimbra Vibra, 2003.

Coimbra Vibra, 2003.

kind of sound-maker – a whistle perhaps, or a rattle stick or a toy drum. Their guardians could decorate their wheelchairs with coloured streamers and work out a choreography of moving wheelchairs on the large square we had assigned to them. Audiences were genuinely moved by this event and applauded loudly; and I know the children recognized the effect they were having – you could see it in their eyes.

Coimbra Vibra provided an opportunity for creativity and expression by a multitude of people working together non-competitively to produce an event full of exciting and original activities. The various processions finally wound their way to the central square of the city. It was now ten o'clock and the audience was hungry for dinner. The organizers had arranged for a dozen food stalls to be set up in the square. There we were entertained alternately by three non-amplified bands on three platforms. At ten minutes to eleven, several police cars and a fire engine entered the square, lights flashing and sirens sounding. Slowly they approached the main podium where we conducted them in a little concert of sirens, horns and bells that would have thrilled Marinetti and the Futurists. At exactly eleven o'clock, all the lights in the square went out. We had arranged this with the civic administration. Then a single lamp slowly rose in the air. One could see that it was a woman in a cherry-picker. Now, in all the windows of the square, candles were being lit. When the woman in the cherry-picker had reached a certain height, she began to conduct a quiet anthem by Henryk Gorecki, sung by the hundred or more singers holding candles in the windows.

I have witnessed many civic celebrations in different countries. Most of them are dominated by loud music and end in a drunken brawl. Coimbra Vibra was something different. It involved one thousand performers and was attended by an audience of five thousand and it ended quietly! It was one of the most memorable events of my life.

ON AUGUST 9, 2004, Eleanor and I drove to Ottawa where she was to sing the premiere of *Tanzlied* with harpist Judy Loman. But before the concert, she had indigestion. I told her it was just nerves. But immediately after the concert she became violently ill with stomach cramps. I rushed her to the hospital where, at 3 a.m., the doctor announced that it was a gall bladder attack and advised her to go back to Peterborough; but she told him she had another concert at the Domaine Forget in eastern Quebec where she was to sing *Adieu, Robert Schumann* with the Orchestre de la Francophonie. She sang very beautifully despite stomach cramps and inadequate rehearsal. We then drove back home (eleven hours non-stop) and the next morning I took her to the Health Clinic in Peterborough, our doctor, of course, being on holiday. There she was told to go immediately to the emergency ward of the hospital. We were there at 10:30 a.m. Eventually they did an ultrasound test and we waited for results in a crowded waiting room. They decided to operate at 10 p.m.! The operation turned out to be much more complicated than they expected and took two and a half hours. For the next two days she lay in bed at the hospital suffering the after-pain of the operation. Finally they allowed her to come home. I looked after her as well as I could, feeling helpless but full of love for her.

A MONTH LATER, in September 2004, I was in Brazil again. FLADEM, the Latin American Music Educators' Association, was holding their conference in São Paulo. I had been invited because my travels throughout South and Central America had helped to stimulate the formation of FLADEM. Among the more interesting personalities at the conference was the composer, Coriun Aharonian from Uruguay. We rejoiced on seeing each other again, and since I had a suite in the hotel, we decided one night to have dinner brought up so that we could escape the crowd. Coriun and I always seemed to agree about politics: 'Carl Orff is a fascist,' etc., though he, being a Communist, stated things a little more blatantly than I might. Coriun is that rare combination of musician and intellectual, and our conversations always ranged over many topics beyond music. On this occasion, it was 'bananas' and Coriun was explaining the proper pronunciation of the word to me. The three 'a's in the word are each pronounced differently. The first is vocal, the second nasal and the third 'distant'. The final 'a' should be produced as if it was a metre in front of the face and Coriun had me holding my arm out and trying to hit my fingers with the sound. The rest of the evening was equally educational.

Later we struggled with the waiter over the wine bill, FLADEM refusing to pay for liquor and the waiter refusing to separate the liquor from the total bill.

After a lively conference – conferences in Latin America are always lively – I returned home to finish writing my *Ninth String Quartet,* a strange work blending old age with the excited voices of children. I had recorded a group of children 'loaned' to me for a couple of hours by a generous elementary school principal. I had the children make lots of vocal noises from laughter and screams to shouts of disapproval as they ran up to the microphone and then off across the play ground. The children were to be a counterpoint to the serious music of the quartet. The work opens with the 'Ariadne' theme that may be found embedded in several of the previous quartets as well as in other works. This time it is sung by a prerecorded boy soprano. The variety of moods that follow are directly stimulated by the children's voices, laughing, shouting and screaming with delight.

Although I have never had children of my own, they bring increasing pleasure into my life as I get older, and I loved the sauciness of their voices laughing at the music of an old man.

I wrote my *Tenth String Quartet* in the winter of 2005. It had been commissioned by Radio France for the Molinari Quartet. It was an extremely cold winter with snowy fields outside my window and temperatures that dropped to 20 or 25 degrees below zero Celsius. There were few birds at the feeders: chickadees and sparrows, and a few blue jays and woodpeckers. I have always been intrigued by the 'thin' soundscape of winter and decided to try to replicate it in the shape and texture of the quartet. I'm not sure whether I succeeded but I think we did manage to imitate some of the bird sounds quite accurately. I refrained from incorporating the frolicsome red squirrels in the texture, although they were always outside my window, constantly looking for the peanuts I would occasionally throw out to them. It was so amusing to watch them scramble after a nut, spin it in their little paws and then eat it; or, as often as not, run and hide it under the snow, then later go burrowing in search of it, hop up on a log, spin the next in their paws, gobble it, then jump into the snow in search of something more to eat.

Another visitor I was not so enthusiastic about was a Norway rat. I'd never seen one here before. I don't know why, but I immediately went out and bought some rat poison. He had made his home under a barrel, obviously pleased to have a constant supply of falling bird seed quite nearby. Why had I taken so much delight in the potentially destructive squirrels, and immediately went for the rat poison for a creature who has never harmed me? The worst of it was watching him consuming it. It took three days to kill him and I felt terrible on the second day as I saw him limping out of his little cave towards the food and then dragging himself back. Now he was gone but the memory of his death haunted me for a long time.

INDIAN RIVER is a small village a few kilometres down the road from my farm. There used to be a post office there, and the postmistress installed a little counter where one could buy cookies and chocolate bars. Children and old men would visit frequently, the latter staying around for a few minutes to read the newspaper or chat with the attractive postmistress. One could flag down the train to Toronto. The train would arrive about six o'clock in the morning and return about seven o'clock in the evening. When it stopped the engineer would climb down and feed the local dogs while the passengers climbed on or off. The post office was eventually closed and the train was discontinued. Now we have to drive to Peterborough to catch the bus to Toronto.

Twenty years ago we used to see wolves in the area, but not today. I am told that when the human presence exceeds four or five humans per square mile the wolves move out. And the human presence around Indian River is mounting at a fast rate as farmers sever one-acre lots along the roads, many of which have recently been paved. It used to be that farmers were only allowed to sever portions of their farms to members of their own family, but that restriction was rescinded so that the one-acre lots are being cut off for people with urban jobs but the desire to live outside the turmoil of the city. It's a tragedy because once farm land is lost it will never be regained.

Although the wolves have gone we still have coyotes, deer, beaver, porcupines, occasional bears and lots of groundhogs and raccoons. Many days pass when I will see more animals than humans, and I like that. In all the years I have lived here I have only seen one fox. But the groundhogs (or woodchucks as they are known) are numerous and are a real threat to my vegetable garden since the long grass protects them and they will climb a fence or chew their way through it. Early settlers used to eat them but today it is easier to eat pork chops. Moose no longer come this far south but they once did and Mrs Simcoe, wife of John Graves Simcoe, lieutenant-governor of Upper Canada (1791–1796) describes eating moose lips with great pleasure. However, I have been unable to persuade my hunter friends to save the lips for me.

As I write this I am watching a flock of twenty-five wild turkeys strut across my back field. I am told they are also delicious to eat but I have no desire to see them killed.

In Switzerland all young people are required, or used to be required, to work on a farm for a semester of their education in order to understand where their food comes from and how important it is to comprehend a world that was never intended for humanity alone – a world that will sink into ruins if we fail to comprehend this message. We could institute a practice similar to this in Canada. Then why don't we? Is nature not exciting enough, or colourful enough, or noisy enough to hold our attention?

I once taught a class in communication studies in which each student was to find and mark out a metre of ground untouched by human intervention, and study all forms of natural activity within it. Then they were asked to add one or more ingredients to it to enhance it without destroying it. The results were in their own small way remarkable and involved petals of flowers, leaves, trellises, water ceremonies, stones ... In a few cases small structures were added but with subtlety not destruction.

We would probably all agree that reaffiliation with nature is important. But if there is no retreat from the technology-driven world it is hard to imagine a victory for ecology. I am not a Luddite. I drive a car, and as these pages have shown, I fly around the world from time to time; but I am still more amazed by the water in a stream or the colours of a sunset than by any technological gadget I am forced to use. I have neither e-mail nor a computer or cell phone, and I intend to leave it this way.

I dread observing the expansion of our cities. Do we really need so many people in Canada? Are we greedy to discover the treasures that await us in the North? So greedy that we would slaughter the wilderness to obtain them? Can't we learn a lesson from fallen empires or from those that are disintegrating before our eyes?

IN THE SUMMER of 2005 I travelled to Japan again, where the Newfoundland Youth Orchestra was to give a performance of *Threnody* and some of my choral works before a Japanese audience. I had written *Threnody* while I was at Simon Fraser University in 1966. The text consisted of eyewitness accounts of the atomic bombing of Nagasaki, by children and adults who had experienced it. I was extremely nervous about how a Japanese audience would react to a Canadian youth orchestra and chorus performing a work about the bombing of their city that killed and injured 65,000 of their citizens and led to the defeat of Japan in the Second World War. The audience reacted in the typically inscrutable Japanese manner. They were very quiet and there would have been no applause at the end of the performance had not Carl Goulding, the conductor, motioned the orchestra to stand up in the traditional expectation of provoking it. After the performance, a young man introduced himself as the grandson of Dr Nagai who had collected the texts from survivors of the bombing that I had used as the libretto for *Threnody*. He invited me to the Dr Nagai Museum. I defy anyone to visit that museum and depart without tears in their eyes.

I remained in Nagasaki for a few days, lecturing at the Catholic

Murray in Japan, 2005.

University and meeting with artists and musicians. At a reception a man approached me and introduced himself as a soundscape designer. He then introduced me to a very attractive young woman. 'She is my student,' he said. 'She work on sound design of toilets.' I tried not to smile but the young lady beamed. 'Have you some special words for her?' asked the professor. Of course, I was speechless, so the professor filled me in. 'Japanese women very embarrassed by sounds made in toilet. She work to find precious sound to cover embarrassing noise. Please advise her.' The lady continued to smile at me. I mentioned that the toilet in my hotel room began to make a flushing sound as soon as I approached it. 'Yes,' affirmed the professor. 'New hotels have introduced this. But she wish to find more beautiful sound.' I pointed out that water *was* a beautiful sound – even dirty water. And I smiled. We all smiled. And then we left the topic. A few days later I was to visit the professor's university and hear the young lady's experimental solutions for the toilet problem.

There is no doubt in my mind that the Japanese understand soundscape design better than any other nationality I have encountered. There is a blending of music and the soundscape in their culture that is unique, and it is derived from the openness of the word for music, *ongaku,* which simply means enjoyable sound. So a waterfall or a chorus of birds can be *ongaku* just as much as an orchestral piece by Toru Takemitsu or Mozart. I have met sound designers in Japan who are designing the acoustics of rooms and gardens with incredibly imaginative simplicity – for instance, the tinkling of small bells that can be heard and seen for brief intervals every ten or twenty minutes. The sound is not loud, perhaps barely audible, but it makes each room unique just as colours, furnishings, and lighting make it visually unique. In Western architecture audio design consists of nothing but wiring every corridor for Muzak. The presence of infrasound in practically every wall is another feature of Western architecture.†

---

† I mentioned this during a lecture at the Canadian Centre of Architecture in Montreal a few years ago. What did I mean? asked the architects. Go and put your ear to the wall and you'll hear the furnace and the air-conditioning vibrating. It is the same with all modern Western buildings. They are all vibrating with infrasound.

In the late spring of 2005, Lawrence Cherney asked me whether I'd like to write another large-scale choral piece. He had a venue in mind: University College at the University of Toronto. I went with him to see the site: an outdoor quadrangle, much like a cloister, and two or three interior rooms rather large and Gothic, immediately suggested something medieval. I began reading various texts trying to find something suitable: *Le Roman de la Rose, Aucassin et Nicolette,* checking out stories in Chrétien de Troyes, etc. Then I thought of Savonarola, then of Joan of Arc; but nothing seemed quite right for the treatment Lawrence had in mind: a choreographed choir or choirs, possibly with one or two soloists. I visited the proposed site again and sat on the stone wall of the courtyard trying to imagine what might work there. All at once, I thought of the Children's Crusade.

In the early thirteenth century there were two crusades involving children, one originating in France and one in Germany. After a little researching, I decided to use the French crusade as my model. In it a young boy named Stephen had a vision of redeeming the Holy Land with love not force. He went to see King Philip at his court in Saint-Denis. The king laughed at him until it was pointed out that Stephen was a gutter child, who had a large following of other such children who wished to go with him. If the king were to authorize the crusade, the streets of Paris would be 'cleaner'. So the king gave the children free passage to Marseilles, where they expected the sea to part as the Red Sea had parted for Moses. Of course, the sea did not part and many of the children drowned while others were sold into slavery. As the chronicles are vague and sometimes contradictory I felt free to embellish the story in my own way, so I introduced a Saracen girl who appears in Stephen's dreams telling him that the children of Jerusalem, both Saracens and Jews, were waiting for their arrival to join them in their mission of peace.

I wanted the work to move from place to place with the audience following. As they moved from scene to scene they would be entertained by medieval characters: priests, beggars, dancing bears and jongleurs. There were neighbouring buildings and pathways in the University College complex that would make this possible. I plotted out a potential itinerary for Lawrence to present to the University College authorities.

They turned it down. Undaunted, Lawrence went to Trinity

College which has a similar quadrangle, a beautiful chapel and a very large dining hall. The work could have been adapted quite nicely to those premises. When Lawrence met with the authorities it was pointed out that film companies paid ten thousand dollars a day for use of the premises. 'Just how many days do you have in mind?'

A last attempt was made at Hart House, but the multiple use of the building, including a basketball gymnasium that was constantly in use, rendered it unsuitable.

Meanwhile I was carrying on with the text and the music. I definitely wanted the work to have a medieval character, but I wanted it to have a contemporary appeal as well. Lawrence was very generous about accepting the swelling scale of *The Children's Crusade* as we continued to try to find a suitable performance location.

IN SEPTEMBER 2005 we produced *Patria 9: The Enchanted Forest* at the Haliburton Forest and Wildlife Reserve. We gave eight sold-out performances and received some very good reviews. Because I had been careful to incorporate as many local people as possible, the local turnout was very high, which promised support for future productions. Peter Schleifenbaum, owner of the Haliburton Forest, had supported us in every way and I was happy for him that so many people attended the production. We were rained out only one night and that, unfortunately, was the one night that Michael Koerner came. Michael has been a supporter of my music for many years, but he had never come to any of the outdoor productions. To my great delight, we had finally persuaded him to attend one of these performances with his entire family. This was the result. I felt sorry for both of us.

Personal patronage is rare in Canada today. It has been replaced by foundations and government agencies. In some ways this is unfortunate, because it fails to encourage the patron's understanding of the creative process. However, Michael is the exception. He and his wife, Sonja, have commissioned several works from me, including the orchestral piece *Spirits of the House* which was written for the opening of Koerner Hall in Toronto in 2011. My 'Symphony Number 1 in C Minor' (a work with an intentionally ironic title), was also commissioned by Michael.

I am not sure that all readers realize how much more expensive it is to produce a work in a wilderness environment than in a conventional theatre. First of all, we have to shape the environment into a theatre stage. Creating seating for the audience is also desirable – unless, as in *The Enchanted Forest,* the audience moves from scene to scene, with much of the action occurring as the audience is standing or moving through the forest. Changes in the weather can affect the success of the production profoundly. On a bad day box office money must be returned, yet actors, musicians and crew must continue to be housed and fed. *The Enchanted Forest* required a cast and crew of well over a hundred people and the unionized members had to be paid in full every night we were rained out. The Haliburton Forest and Wildlife Reserve is more than two hundred kilometres north of Toronto, and the audience has to be lured to make the pilgrimage to see the production.

While we continued to produce *Patria* productions at the Haliburton Forest – *The Palace of the Cinnabar Phoenix* and *The Princess of the Stars* were both performed there – we were amassing an enormous debt that finally terminated productions, except for the *Patria* Epilogue: *And Wolf Shall Inherit the Moon,* which is paid for by the participants themselves.

In the fall of 2005 I taught a course at Concordia University in Montreal entitled 'The Theatre of the Senses'. I wanted to introduce the students to the idea that the audio-visual entertainments of the modern world are dismissing the other senses which were at one time present in the ceremonies of our lives. The mass, for instance, involved all the senses: touch, taste and smell as well as sight and sound. You see the altar and the priest. You hear the choir. You smell the incense. You kneel on the prayer-stool and you taste the sacrament.

Drinking wine, if one does it properly, also involves all the senses. We hear the wine as it is poured. We see the colour of the wine. We smell its fragrance. We touch the glass with our lips and we taste the wine sensing its potentially intoxicating effect.

But the students needed to be reminded of how the senses interact or could interact in art, and so I gave them exercises in sensory awareness. I had them create 'smellodies' by arranging sequences of different smells in a series like the notes of a melody. We also created tactile walks. Blindfolded and barefoot, we walked over different materials.

Some of the textures were also warm or cold from heating pads or crushed ice. The sensation of such a walk for a blindfolded person was very strong. I sent the class out to examine the ornate woodwork and stonework of ancient Catholic churches, of which there are quite a few in Montreal. I wanted them to appreciate how these buildings attract our sense of touch while modern buildings avoid textural detailing that might persuade us to linger. Modern buildings are erected for the swift traveller.

A few years earlier I had tried something similar at McGill University. I had the students compare listening to different pieces of music with tasting different food. Each student was to prepare a menu explaining why a particular piece of music would go with a particular course of a meal. After discussing each student's selections we chose the most interesting and as a final assignment the students prepared the music and the food for a six-course meal attended by a dozen faculty members. There was no talking while the food was served and the music was performed. Much of the conversation between courses was devoted to a discussion of the *correspondance* between the music selections and the taste of the different courses.

I have often wondered whether a commercial restaurant might one day pick up the idea as a replacement for the unending competition between the roisterous customers and the boisterous music.

One day at Concordia University I brought a basket of apples to school and gave a lecture on the apple as a multi-sensory object uniting tactile and visual beauty with smell, taste and sound. Each student held an apple as I commented on its features. Then as they bit into it I read them a poem by Rilke.

> Full round apple, pear and banana
> ... all this speaks
> Death and life into the mouth ...
> Read it from the face of a child
> Tasting them. Is something
> indescribable slowly happening in your mouth?
> Where otherwise words were, flow discoveries,
> out of the fruit's flesh.
> Oh experience, sensing joy – immense!

I am not sure if the Concordia course was a success. Some students stubbornly clung to the notion that art involved two senses only, as they were being taught in their studios and music rooms; but we did manage to put on a little show of our work in an unknown building off-campus to which we took the audience by bus, blindfolded, and I think the experience affected many of them strongly.

One other event from the fall of 2005 in Montreal remains with me. This was a little concert organized by Wolfgang Bottenberg and his wife, Joanna, of *Lieder* by Schumann, Liszt and Brahms before an audience of twenty-five or thirty invited guests in the spacious living room of their own home. This is the way these songs were intended to be performed, before an intimate audience of friends and devotees, not in a huge hall and certainly not on recordings. One must watch the singer in those practised and touching gestures, so light but as carefully planned as a bouquet of flowers. We listen to the curve of the song and watch the singer's searching eyes....

I reminded the Bottenbergs that they might have performed the *Lieder* in candlelight, as they would have been at the time of their creation. The softer light and darker shadows would have given the texts of the songs an opportunity for a deeper interpretation. There were hors d'oeuvres before the concert and tea and cake afterwards to make the experience multi-sensory. An almost exclusively German-Canadian audience had been invited, including Winifred Wagner, the grandchild of Siegfried Wagner, a silver-haired Rhine maiden two metres tall.

In January 2006 I went to Paris at the invitation of the acoustical engineer Christian Hugonnet, who had inaugurated an event called 'La Semaine du Son' in which various organizations dealing with different aspects of sound confederated into a kind of festival ranging from music education to noise pollution, music therapy and sound in the cinema. Each organization makes its presentation at various sites in Paris, and also in several other cities, and the activities – concerts, lectures and demonstrations – are all advertised in one brochure. It is certainly an endorsement of the communal exploration of the soundscape advocated in *The Tuning of the World*. I gave lectures both in Paris and in Chalon-sur-Saône and had the audience doing various listening and sound-making exercises in each place, to which they responded with more enthusiasm than I had expected. Encouraging the participation of the audience is something, I am told, that never or rarely happens in France; and certainly it never happened in any of the other lectures I attended during the Week of Sound, where the speaker (always with a microphone) riddles the audience without ever soliciting a question or a response beyond the spotlight. I have always been suspicious of technology and try to eliminate it when it seems unnecessary. The microphone is a weapon of dictatorship.

On the way home, I had to make a stopover in Montreal. In the lavatory of the airport, a man was sitting on the pot, carrying on an intimate cellphone conversation with a woman (his wife? his girlfriend?). He continued to talk while he wiped his bum and flushed the toilet.

Christian Hugonnet invited me to return to La Semaine du Son in January 2010. The activities had expanded to fifteen cities all across France, and Christian wanted me to visit twelve of the participating cities within fourteen days! Each day my guide Agnès Puissilieux and I mounted one of those incredibly fast French trains and streaked our way to Marseilles or Lyon or Dunkerque, sometimes staying overnight, sometimes returning to Paris. Needless to say, I had little impression of the places we visited; but the strangest experience of all took place in the Conservatoire in Troyes, an important medieval city, though the closest I got to seeing it was the beautiful book the principal of the Conservatoire gave me on my arrival. We chatted for an hour in his office, or rather, he talked about the accomplishments of his school while I nodded approvingly. Then looking at the clock he said: 'On commence maintenant,' and he led me through the corridors to a large hall with an empty stage. In the first two rows of seats were about forty children six or seven years old. In the next rows were about fifty teachers and professors. I was ushered onto the stage and left there. What did they expect me to do, talk to the children or talk to the professors?

I chose to work with the children and my first exercise was a hard one, even though it may sound simple. 'When I signal you I want you all to stand up without making any sound … not yet! Wait for my signal!' The children tried eagerly to do the exercise. We tried it several times and it improved a great deal as the children got into the habit of listening to what they were doing, which is, of course, the purpose of this and many other simple exercises I have devised to assist in clairaudient listening.

I then asked the children whether the teachers should do the same exercise. 'Oui!' they screamed while the teachers frowned. But we tried, or at least most of the teachers tried, though some sat firmly glued to their seats.

The ice was broken. I had the children come 'silently' on stage and we did a lot of listening and sound-making exercises while the professors watched, and I hope understood that what we were doing was part of the foundation of all music and just as important as *do re mi fa so*.†

ON A NIGHT in May 2006, I arrived in Mexico City at 2 a.m. I was met by two rough-looking men who drove me to the Holiday Inn Talplan. When I awoke in the morning I opened the handsome, leather-bound directory of hotel services to read:

> We are conscious that the Holiday Inn Talplan is the beast option for you that likes of the good attention and of the excellent hospitality. If it wishes some drink of its preference please ask for it to exist ...

I had been invited to Mexico City to give a workshop in soundscape recording at Radio Educacion. The previous year I had been the invited speaker at the Quinte Bienal Internacional de Radio, which was organized by Lidia Camacho, director of Radio Educacion and her team of handsome black-haired maidens. I liked Lidia immediately. She told me that reading *The Tuning of the World* was one of the turning points in her life and she wanted Radio Educacion to produce soundscape compositions of all parts of Mexico; so she invited me back to work with her producers on the development of this ambitious plan. I did a lot of listening exercises with them and had each of them keep a sound diary. Every day I would have one or two of them read a passage from their diary and we would discuss it. I also gave them exercises in recording. For instance, one exercise was to record the sound of ten or twenty different doors opening and closing. It was truly amazing to listen to all the variations of a sound we hear every

---

† The exercises are found in the books *A Sound Education* and *HearSing*, both published by Arcana Editions.

day but ignore. I told them how in Japan part of a girl's education is learning to open and close a sliding door as quietly as possible.

Another exercise I gave them was to record the most beautiful sound in Mexico City. You can imagine the variety of sounds they recorded – all the way from fountains to the voice of the beloved. I also provoked them to think by making statements like: 'In radio there is no up or down.' Stereophonic microphones can record left and right but there are no microphones to delineate the cascade of a waterfall or separate an airplane in the sky from a car on the ground. Does this mean that radio is incapable of rendering heaven or hell?

Some authors have very good ears for sound and some authors are deaf. Two authors with good ears who lived about the same time were George Eliot and Richard Burton. Burton's *Personal Narrative of a Pilgrimage to Al-Madinah and Meccah* is perhaps the only document in English that gives us information about the soundscape of the Middle East in the days of camel caravans. In it, Burton speaks about 'sound sweetened by distance', referring to the muezzin's call to prayer, the camel bells of the distant caravans and the tinkling bells of sheep and goats being driven home at night. Actually all sounds are sweetened by distance, even rough or aggressive sounds. Burton learns that the voice of the muezzin defines the limit of civilization from the wilderness just as the church bells of Europe separate the wilderness from the civilization of Christianity.

The other writer, George Eliot, who grew up in quiet rural England, in *Middlemarch* gives us the memorable phrase: 'the roar on the other side of silence', meaning that we prefer not to hear the unhappiness of others. But could the phrase have also been inspired by the microphone, invented just a few years before? The microphone made it possible for the first time to transmit sound in silence and amplify it on release. This was to become a new experience in listening, adding its roar to the noises of the city. Burton speaks about the beauty of distant listening while Eliot dreads the amplification of sound that would eventually drown out the distant listening so familiar to her from her childhood. I live on a farm where distant listening is still possible. In the city there is no distant listening. All sounds are close. The only way to make a sound expand over a large territory is to increase the volume which, when pursued vigorously, will inevitably lead to 'the silence on the other side of the roar' – i.e., deafness.

JUNE 15, 2006: 9:00 P.M. I am home from Mexico City. I am alone on the porch. A few mosquitoes. What else? Someone is pounding a pylon with a sledge hammer in the distance. The sky is darkening with rain clouds. From Douro Park, a mile away, I hear the occasional cheer from a baseball game. A variety of birds are heard, near and far, diminishing and falling silent one by one. In the distance, there is only the occasional buzz of a redwinged blackbird. Suddenly a hummingbird whisks by, turning to look at me on his way to the feeder. It begins to grow dark. Still no frogs. The spring peepers are late this year. Now the bats are coming out of the attic gables. A squirrel chatters. The evening has reached that moment when the land begins to exude its perfumes. The hummingbird returns and perches on the clothesline, pretending to be a clothespeg. The mosquitoes are getting worse and I decide to go inside. It is from soundscapes like this that I draw my inspirations – and they are all free.

One July morning, I went into Toronto to visit John and Helen Weinzweig who were in a nursing home there. John's mind was still alert; Helen's was wavering (she couldn't recall the title of one of her own novels). We talked about old times of course, and the conversation was lively. Then we went to lunch. I was surprised at how little John ate, for he had always been a tall and robust man. After lunch he wanted to lie down immediately so I helped him into bed, and as I tucked him in, I felt how much it was like tucking in a baby for his afternoon nap. He went to sleep almost immediately. A week later his son, Paul, called to inform me that the sleep was now eternal.

I HAD BEGUN to skirmish with another quartet, a commission from the Lafayette String Quartet in Victoria. I wrote and rewrote the first part of the first movement six times, trying to find a notation flexible enough for the pleading sound I wanted to create at the opening of the work. I spent several days lying on the couch thinking, then getting up to scribble something which, on second thought, I would strike out. Normally, I like to write out the whole work quickly, let it sit around for a few months, then go back and rewrite it completely, saving only what Ezra Pound used to call the 'gists and piths' of the first version; but, in this case, I couldn't even get past the first page.

Of course, I did eventually complete the *Eleventh String Quartet,* and I think it is one of the better pieces, particularly because of the first and last movements. In the last movement, I incorporated a very soft recording of an Aeolian harp and had the strings also produce similar sounds. Aeolian harps were very common during the nineteenth century and are mentioned by Berlioz, Schumann and E.T.A. Hoffmann, among others. So instead of a vigorous ending, the *Eleventh String Quartet* drifts slowly and softly to silence. I know of no other piece of music to which it can be compared.†

At the end of October 2006 I contributed (once again) to the noise pollution of the world by flying to Japan where the World Forum for Acoustic Ecology was to have its meeting at Hirosaki in the northern state of Aomori. Before that, I stopped in Tokyo where the Tokyo Symphony Orchestra gave an excellent performance of *Manitou,* which Suntory Hall had commissioned a few years before. Several good papers were read at the soundscape conference concerning a wide variety of issues. On the final day, we visited a Kabuki theatre, said to be the oldest in Japan, where the audience is seated on the floor. The first half was ancient Kabuki but in the second half men dressed in women's clothing (traditional in Kabuki), pranced around to Japanese rock music that quickly drove me out to sit in the park nearby, where I was soon joined by Sabine Breitsameter, who was later to undertake a new translation of *The Tuning of the World* into German.‡ At dinner, I modestly suggested that the WFAE might write a polite letter to the theatre management pointing out the dangers of high-amplitude sound, but my 'modest proposal' merely elicited a few smiles and nothing was done. I should have proposed that we fry the audience at an even higher volume and then eat them.

---

† 'Then began the Aeolian Harp of the Creation to tremble and to sound, blown on from above; and my immortal Soul was a string in that Harp' (Jean Paul Friedrich Richter).

‡ The original translation was full of inaccuracies and was incomplete. The title *Klang und Krach* (Sound and Noise) was misleading. Moreover, it had just appeared when the publisher went bankrupt. I was never paid any royalties. The new translation was complete and was given a more appropriate title, *Die Ordnung der Klange* (The Arrangement of Sounds), which suggests that we have an opportunity, even an obligation, to participate in their arrangement.

During the inevitable bus tour to view the sights that seems to follow all conferences, the bus stopped at a rural hotel for us to visit the washrooms. I was the first to descend and as I stepped into the foyer, a woman shrieked! I had forgotten to take off my shoes before touching the tatami mats. I clumsily took them off and shuffled across the foyer in slippers. As I was about to enter the men's room, the attendant roared at me. I had forgotten to exchange my slippers for the toilet slippers, identical with those I was wearing, but red instead of white. I have the highest regard for the rituals of Japan and I feel like a brute every time I break them.

JANUARY 22, 2007. Another stigma of old age: memory problems when names of persons you know escape you, so that introducing them is a supreme embarrassment. Yes, of course you also forget the names of your perennial enemies, which I suppose is good, putting an end to the venomous slingshots you would actually like to continue to fire at them. But when you forget the names of your friends, or the names of those who have assisted you in your accomplishments, why that? Yesterday I couldn't recall the name of Montaigne, whose wisdom has been a treasure chest for me ever since I crossed the border into old age.... Why must we lose contact with such close friends? Yes, of course, in the end, it is all extinguished and I can see the value of forgetting everyone you have ever read about or met as you lie on the bed of expiration. But when you are still standing isolated on the platform in front of a hundred expectant students, the omission or misquoting of a single item could lead to one's dismissal as the oracle of the subject one has been invited to speak about ... *that* is serious. It signals an era of contracting back into oneself, or into one's library where one can still hunt for the missing quote unobserved.

I finished the first complete draft of *The Children's Crusade* in early September, 2007. During the last few days I worked from eight in the morning until ten at night with short breaks for meals. We were still looking for a performance venue when Lawrence Cherney, who had commissioned the work, decided to present a few sections of the new work in an open workshop to try to stimulate interest in a full production. He asked Eleanor James to direct the chosen sections and contracted Jerrard and Diana Smith to design the production. Lawrence had seen Eleanor direct some operas with amateurs in

Peterborough and was familiar with the Smiths' work through numerous *Patria* productions. The workshop went well, or so we thought, but evidently others thought differently. The directors of the Luminato Festival of Toronto came to the workshop and decided to pick up the show but on condition that an internationally renowned director would replace Eleanor. Of course, that director would appoint his own team of designers, so Jerrard and Diana were fired. I was so angry at the way this was handled that I avoided having anything further to do with the production, which was, nevertheless, enthusiastically received by audiences and critics alike. I know my productions are very complex, and I have on more than one occasion been grateful to Lawrence for trying to realize them. One day, perhaps, *The Children's Crusade* will be realized in the manner in which I had envisioned it.

IN THE BEGINNING, humans and animals were the same, for humans were also animals. They shared the world together and spoke the same language. They met in the Wheel of Life, where each animal had its own special place. This is the theme of *And Wolf Shall Inherit the Moon*.

The leaders of the human clan were Shalana and Hatempka. But eventually some humans began to think they were superior to the other animals. They invented a language of their own that the other animals could not understand. They took the best land for themselves and drove off all intruders.

It was then that Shalana and Hatempka deserted the human clan and went to live in the forest alone. Shalana died there but his voice remained alive for all those who could hear it. Each year a few humans, loyal to Shalana's dream to reunite humans with all other creatures, meet in the wilderness of Haliburton Forest to perform the eight-day ritual drama, Epilogue of the *Patria* cycle.

AUGUST 20, 2007: The Wolf Project, our abbreviation for *And Wolf Shall Inherit the Moon*, the *Patria* Epilogue, is just over and I am exhausted although I only went in for Great Wheel Day, arthritis in my knees having resisted my ability to clamber over rocks and fallen trees as I was once able to do.

Great Wheel Day is the final day when all the clans come together from their various campsites, which are actually kilometres apart from one another, for a performance of the final ritual, which begins in the Great Wheel of Life in the afternoon and continues late into the night when Wolf and the Princess of the Stars canoe up Wildcat Lake, Wolf to inherit the moon and the Princess to reclaim her crown as the missing star in the Corona Borealis – just as it was announced in the Prologue of the *Patria* cycle, *The Princess of the Stars*.

I love the excitement in the afternoon when all the clans gather in their animal costumes and masks to walk to the Great Wheel of Life where the drama begins and the whole story of the *Patria* cycle is reviewed. We have now been performing this work for over twenty years. There is no audience. We are the creators, performers and audience.

It rained off and on during Great Wheel Day this year but we never cancel the performance because of the rain, we just stumble on and, in the end, have a good laugh at our persistence. This year there were a number of new faces, as there always are, but it is the illumination of the seasoned veterans of ten years or more that always gives me the most pleasure. I ask some of the new people what they think of the experience. 'It's awesome!' 'Incredible!' 'Like nothing I've ever experienced,' are the replies. Everyone, from the youngest child to the oldest adult, throws their complete energy into the whole week to be repaid by some of the most memorable experiences of a lifetime, created, for the most part, by themselves!

In many ways, I regard *And Wolf Shall Inherit the Moon* as the triumph of my career, not because of the music or the text, but because, by its survival for over twenty years, it defies the rules and habits of the arts industries. We have created a complex myth in the annual retelling of which there is a place for everyone, including children, some of whom have literally been born into the project.

We have never asked or even contemplated asking the arts councils for money. Yet we are solvent and even raise enough money by fees to help pay the travel costs for participants who have come from as far away as Greece, Portugal and Brazil.

THROUGHOUT THIS BOOK I have mentioned the various music-theatre works that belong to the twelve-part cycle of music dramas I have titled *Patria* (homeland). The sweep of the *Patria* cycle is enormous. I have discussed the creation and production of some of the works in the cycle but here is a complete list.

Patria Prologue: *The Princess of the Stars*
Patria 1: *Wolfman*
Patria 2: *Requiems for the Party Girl*
Patria 3: *The Greatest Show*
Patria 4: *The Black Theatre of Hermes Trismegistos*
Patria 5: *The Crown of Ariadne*
Patria 6: *Ra*
Patria 7: *Asterion*
Patria 8: *The Palace of the Cinnabar Phoenix*
Patria 9: *The Enchanted Forest*
Patria 10: *The Spirit Garden*
Patria Epilogue: *And Wolf Shall Inherit the Moon*

I have already commented on some of the *Patria* works and have written a book describing each work in detail,† but I have listed them here for the reader to gain an impression of the magnitude and complexity of the complete cycle. They were never intended to be performed in sequence. Each work is complete in itself. What unites them is that several of the characters make appearances in more than one work, and certain themes introduced in one work are developed in others. Thus they form a cycle in which the principal characters, Wolf and the Princess of the Stars, appear and reappear in different guises and places: in *Wolfman, Requiems for the Party Girl* and *The Greatest Show* they are in the twentieth or twenty-first century; in *The Black Theatre of Hermes Trismegistos* they are in the Middle Ages; in *The Crown of Ariadne* they are in ancient Greece; in *Ra* the entire audience is in ancient Egypt; in *The Palace of the Cinnabar Phoenix* we are in ancient China while in *Patria* 9, 10 and the Epilogue we return to the Canadian wilderness. *Asterion* is a labyrinth that belongs to all periods and to no period. In all of these works we

† *Patria: The Complete Cycle,* Coach House Books, Toronto, 2002.

encounter the hero and the heroine, sometimes as protagonists, sometimes as deuteragonists, sometimes as mere observers. In *Ra* and *The Spirit Garden* members of the audience become actors in the drama. In these works Wolf and the Princess are present in spirit only. It is important (at least to me) that the cycle begins and ends in the wilderness of Canadian lakes and forests. We are drawn out of the city as curious urbanites to experience *The Princess of the Stars*, and we are offered the even more daunting opportunity to return to the forest and participate in the *Patria* Epilogue as performers and creators. Thus each of the *Patria* works requires its own environment for presentation. The works are also performed at different times of the year or day or night.

Wolfman and *Requiems for the Party Girl*, the first works of the cycle, were created for a seated audience in a regular theatre; but *The Greatest Show* broke away from that, introducing an itinerant audience and actors who moved about the fairgrounds. The later works each required a unique environment and a different relationship between performers and observers: a forest, a lake, a floating theatre, etc. This has made the productions more expensive than those presented in traditional environments because we have to house and feed the entire cast and crew as well as move our stage and properties to remote and sometimes almost inaccessible environments.

At least all the works have been performed once or more than once with one exception: *Patria 7*: *Asterion*. The word Asterion means 'star creature' and was sometimes used instead of Minotaur in the Cretan myth of the Minotaur and the labyrinth. The position of this work in the cycle, just after *Ra*, is appropriate, for much of *Asterion* is performed in total darkness, as were many of the scenes in *Ra*. At this point in my life I don't expect to see *Asterion* ever performed completely for the stage set is a complex labyrinth full of mysteries and dangers through which one travels alone!

We have, at least, sent individuals through portions of the labyrinth that have been constructed and all have attested to the intensity of the experience. Failing completed corridors and passageways, we have guided individuals by hand through various encounters, and that also can be quite an intense experience.

'If you wish to outline an architecture which conforms to the structure of our soul ... it would have to be conceived in the image of a labyrinth,' wrote Nietzsche in *Aurore*. So in *Asterion* you are passing through yourself – an experience we rarely indulge in and therefore one that can be both inspiring and terrifying. Can you imagine the impact of seeing daylight after such a long and often frightening experience? In our production of *Ra* I remember people weeping when Anubis embraced them in the dawn light, saying 'You have passed through.' In *Asterion*, unlike *Ra*, you are completely alone. One day, perhaps, the labyrinth will be complete but as I grow older I wonder whether I will live to see it. Perhaps it is a construction that will remain in the imagination alone.

POSTLUDE

WHEN I WAS A CHILD, Toronto ended at Eglinton Avenue. Beyond that were hay fields and farms. The population was about four hundred thousand. But soon it was to increase with immigrants from the Second World War and later from the Hungarian Revolution. It wasn't long after the Second World War that our former 'enemies' from Italy and Germany were also finding new lives in Canada. The result was a genuine enrichment of European culture as well as an enormous improvement in restaurant food. Our orchestras also improved remarkably. Audiences patronized European music because it had been such a strong force in their lives in 'the old country'. This increased interest in culture led to the Massey Report (1951), and ultimately to the formation of the Canada Council (1957) to assist in the promotion of 'European' culture. Yes, European, because that is primarily what was being demanded. Canadian music crept in with the expatriation of European culture because most of it was inspired by European models anyway. The magnificent European orchestra seemed to us to be the means by which the greatest musical expression was possible, and Canadian composers were encouraged to write European-style music with the hope that it would one day share the stage with Beethoven and Brahms, or at least with Stravinsky and Shostakovich. This dream has never really been realized, due largely to the fact that the non-Canadians who conduct most of our orchestras see no advantage in learning repertoire that arouses little interest outside of Canada. This situation caused John Weinzweig, one of our most courageous and outspoken composers, to proclaim: '[Canada's] composers have a special distinction. We are the most unpublished, unheard, unperformed and unpaid composers in the western world.'†

Later the waves of immigration shifted and are now flowing in from many other parts of the world. European culture is being replaced

† Weinzweig: *Essays on His Life and Music*, John Beckwith and Brian Cherney, editors, Wilfred Laurier University Press, 2011, p. 60.

by multiculture. Orchestras and ensembles performing European music are finding it increasingly difficult to rely on money from government, the arts councils and especially from the CBC, which has drastically cut its fund for European-style Canadian music.

Canada may be one of the most desired destinations in the world, but who are we and why are we together? It is an embarrassing question. Are we trying to overtake and overpower the United States, whose little brother we have been for the past two hundred years? Yes, it must be that. Look at how big Canada is on the map. We could rule the world if we only had more people. Unlike refugees in the past, whose destinations were small towns and farms, today's new Canadians congregate in the big cities.

My grandparents and great-grandparents came from Scotland and Germany and they were farmers. Both my father and mother were brought up on farms until my father was offered a job as an accountant for Imperial Oil, but the perspective of my parents remained largely rural. They understood where food came from and what it meant to go hungry during years of drought. My father respected the thinking and mythology of the Dakota tribes who lived close to him as a child. He often spoke to me of their wisdom.

In 1975 I deserted the city to live on a farm near Maynooth, Ontario, a decision I have never regretted. Later I moved to Indian River, Ontario. Since that time I have lived in the country except for brief periods of urban life, mostly outside of Canada. Life on the farm brought me into immediate contact with nature, with the passing of the seasons, bringing brilliant sunrises and sunsets, snowstorms and rainstorms, and the soundscape of nature in all its vibrations.

I planted a garden and discovered where food came from and how much better it tasted when one grew it oneself; and I discovered how many native plants one could eat that are not seen in supermarkets: Jerusalem artichokes, fiddleheads, cowslips and cedar-leaf tea.

I watched the stars at night and listened to their music, and wrote down the sounds I heard. I was lifted out of this world and soared on cosmic rays, singing with the angels; and from time to time I was allowed to touch the mists of the Unknown Being.... And when I die I pray that I will return to the empyrean of the sky or ...

In July 2008, I recorded a dream in my diary.

My seventy-fifth birthday is approaching so it did not surprise me that I should have a dream about it. The dream was an elaborate birthday party at the Holiday Inn, the kind where everything is fixed and phony. The birthday songs were sung, photographs were taken with a bevy of smiling cheerleaders, a birthday cake arrives and I am about to cut it when the phone rings and the receiver is handed to me. 'Happy birthday, Murray,' says a voice. 'I'm phoning from Mars to wish you all the best returns on this special day. We're all thinking about you up here. When are you coming up to see us?' Then the hostess takes the receiver away and a crowd cheers as I cut the cake.

ABOUT THE AUTHOR

Born in Sarnia, Ontario, in 1933, R. Murray Schafer is an internationally acclaimed composer, environmentalist, educator, scholar, visual artist and writer. He has taught at Memorial and Simon Fraser universities, and has received honorary degrees from Trent, Simon Fraser, Carleton, Toronto, and Concordia universities in Canada and Mendoza (Argentina) and Strasbourg (France). His music is widely praised and performed all over the world. He lives on a farm east of Peterborough.